Birdwatchingwatching

Alex Horne's first ever comedy gig came after winning a Christmas Cracker joke-writing competition. Since that inauspicious beginning he has managed to establish a remarkable reputation among critics, comics and audiences as a gifted gagsmith, prolific writer and one of the most creative solo performers at work today. He was nominated for the Perrier Award at the Edinburgh Fringe Festival in 2003, and in 2004 he won the Chortle award for Best Breakthrough Act. He is married, has met Ken Dodd three times and the Pope once. This is his first book.

Birdwatchingwatching

One Year, Two Men, Three Rules,
Ten Thousand Birds

Alex Horne

For Rachel, Beyoncé and Shakira

Published by Virgin Books 2009

2 4 6 8 10 9 7 5 3 1

Copyright © Alex Horne 2009

Alex Horne has asserted his right under the Copyright, Designs
and Patents Act 1988 to be identified as the author of this work

This book is sold subject to the condition that it shall not, by way of trade or
otherwise, be lent, resold, hired out, or otherwise circulated without the
publisher's prior consent in any form of binding or cover other than that in which
it is published and without a similar condition, including this condition, being
imposed on the subsequent purchaser.

The publisher has made serious efforts to trace the copyright owners of all
material reproduced in this book. Should any have inadvertently been overlooked
the publisher would be happy to acknowledge any rightful copyright owner and
would be grateful for any information as to their identity.

First published in Great Britain in 2009 by
Virgin Books
Random House, 20 Vauxhall Bridge Road,
London SW1V 2SA

www.virginbooks.com
www.rbooks.co.uk

Addresses for companies within The Random House Group Limited can be
found at: www.randomhouse.co.uk/offices.htm

The Random House Group Limited Reg. No. 954009

A CIP catalogue record for this book is available from the British Library

ISBN 9780753515761

The Random House Group Limited supports The Forest Stewardship Council [FSC],
the leading international forest certification organisation. All our titles that are
printed on Greenpeace approved FSC certified paper carry the FSC logo.
Our paper procurement policy can be found at www.rbooks.co.uk/environment

Mixed Sources
Product group from well-managed
forests and other controlled sources
www.fsc.org Cert no. TT-COC-2139
© 1996 Forest Stewardship Council
FSC

Typeset in Swift-Light by Palimpsest Book Production Limited,
Grangemouth, Stirlingshire

Printed and bound in Great Britain by
CPI Bookmarque, Croydon CR0 4TD

Contents

Introductions

My dad is a birdwatcher.

That's a sentence I've struggled with for the last twenty years. My dad watches birds, often for hours at a time. Why?

Before I attempt to come up with an answer, there's one thing I need to get sorted right away. This is a book about me and my dad. But it's also about me hypothetically becoming a dad, so I don't really want to refer to my dad as 'dad'. That wouldn't do at all.

I also don't want to call my dad 'Hugh'. That is his name (well, it's his middle name, but for some long forgotten reason everyone calls him Hugh rather than the James his parents intended), but I just can't call my dad by his real name. I'm sorry, but I can't write a book about Hugh when Hugh is actually my dad. And for those of you who are thinking ahead, yes, Hugh Horne is quite a funny name. He's a GP, and so his full title is Dr Hugh Horne, perilously close to Dr Huge Horne, a nickname few of his patients were able to resist. (I should add that I didn't discover that my surname was a euphemism until I was fifteen years old, when a teacher – who was also a priest – got the giggles while reading out the register.)

Thankfully, my dad (that's one of the last times I'll refer to him thus, so enjoy) managed to rename himself without even trying. Like all dads, he's useless with modern technology. He can't text, for example. He tries, but consistently ends up sending messages filled with twenty-first century Freudian slips, devoid of punctuation, and more often than not using 'in' instead of 'go' and 'of' instead of 'me', which isn't helpful when the text is meant to be about 'me' 'going' somewhere.

One particular text sent to my brother Chip (we won't go into his name just yet) was unsurpassed in its 'dadness'. In capital letters of course, and unintentionally aggressive in tone, but with virtually no mistakes until the final three words:

LOVE FROM DUNCTON

Chip understood what he meant, but this was too good an opportunity to miss. He immediately forwarded the message to his brothers, one of whom (me) phoned up our father and asked why he had signed off his text 'DUNCTON'?

'I was trying to write *dad*,' he offered apologetically. 'It must be this new predictive texting.'

'It doesn't predict that you're going to use a word that doesn't exist,' I countered logically, if a little harshly. 'That wouldn't be a helpful system at all.'

But Duncton does exist. It's a place in Sussex that my dad (that's the last time) occasionally frequents (you've guessed it) for birdwatching purposes. It turned out that he'd typed the word 'Duncton' more often than the word 'dad', which didn't make us brothers feel all that good. Still, Duncton he wrote, and so Duncton he became. And from now on, I will refer to him as Duncton, both here, at home, to friends, to family and especially in texts.

So, Duncton is a birdwatcher . . .

But Duncton was never a particularly fanatical birdwatcher. He didn't watch birds with any regularity, or belong to any clubs. He didn't go on birdwatching holidays, attend birdwatching lectures or charter a plane to the Isles of Scilly to catch a glimpse of the UK's first recorded great blue heron. He was simply an everyday birdwatcher. More accurately, he's a *birder*. The word 'birdwatcher' sounds too deliberate. It suggests that he only watched birds when on a 'birdwatching trip'. Of course he did go on many such outings, but Duncton didn't devote specific time to birds, he was just constantly aware of them.

So, Duncton is a birder . . .

I ought to introduce myself properly here too. I'm a comedian. And that's a sentence I've struggled with too, for the last seven years. As soon as you tell someone you're a comedian they ask you one of three things. Have I heard of you? Are you funny? Can you tell me a joke? Only the first of these has a simple answer, and that is no. Unless you have heard of me, in which case the answer is yes. Am I funny? On stage, yes. That's why I'm a comedian. But I'm not funny all the time. That wouldn't be funny. And can I tell you a joke? I could. But I'd prefer to tell you about Duncton.

During my childhood, his hobby manifested itself in small but persistent ways. The tedium of a long journey would be broken by Duncton suddenly squawking, jerking his head round and shouting 'Kestrel! Kestrel!' Kestrels aren't especially rare, but he'd be so excited by the sight of one hovering above the motorway ('It's as though it's dangling on the end of a piece of string!' he'd cry) that he couldn't help but share it with his family, thereby putting us at risk with his erratic driving. On walks over the Downs near our home in West Sussex he would stride far ahead, clutching his binoculars like a child might a cherished bear. We would only catch him up when a particularly indistinct LBJ[1] caught his attention, causing him to stop and stare at what looked to the rest of us like an ordinary bush. Mealtimes at home would be interrupted not by a programme on TV, but by a goldfinch on the bird table.

---

1 LBJ is birders' speak for 'little brown job' – any small brown bush-dwelling species that inexplicably gets a birdwatcher's juices flowing.

My 'Writing Book'
May 1984
aged 5¾.

we went to the king's walk it
was ten miles and are Friends and
There was Ten hills as well we could
not it to get home daddy wanted
to go bind watching due it was lunk time
fish and chips for lunch and after lund
we went bind watching and all we saw
six kestrel.
✓good.

I didn't think Duncton's behaviour abnormal, until my tenth
New Year's Eve party, and a brief moment my parents have probably long forgotten. Perhaps unusually, new year festivities have
often been momentous for me. Before I was trusted to go out
by myself, they involved a party at one of our friends' houses
in Midhurst, where we lived. Conveniently, every family we knew
seemed to have three similarly aged boys, all of whom would
spend the evening upstairs, playing games and then fighting,
while the adults did what adults did at parties in the late eighties
(probably playing games and fighting too) downstairs. I should
make it clear that mine wasn't a scandalous childhood. This is
no confessional memoir. The word 'fighting' in the previous
sentence should really be 'squabbling'. But there are a couple
of confessions I'd like to get off my chest as the story unfolds,

4

and which I've never made before. The first is that it was at one of these New Year's Eve parties that I first got drunk (as opposed to not really liking the taste of alcohol and pretending to be dizzy).

As the gap between the eldest children and youngest adults mysteriously narrowed, the generational groups began to mix more at these get-togethers, so that on one occasion I found myself in the kitchen, fetching my friend Ben's dad Mike a snack. Seeing an open bottle of red wine on the table, and carried away by the occasion, I glugged down a few hearty gulps before returning with a plate of mini cheddars. I then continued to generously offer to distribute food while steadily getting merrier in the kitchen.

There is no dramatic ending to the story. I wasn't sick in front of everyone. I might have had a sore head the next morning, but no more than anyone else. It was probably quite a safe way to experiment with alcohol, and thinking back, my parents almost certainly knew I was getting quietly sozzled and were happy and amused to keep an eye on my progress. At the time, of course, I thought I was being both mature and naughty.

But back to the incident of 31 December 1988. As midnight approached everyone gathered together in the biggest room. There was just time for one last party game before the year ticked over. Someone suggested charades. Someone else suggested a game of charades in which you pretended to be a person in the room. Everyone thought this was a tremendous idea. Like I said, this is not a drugs-hookers-binges memoir.

One of my parents' friends, almost certainly Mike again, spent the next few minutes pretending to be Duncton, to the delight of everyone present. It was the perfect portrayal of the stereotypical twitcher: sleeves rolled up way above the elbow, mimed binoculars repeatedly raised, head cocked, walk stealthy, and then the *pièce de résistance* – he almost exploded when he caught sight of a bird![2] Not, of course, one with wings, but one of my friends' mums – one of the Midhurst birds. This almost took the roof off the place. 'It's Hugh!' they all shouted and everyone laughed.

And that was it. The moment was soon lost in the confused countdown to the final year of the decade and a rousing chorus of the few words of 'Auld Lang Syne' that everyone knew and repeated ad nauseum. But for me, this was a turning point, as pivotal as those first swigs of wine. It was my very first indication that there might be anything odd about being a 'twitcher', my first brush with the double meaning of 'birds' and the first time I saw that there was something amusing about bird-watching.

From that moment Duncton's hobby became the focus of my curiosity. As I grew more independent of my parents and did what my friends said was cool, I stopped watching birds and started watching football. But all the while, as Liverpool shrank, Man Utd grew, and I slowly realised I'd backed the wrong horse, Duncton remained a birder. As I lurched through puberty, my emotions towards this eternal paternal birdwatcher moved from shame and embarrassment in my early teens, to pride and amusement as I realised my 'quirky' family might make me seem more interesting to girls, then confusion and genuine disbelief as I

---

2 OK, let's deal with this now: Duncton is *not* a twitcher. A twitcher is someone whose sole birdwatching aim is to see as many different species of birds as possible in their lifetime. Duncton, as I've said, is a birder, someone interested in seeing the birds in his local area, year in year out, without chasing across the country to 'get' a new species. The term twitcher was coined by one of birdwatching's great pioneers, Howard Medhurst, a.k.a. The Kid. Lacking his own transport, The Kid would often travel for miles on the back of his friend Bob Emmet's motorbike to seek out a rumoured bird, and would frequently arrive so cold and excited that he would, literally, twitch. This happened with such regularity that the burgeoning birdwatching community soon adopted the term 'twitching' to represent the activity of chasing birds around the country.

left school and embarked on my own bird-free adult life. *Why does Duncton watch birds?* When I started making a living out of comedy, this question was always at the back of my mind. I was sure something funny lurked in the answer. If humour comes from incongruity, then birdwatching must be a rich source of material.

Almost two decades after that party, I was twenty-seven years old and rapidly approaching the same age Duncton was when he had me. He would soon be twice as old as I am. That works mathematically. And it hasn't always been the case – when I was five he wasn't ten.

On New Year's Day 2005, I got married. Two days later my wife, Rachel, and I flew to Costa Rica for an unforgettable honeymoon in what seemed to us like paradise. Before we left, Duncton gave me a small wedding present, a compact pair of RSPB binoculars, nothing fancy, just a lightweight piece of birding equipment so I wouldn't miss the sort of birds he knew I'd have the chance to see in this avian nirvana. By the end of the trip, I'd lost both lens caps, broken the strap and used them more than any other item in our suitcase. Surrounded by iridescent hummingbirds, ridiculous-looking toucans, pelicans diving for fun and fish and love-struck pairs of scarlet macaws, I stopped and looked at birds for the first time in twenty years. I got excited by feathers, my ears pricked involuntarily when I heard an unusual call; I even wrote a list of the species I'd seen, prompted by the sight of a rare bird in the heart of the cloud forest that our guide insisted was called a resplendent quetzal.

Having outgrown the label of newly-wed, and aware that I was nearing the pertinent age discussed above, thoughts and conversations inevitably turned to fatherhood. Rachel and I weren't in any particular rush to have kids but we knew we both wanted to start a family at some point. Naturally, I hope, I was scared. I knew nothing about babies. I had no idea about birth weights and what might be a good one, whether it's ever OK to shake them, and at what age I should reasonably be alarmed if my offspring were not talking. But the one man I wanted to turn to for advice was spending more and more time typing the names of obscure birdwatching sites into his phone and less and less time communicating with his own sons. Recently retired, Duncton was now 'out birding' on an almost daily basis.

There was only one thing for it – I would have to join him.

My plan was simple. Not only would I spend time with Duncton, ask him about fatherhood while attempting to finally understand why he does what he does, but there was also the faint possibility I might 'get into' birdwatching. For, as well as worrying about my ignorance on the baby front, I was also beginning to fret about not knowing anything about anything. A dad, I thought, should be able to tell his children what things are. That's what mine did for me.

'That,' Duncton would say, as a bright yellow bird fluttered up to the bird table, 'is a grey wagtail.'

'But it's yellow!' we would object.

'Not as yellow as a yellow wagtail,' the oracle would reply.

Unfortunately, very little of that invaluable information sank in. I didn't know the difference between a coot and a moorhen. I was useless. So I immersed myself in the birdwatching books I'd ignored for so long on Duncton's shelves. From the calm journalism of Simon Barnes, Stephen Moss and Mark Cocker to the more impenetrable excitement of Bill Oddie, Dan Koeppel and Kenn Kaufman, I absorbed the history of the hobby, studied the main protagonists and gradually learned to speak the language. Soon, however, it became clear there was only one way I could really get under the skin of birdwatching: by birdwatching.

Tentatively, I asked Duncton if I could join him on his outings. Aware both of the commitment needed to do his hobby justice and my own slightly impatient nature, Duncton suggested a trial period. And so, inspired by the more competitive world of birding in America,[3] I agreed to join him on what would be a first for both of us: A Big Year. From 1 January to 31 December 2006 (exactly the same size as a normal year, only more exciting) we would each attempt to see as many species of bird as possible. The contest appealed to my sense of sport and scale, and while the formality was alien to Duncton's relaxed approach to birding, he was so amazed and excited by his son's new-found enthusiasm that he was more than happy to take part. It was agreed that I would use a small microphone to record what I hoped would be the hilarious banter bandied about in bird reserves up and down the country[4]. If I was going to spend a year watching birds, I reasoned, I'd have to get at least a couple of funny stories on the way.

This, we agreed, was to be a proper contest, the winner being the man who saw the greatest number of species after twelve months. Several birders have committed their Big Year stories to paper. After an American Jack Kerouac-like figure by the name of Kenn Kaufman kicked things off with a hitchhiking trek across America, immortalised in the great *Kingbird Highway*, bird writers like Mark Obmascik and Sean Dooley followed his footsteps with terrific international Big Year books. But after buying and reading just about every major book about British birdwatching (not about British *birds* – there are about as many books about birds as there are birds themselves), I hadn't actually read the

---

3 Birdwatching in the United States is now more of a sport than a hobby. On New Year's Day each year, thousands of teams set off on an annual 'Bird Race': 'In a good year the contest offers passion and deceit, fear and courage, a fundamental craving to see and conquer mixed with an unstoppable yearning for victory,' writes Mark Obmascik in *The Big Year*.

4 As it turned out there wasn't an awful lot of hilarious banter. It was mostly men sitting in silence, and that silence occasionally broken by someone saying, 'Oh, there's a skylark . . . Is it? No, it's gone.' But what little there was, I captured!

story of a British Big Year until Amazon took it upon itself to recommend one to me.

I was supposed to be buying Christmas presents for my brothers, but Amazon had other ideas and suggested, quite convincingly, that I really ought to invest in *Arrivals and Rivals: A Birding Oddity* written by a birder (and moth expert, taxonomist and scientist) from Harpenden called Adrian M Riley. I'm easily persuaded – Amazon seems to know me very well – and when it arrived I wasn't disappointed. This was exactly what I needed before setting off on my journey. With the subtitle 'A Year of Competitive Twitching', this book, written with raw enthusiasm by a fellow Big Year competitor, would be my reference point, pace setter, compass. Duncton was the man I was trying to both understand and defeat, and Adrian M Riley would show me how.

The rules of our Big Year were simple. We were governed, of course, by the fundamental birdwatching covenant:

•Birds seen must be wild, free and alive

They can't be pets, captives or dead. We couldn't phone up the local Chinese takeaway, order a Peking Duck, and tick off another species. A bird in the hand was not worth two in the bush.

We also added some rules of our own:

•We had to actually see the birds

This may sound obvious, but it is common practice for birdwatchers to tick off birds they can only hear. Such is the knowledge of an even half-decent birdwatcher that they can identify a bird hidden in a grove from its chirping alone. Not so for us. Possessing none of this awareness myself, I would have to actually clap eyes on the creatures for them to be ticked.[5] We also,

---

5 Once, when I was explaining these rules to a friend, I said I would have to 'make eye contact' with the bird. That was not the case. It didn't matter if the bird wasn't watching me watching it.

incidentally, banned the other senses. If one of us could feel and taste a bird, but not see it, that wouldn't count. Clearly this would rarely be relevant, but if Duncton was to fall asleep in the garden and accidentally swallow[6] a goldcrest, he would not be allowed to add that goldcrest to his list, unless he was able to first eject it unharmed, an ugly and unlikely scenario considering the delicacy of the bird (it's the smallest in Europe).

And finally:

• We could travel anywhere in the world to see our birds

Birdwatchers often limit their Big Year to a local patch,[7] be it their country, county or even their garden. Considering that I, a non-birder, lived in northwest London, while Duncton, a birder, had the whole of Sussex to roam around, I made the executive decision to remove border controls from the challenge. This, I thought, was a fairly canny move, given that my job as a stand-up comedian allows me (well, forces me) to travel extensively. I also knew that in August I would be attending the wedding of a friend of my wife's in Caesarea, Israel, bang in the middle of the migratory route of birds flying south for the winter. I was thinking tactically. I wanted to win this thing.

So that was that. We were ready. And on the morning of my first wedding anniversary I started birdwatching.

---

6 A not unusual example of a bird's name also being a verb. See also *duck*, *snipe* and *tern*. Common too is the phenomenon of a birding term having some sort of sexual connotation. If you want to play Horne's Birdwatching Euphemism Bingo feel free to do so. Simply underline any word or phrase you encounter that could in any way be construed to be rude, then cross it off the checklist at the back of the book and see if you can get all twenty.

7 A birder's patch is the area he visits most regularly. Whether daily, monthly or annually, this is his haunt and those are his birds.

CHAPTER 1

Fork in the Road

'Like so many birders, and particularly those trying to compile large year lists, the first morning of January usually heralds the start of a maniacal rush towards the pursuit of filling the pages of one's notebook.'

– Adrian M Riley, *Arrivals and Rivals: A Birding Oddity*

Alex: 0 species
Duncton: 0 species

1 January

One good thing about getting married on New Year's Day is that you'll never forget your wedding anniversary. Well, you shouldn't forget your wedding anniversary. Right up there with the Fifth of November, it's one of the easiest dates of the year to remember.

One bad thing about getting married on New Year's Day is that you will rarely celebrate your anniversary without at least a small hangover. This was definitely the case on our first such occasion, on the morning of which Rachel and I woke late in the sitting room of a friend's house in Olympia. Only after a good couple of hours and eggs were we able to contemplate the day, let alone the year, ahead.

During the course of the previous night of the previous year, the thorny issue of resolutions had inevitably reared its ugly head. Several of our friends heroically wielded phrases like 'get fit', 'stop smoking' and 'try to get a girlfriend or a foot on the property ladder or generally be less shambolic' in an attempt to make that ugly head turn away. I, however, felt smugger than usual, with my simple promise to 'go bird-watching'. This year I felt sure I'd keep my pledge longer than any of my friends.

After the excitement and expense of the previous year's wedding and honeymoon in Ireland and Costa Rica, we'd decided to spend the first few days of our second year of marriage a little closer to home. So, finally extracting ourselves from our hosts' comfortable, comforting sofa, we set off on a leisurely drive down to Warwickshire where we'd booked a couple of nights in a modest bed and breakfast in the middle of nowhere. As well as my Christmas jumper and spotless walking boots I'd packed a couple of new books. Along with Adrian Riley's account of his Year, I'd nicked my older brother Mat's old 1983 *Collins Bird Guide*, as recommended by both Duncton and the cover quote ('Easily the most authoritative and best illustrated pocket bird book ever published' *Daily Express*). I also had a hardy, pocket-sized writing pad called *'The Alwych All Weather Notebook'*. The Alwych website claims that their 'flexible cover and durability' make these books ideal for birdwatchers, policemen and milkmen,[8] so I proudly shoved it into my back pocket, determined to fill its light cream pages with my many sightings over the next twelve months.

Unfortunately, our hour-long, New Year's Day journey out of London was as stressful as ever, and not helped by my attempts at spotting my first birds of the year. As we struggled to find our way to the A40, Rachel's patience was tested for the first of what would be many times in 2006 by my proclamations of 'That's a seagull!' which should really have been 'That's definitely the right way to Warwickshire!'

In the driver's seat, I was becoming frustrated with both road and bird signs. It was dawning on me that actually this 'birdwatching lark[9]' might not necessarily be as easy as I'd thought. In the first few hours of the year I'd seen several birds, but not one I could definitively identify. A couple of small brownish ones had flitted past me so quickly they might well have been leaves or Snickers wrappers, one so high up it might have been a plane. And then there was this seagull. It definitely was a seagull. But I knew this wouldn't be enough for Duncton. There are several types of seagull. Which one was this? It was white. Ish. Size-wise it was big. Ish. But then I couldn't really tell how far away it was. It might have been miles away and massive. Or the other way round. And I only had a second or two to glimpse it before taking the wrong exit from that roundabout. Things weren't going well. Even the inevitable pigeon I saw on Shepherd's Bush Green would

---

8 The latter two being particularly manly occupations in my opinion.

9 A not unusual example of a bird's name also being a noun. See also stilt, stint, kite, bunting, hobby and yellowhammer.

be entered in my notebook with a question mark later that afternoon. Again, I knew it was a pigeon. Everyone knows what pigeons look like. But what sort of a pigeon? My bird guide listed no fewer than four varieties, as well as about fourteen doves that all looked pretty much the same. It was probably a feral pigeon, but if I was going to commit him to my book I'd have to be completely sure. Any reasonable doubt and I couldn't send him down.

My first official bird was a magpie. Again, everyone knows what a magpie looks like and unlike the pesky pigeon there were only two types of magpie in my guide (the common magpie and the azure-winged magpie). While I didn't know exactly what colour 'azure' was, I was pretty sure this one wasn't. This was definitely a common magpie. My first bird! Unluckily for me, according to British lore this particular bird seen without its mate foretold 'sorrow'.

Thankfully, many years earlier my mum had taught me how to deal with just this situation. I was able to avert misery by saluting the magpie (swiftly and safely) and asking after his wife. That's what my mum has taught me to do. I suppose that constitutes one very basic parenting lesson. My mum is not, incidentally, a birder. She likes birds and knows a lot more about them than me, but she is definitely *not* a birder. She knows the basic species and occasionally even dons binoculars, but she's unquestionably *not* a birder. I've always assumed she likes the fact that Duncton *is* a birder – that he can tell us all what's what on the bird feeder, in the sky or making that racket – but I know she's happy not to share his obsession. Hers is a more measured interest, a natural curiosity rather than an immovable character trait.

Before Duncton and I embarked upon our Big Year, I think Mum and I were each fairly sure I was more like her than him – I was also definitely *not* a birder – so she could watch our birdwatching with amusement as well as her customary encouragement; I was going to discover exactly how it does feel to spend time with a natural born birder. And although I was at first concerned about devoting myself to Duncton and ignoring Mum for a year (a worry that I'm sure I wouldn't have entertained before the prospect of fatherhood appeared on the horizon), as the months passed I found it increasingly reassuring to talk to her about anything other than birds. If I'm at home, it's not the bird table I gravitate towards, it's *Countdown*, *The Times* crossword or Brewer's *Dictionary of Phrase and Fable*; things that don't necessarily make me 'cool' or 'hard' (no need for the word 'necessarily' there) but that Mum and I have always enjoyed and, I'm sure, always will. I don't really need to spend a year trying to understand her interests, since I share many of them.

I suppose a superstition like saluting magpies comes under that category. And if you quickly have a look in your own reference books you'll see that other ways of forestalling lonesome-magpie-inspired distress include blowing kisses in his direction, asking him the whereabouts of his brother, and keeping your eyes on him until he's out of sight – not a sensible option when driving (a memorable pigeon-obsessed comedian by the name of Phil Zimmerman also suggests carrying round a spare magpie in a plastic bag which one can flourish whenever necessary).

On the occasion of my first bird sighting, my mother's simple method seemed to work. Before long we found our way onto the A40 and sped off towards my birdwatching future.

As we soared through the valley between Junctions 5 and 6 of the M40 – probably my favourite two junctions on any motorway, including the Birmingham Toll Road at night – where Berkshire and Buckinghamshire stretch their legs and you can finally breathe a sigh of relief at having left the city well behind you, my eyes were drawn to what I could only describe as an enormous bloody bird wheeling around above us. I could only describe it thus because at that height, on a clear winter's day, with the sun at its back and to my naked eye, it was little more than a silhouette. A pretty bloody big one at that.

Despite this lack of clarity, and much to my surprise, the words 'That's a red kite!' instantly slipped from my mouth. I was shocked. Rachel told me to concentrate on the road. I glanced up again. It was definitely a red kite. 'Look, you can see its forked tail!' I muttered. Once more Rachel encouraged me to look ahead rather than up. Something terrifying was happening. Within a matter of hours, I was becoming a birdwatcher.

When we finally arrived in the village of Luddington, I reached straight for my bird guide and looked up red kite. There it was – the forked tail. That must have been my bird!

I phoned Duncton.

'Hi.'

'Chip!'

'No.'

'Alex!'

'Yes. Second time lucky. Not bad. Happy New Year.'

'Yes, Happy New Year. We're all well here. Had a very nice evening last night with the Reynolds. Marion was there, and Pam and Adrian – the usual lot, you know. The Phillips came along. John was there too because he's back from Exeter . . .'

I didn't have time for this.

'Duncton – I don't have time for this. I saw a bird.'

'Ah! Well done! Whereabouts? What did it look like? What was it?'

Now I had his undivided attention.

'Yes, well, it was on the M40 . . .'

'Red kite.'

'Quite big . . .'

'Red kite.'

'Forked tail . . .'

'Red kite.'

'I was thinking it might be a . . . Oh yes, a red kite. Well that's that then. Thanks Duncton. Have you had any luck?'

'Well, not really. I think I'm up to about sixteen.'

Later that evening, I contemplated my own grand total of two species. On the one hand, I wasn't doing very well. I couldn't even confidently identify a pigeon. On the other, acting on instinct, I had managed to spot a red kite in a split second from a long way away. And in the moments that followed I'd thought to myself, I can do this! I'm a birdwatcher! This is easy!

As I drifted off to sleep, I realised this probably wasn't a bird-watching miracle. Recollections of other long ago journeys west drifted by, and Duncton's familiar voice shouting, 'Forked tail! Red kite!' The image of that kite had been stamped on my brain a long time ago. Duncton's birdwatching habits had made some impression on me. But how ingrained was it? What would come flooding back when I got out in the field? Was birdwatching like riding a bike? Or was it like flying a plane, training for several years, then sitting a vast array of tests, and even then taking continual examinations to maintain the required level of skill and knowledge?

2 January

My first birdwatching outing of the year was a disaster. Not a full-scale disaster, but a personal debacle at the very least.

Rachel and I like walking, so even without my birdwatching challenge we probably would have gone on a 'good walk' on the second day of our break. The only difference was that this time I was carrying a bird guide and some binoculars. Would this be a case of a 'good walk' ruined?

I went camping and I saw lots and lots and lots and lots and lots and lots and lots and lots and lots of birds and then we went into the tent to go to bed and when we got up we went birdwatching and then it was lunch and it was fish and chips and then it was pudding and after that we all had a rest. ✓

During the first five or six years of my life, apparently, barely a day passed without me staring in wonder at something with wings. This seems odd to me now but I do remember thinking golden eagles were my absolute favourite bird. I'm sure I didn't really know anything about them but they sounded tremendous so I liked them. A little bit like Liverpool and fish and chips.

As we headed through Ilmington towards Meon Hill, the first bird we encountered was in the garden of a typically quaint Warwickshire cottage. Atop a pristine dovecote was a white dove. We admired it for a while, I scribbled its details down, and we carried on walking.

A few doors later we came to a fairly posh allotment, run, it seemed, by various chickens. Lots of various chickens. Some brown, some black, some white – even an auburn one, according to my notes. Again I took down their particulars. This wasn't so bad.

Then, at the foot of the hill itself we found a pond, romantically called The Dingle. 'Wow,' I said, 'look at all those birds.' Rachel wasn't necessarily impressed but we did indeed look at all those birds. 'Ducks and a goose' I wrote in my book, pretty pleased with myself. I even counted them. 'About 200 of the former and just the one of the latter, running,' I scrawled in what I thought was really quite scientific language. I should make it clear that the point of the Big Year was not to count individual birds but different species. There are, after all, an estimated 500 million birds in the UK, about eight for each person. I knew I didn't need to say how many ducks and geese I'd seen, but I was getting into this observation thing.

What I didn't know just yet, however, was that not one of these birds would count on my list. When I took out my bird guide over a spot of lunch at the summit of Meon Hill, I was hugely disappointed and just a bit humiliated not to find any of the birds I'd seen listed in the index.

White doves and chickens are captive birds, the first a pet, the second a meal, both contradicting rule number one of our birdwatching code. Most ducks aren't captive, but I had still got it wrong. I hadn't realised that a duck was a *type* of bird, not a *species*. As we'd gazed down on The Dingle, Rachel had actually said, 'Those are mallards,' to which, regrettably, I'd snapped, 'No, they're ducks.' Again, I am embarrassed now, but I hadn't realised mallards were ducks. 'Mallards' would have counted. 'Ducks' didn't.

Finally, 'a goose'. Again, not specific enough. It was, in fact, a Canada goose, but at this early stage of the year I didn't know such detail was needed. In real life (well, human life – bird life is of course real, but at the same time, it's not *really* real life . . .) I find it almost impossible to tell Canadians from Americans (usually the former are a bit quieter but even that's not always the case). If I'd known I'd had to give the nationality of every bird as well as its species I might never have undertaken the mission so readily.

On my despondent way down the hill I did see my first blackbird of the year, but even that was soon jeopardised by the sighting of another bird that was also black but definitely wasn't a blackbird. I started to doubt that the first one had been a blackbird. Surely, if there's more than one type of bird that is black, calling one a blackbird is unfair on the rest?[10]

And this second 'black bird' was blacker than the blackbird! The blackbird's beak was orange! This one's was, yes, black! Ridiculous. To me this represented bad planning on the part of the original namer of birds. If there were only ten different species, each one a different colour, then it might have been reasonable to name each one by its colour and the word 'bird'. But there aren't. There are loads of different species of bird, and little variation in colour. I hastily sketched this black bird, and got in a bit of a huff. And the two flitting brown things that disappeared as soon as I raised my binoculars didn't help that huff. 'Two brownbirds' I noted indignantly.

Even the moorhen and coot conveniently bobbing along the stream near our hotel did little to perk me up. I was glad to finally work out which was which (mooR hens have Red beaks, cooTs whiTe, that's how I remember it now), but I couldn't help thinking the few birds I had ticked off were the ones seen by us all everyday. I didn't feel as though I'd made any progress at all.

---

10 It's the same with insects. Flies aren't the only ones that fly, but they got the catchiest name. Daddy-long-legs were hard done by. Is that even a real name? How did that get through the naming net? Daddy-long-legs? Or do adults call them something different? Someone please help me.

3 January

I pondered this early rut with our friends Phill and Fiona on our third and final day in Warwickshire. We'd met them for lunch and a wander round their local town, Luddington, and birdwatching proved to be a fecund topic of conversation. I've discovered that no matter how far removed they think they are from the hobby everyone has something to say about birds. Whether you have a twitching uncle, live near a bird reserve or occasionally feed the ducks, birdwatching will at some point or another stick its beak into your life.

Phill is quite a romantic sort of chap. He directs plays and is passionate about the good things in life. Birdwatching, he told us theatrically, was good for the soul. In an excited and quite high voice he told me about a sparrowhawk he'd seen over Christmas. I asked him how he knew it was a spar-rowhawk. He told me it looked a bit like a hawk and a bit like a sparrow.

Fiona, meanwhile, said she thought birdwatching was like trainspotting.

Pausing by the lock behind a church, we watched two swans swim stoically past. I got out my notebook and jotted down 'Two swans on the Luddington Lock'. Maybe Fiona was right (my soul certainly didn't feel markedly improved).

They were, in fact, mute swans. You do occasionally find whooper swans and Bewick's swans in the UK, but if it's got an orangey beak with an odd black nubbin affair on the top, then you're looking at a mute swan. And yes, I know it's noisy – honking or hissing, depending on its mood – but it's definitely a mute swan. Most swans in Britain are mute swans.

Some people are terrified of swans on account of the rumour put about, I guess, by the swans, that they can and will break your arm in an instant. Every schoolboy knows that at the slightest provocation a swan will get you in a headlock, give you a Chinese burn then snap your upper limb in two. Many people also think that swans are beautiful birds. But what people like best is the tremendously anachronistic fact that The Queen Owns Them All! Lucky Queen! And she can eat them too, something she does as often as possible. 'Swan soup, your Majesty?' 'Yum yum, James!' is, I suspect, a typical exchange between the Queen and her head waiter (James) most evenings in the palace.

Two other sightings of note that morning were a canoeist, braving the swan-infested waters, and a colourful duck that wasn't a mallard. The trouble was that they were sitting side by side on the water, so to have a good look at the bird meant staring hard at the now self-conscious novice. In the end, the situation became too much for everyone and we scurried off. I couldn't say what I'd seen. A shelduck maybe? A pochard? Who knows? Not me.

After a brave final lunch of ox's cheek and calf's liver in Lower Quinton (an interesting combination but on balance, I'd rather have had ham and chips), Rachel and I looked, once more, for the M40, this time to head back to London and our normal lives. Picking our way across the countryside, we were to have our final birding incident of the trip.

Rounding the corner on to a straight stretch of road, yearning for a sign to help us on our way, our eyes fell upon a large shape sitting right in our path, a hundred or so yards ahead. 'It's a goose,' I said. 'Canada goose,' Rachel corrected me. We were both wrong.

I slowed down to get a closer look and protect the car. It wasn't a goose. It was more like a griffin. 'What *is* that?' cried Rachel, not taking her eyes off the beast. It was then that I realised Duncton was right about one aspect of birdwatching. To be a proper dad I needed to know these things. One day it wouldn't be Rachel asking me, but a smaller version of Rachel in the seat behind her. And right now, I didn't have a clue.

The mythical bird turned towards us and stared us down. Even he could tell I didn't know what he was. I looked away and groped around behind me for my binoculars and bird guide only to discover I'd amateurishly stowed both away in the boot. Before I could start to manoeuvre over seats and towards the rear of the vehicle, the brutish creature spread his bulky wings, flopped over the hedge, and disappeared.

On our way back to Kensal Green, Rachel and I compared notes. We both agreed it was sort of a mottled brown colour and quite tufty. 'It had big, chunky legs,' said Rachel. 'It looked hairy and arrogant,' I added. Back home I wasn't allowed to look at the bird guide till we'd unpacked and when I finally turned to the 'Birds of Prey' section I saw, to my dismay, that the most likely candidate was a red kite. The image fitted – I hadn't seen the forked tail this time, but it was mottled and brown and the legs were definitely furry. What's more, all the other details fitted perfectly. It was dining on some carrion left on the road, and that road was close to the M40, where kites tend to dwell.

But then again, it might not have been a red kite! It could have been an imperial eagle! They are also big and tufty and fairly hairy and arrogant.

The more I looked at the picture of the imperial eagle, the more convinced I became that this was exactly what I'd seen. It wasn't particularly red, and it was especially imperial. It might even have been a vulture! After all, it was big. As big as a dog, at least. And a big dog too – not a spaniel – one of those large terrifying ones. Or a small horse. A small, terrifying horse.

I closed the book. In my heart of hearts I knew it was almost certainly a red kite. I'd already 'got' a red kite. But there was still a chance that it was, in fact, something spectacular. A genuine birdwatching find. A golden eagle maybe. Or a condor. It was my responsibility, I felt, to learn these things. Not just for me, not just for my hypothetical children, but for the bird-watchers, for the birds, for Britain.

4 January

Kensal Green is an idiosyncratic segment of London, trapped between the rough reputations of Harlesden and Kilburn and the more trendy expensive likes of Queen's Park and Notting Hill. What it is not, is green. Or Kensal for that matter (the word comes from 'King's Holt' meaning 'King's Wood', which disappeared a very long time ago).

Immediately after our wedding Rachel and I moved in to the ground floor flat of one of the many Victorian terraced houses that criss-cross their way from the Grand Union Canal up to Willesden, which meant that although there was no grass to speak of, we did have the tiniest of gardens. 'We need some outdoor space,' we'd said to our estate agent. 'I've got just the thing!' he told us many times, before eventually showing us something that was sort of almost pretty much 'the thing'.

I'm no gardener but I liked looking after our ten-foot-square patch of land. A fig tree whose roots were actually planted in the garden next door had leaned over the wall and reached out towards our kitchen, offering shade and, in the summer, wizened figs that I insisted on testing every other week, to the bitter dismay of my tastebuds. Beneath its broad, flat, hand-like leaves we set some irregular slabs of fossilised sandstone, surrounded by a border of bits and bobs that we'd picked and mixed from the nearby B&Q. And when I say, 'we set', I mean that we paid a man to come and do what I couldn't. As Jez the Gardener wielded spades and cement, I watched enviously from the kitchen, thinking 'I could do that,' but knowing that if I tried I'd only end up calling in a real man to mend my mistakes. Employing an expert now was cutting out the middle man. And that middle man was me.

At the beginning of 2006, I didn't want to be a middle man any more. I wanted to be a man in my own right. For some time I'd been paranoid that I wasn't as masculine as I should be. Lying in bed, waiting for sleep, I'd think, I look pathetic. I'd be in the foetal position, duvet drawn up to my neck, cosy, but not manly. A real man, a proper man, would sleep on his back, probably with his eyes open, on some sort of hard wooden mattress and only a scratchy sack for warmth. Occasionally when I was in the shower, washing myself with some of my wife's opulent Imperial Leather Shower Gel, I'd catch a glimpse of myself in the mirror, gleefully covering my unmanly body with the lather, and again be ashamed at just how feminine I looked. A man of any worth wouldn't behave like this. He'd just wander – maybe even stagger – out into his yard, find a rusting trough and scrub himself with a brick.

After I'd bade a swift[11] goodbye to Jez with as firm a handshake as I could muster, I grew quite obsessed with the process of planting and waiting, then watching as shoots poked their pointy heads out of my ground, before being strangled viciously by invidious weeds. I was particularly proud of a chilli pepper tree that survived this murderous process and eventually produced bright red fruit, almost as tall as the plant itself, which we proudly picked and sliced and added to everything we ate.

The garden was my responsibility. I made regular trips to the hardware shops where I rubbed shoulders with proper men and bought two small sheds (my friends insisted they were just plastic

---

11 A fairly unusual example of a bird's name also being an adjective. See also ruff and puffin.

cupboards, I maintain to this day that they were sheds), tentatively I drilled nails into the walls and hung wire for our climbers to grip. When leaves blew onto the patio I was there to shoo them away with my brand new, definitely masculine, broom.

And then one day some birds discovered the figs. I wasn't there when they first arrived, but returning home after lunch in my favourite café [12] I found several splashes of bird faeces on my beloved sandstone. As the fruits started swelling, so did the number of these lumpy white puddles, and most evenings I'd be out scrubbing the ground with water and determination, while Rachel watched, trying not to giggle.

Eventually my patience snapped and after some brief research on the internet I selected my most embarrassing CDs (The Spice Girls, Genesis, Motörhead) and tied them to the branches. The garden looked slightly less immaculate, my Anglo-Italian neighbours were perplexed, and Rachel thought I was even more ridiculous, but it did the trick. Whether it was the threat of the music or the light bouncing alarmingly off the swinging discs, the birds no longer dared set foot on my patch. Or shit on my patio.

A year later, my priorities had changed, and I now regretted this hasty action. On returning from our trip, I looked out at the garden and knew what I had to do. Wondering how much lasting psychological damage I'd done to any potential avian visitors with this brash light and sound display, I mounted a chair and chopped down the offending CDs. By way of an apology I then got in my car and raced to B&Q, where I ignored the manly aisles of nails and chainsaws and went straight to the hitherto ignored section containing garden ornaments and bird food.

Although embarrassed to be seen in this decidedly fanciful corner, I must admit that my eyes lit up at the display that

---

12 It's an Ethiopian place called The Bole Diner and Café and is still there. Do pop in if you're nearby (and hungry or thirsty).

greeted me. For, to my surprise, five shelves had been entirely devoted to bird accoutrements, a treasure trove of bird delights featuring everything from daisy-shaped food dispensers to what looked like squares of savoury fudge, injected with dead flies. After much deliberation I chose the 'RSPB Bird Care Defender II Seed Feeder', persuaded mostly by the use of roman numerals after the word Defender. It's clearly better than the Defender I, I thought. This is the seed feeder for me!

The Defender II was simply a perspex tube mounted on a metal pole, but its packaging promised so much more: *Feeding the birds is a popular and rewarding activity . . . most likely visitors will be house sparrows, tits, greenfinches, goldfinches and siskins.*

This was exactly what I needed. I was now going to be providing the birds with ammunition with which to sully my patio, but I hadn't seen any of these birds yet, and to be able to add them to my list without leaving my home was an opportunity not to be missed. Siskins in particular caught my attention. I liked the idea of having a cup of tea with a friend and casually pointing out a siskin on my Defender II.

Of course, the siskins wouldn't alight on an empty Defender II. Duncton had thoughtfully provided me with some 'Energy Packed Hi-Energy Seed' as a good luck gift after Christmas. If it was 'Hi-Energy' before and then 'Packed' with yet more 'Energy', this was powerful stuff. The ingredients included kibbled maize, sunflower hearts, peanut granules, millet, canary seed, pinhead oatmeal and hemp seed. While I didn't know what most of these were, I was fairly sure they'd been banned in modern athletics. 'The highest energy value of any seed mix in the range' boasted the label. I'm going to have some pretty hyperactive siskins, I thought to myself.

After an hour-long struggle with a mallet, scaring off a pair of blackbirds in the process, the mighty Defender II was finally mounted and filled to the brim with Hi-Energy Energy food. I also retrieved a house warming present that I had secreted in one of the sheds – an 'Original Tom Chambers Pitch Roofed Seed Feeder for Garden Birds: The Seed Shack'. Two friends had presented me with this miniature food barn, adorned with a hand-painted picture of a generic bird and the message 'Come here Birds! Eat and Tweet at Key and Donk's Hut'. If this didn't make up for my CD torture, nothing would.

5 January

After a young brother and sister died in Turkey from bird flu, the papers were today full of doom-laden predictions about the virus. Headlines like, 'UK Told Don't Panic over Turkey Bird Flu Threat' in the *Daily Mail* did little to ease anxiety.[13]

The article went on to say that the 'deadly' H5N1 strain, as it is always referred to, has 'crept closer towards central Europe' after killing at least seventy people in Southeast Asia. It quoted a reassuring yet evil sounding microbiologist, who said: 'We can all do our bit to keep bird flu away from these shores. If you see a dead bird, stay well away from it and report it immediately to a vet . . . If the virus does mutate, it could go through the human population like a dose of salts.'

Was I doing my bit to keep bird flu away from these shores? Should I tear down my Defender and re-mount my CDs, in a bid to combat the inevitable pandemic? And what is a dose of salts and how fast do they go through a human population?

I made myself a calming cup of tea and tried to think about something else.

---

13 The fact that it wasn't quite clear whether they were talking about Turkey the country or Turkey the bird probably didn't help either. Also, 'bird flu' is an inherently ridiculous name for a deadly disease. First, because it sounds like the female version of 'man flu'. Second, because it also sounds like a childlike sentence: 'Bird flew.' It's a silly name.

6 January

Three days after installing my majestic bird feeders, I hadn't seen a single bird on either. I grew impatient. The only animal I had spotted was a sly black and white cat which seemed to be watching the seeds with as much interest as me. I was fairly sure he was also the one responsible for digging up the bulbs I had planted the previous year. I began to hate that cat, considering it less someone else's pet and more my nemesis.

Worried that perhaps I'd filled the Defender II incorrectly – not leaving a hole for the birds to get at the seeds, for instance – I checked the packaging once more and noticed some fine print: 'It can sometimes take several weeks for the birds to have the confidence to start visiting a feeder.' Several weeks? I didn't have that sort of time. Luckily, I did have a weekend of gigs lined up in Leeds, so I could stop worrying about the shy birds and their feline adversary for a short while at least.

Being a comedian is a lot like being a travelling salesman. You drive around the country, stay in bland hotels and try to show off your wares to people who are sometimes interested, sometimes not. One main difference though, is that we work at night, so hardly see the towns we're visiting. We could be anywhere. So a whole weekend at one venue is, in theory, a refreshing change, a chance to explore a new place, learn about its culture and history and meet a few of its people.

In reality, once you've checked in to your convenient Holiday Inn or Travelodge, it's far too easy to watch a film or go to sleep and I rarely see more of the town than the cinema, the local shopping centre or my room.

I was determined that this trip would be different. On Saturday morning, after the gig the night before, I actually got up for breakfast and then, armed with a map, drove excitedly out to a place named Fairburn Ings for my very first solo trip to a nature reserve. Obviously I hadn't mentioned to the other comedians that I'd be spending the day birdwatching, fending off a tempting invitation to an eat-far-too-much Chinese buffet lunch with a white lie about meeting 'a friend', but inside I was genuinely looking forward to the day ahead.

Strolling tentatively towards what I assumed was the site's reception area, I was heartened to note that entrance to this particular RSPB reserve was entirely free. That, I thought, was a very good thing. If I did end up liking birdwatching, it'd be a cheap hobby. We'll examine football more closely later in the year, but I do have trouble justifying the £40 price tag for a premiership football match that far too often ends in disappointment. And I'm well aware that as a Liverpool fan I'm spoilt compared to supporters of most other clubs, but it does seem a lot of money to spend watching people (most of whom are, terrifyingly, now younger than me) half-heartedly kicking a ball about.

Having said that, in May 2005 I paid more than £800 to watch a single football match and didn't regret a penny. Through a combination of luck, fate and good life choices, my new brother- and father-in-law were also Liverpool fans, proper Liverpool fans with Liverpool season tickets. After Liverpool had thrashed Chelsea 1–0 over two legs in the semi-final of the European Champions League, my father-in-law Terry said I could take his ticket for the final in Istanbul in an unrivalled act of generosity. On 25 May 2005 the mighty Reds came back from 3–0 down at half time to beat the Italian giants AC Milan on penalties in what is widely considered to be one of the best football games of all time and (slightly less widely) the most important event in the history of the world.

The journey back home from that game was nightmarish. We had to walk over fields of broken glass to the coach park. We had to try to find 'our coach' in a coach park full of a thousand identical coaches. We were herded like cattle into a boiling hanger at the airport where all flights had been cancelled. We had to scrummage our way onto any available plane without really knowing where it might be heading.

We arrived back hours late. I missed my train. I got on another train. I was fined a further £100 for being on a slightly later train than my ticket suggested. I didn't sleep for thirty-six hours. But throughout this ordeal I was as happy as I'd ever been in my life. Everyone was that happy. We hadn't been allowed to drink alcohol in the stadium or been able to afford it at the airport, but no one stopped singing, joking and laughing during that night, the following day, indeed for the next weeks, months and years. Fans still chant nostalgically about that night. I can still make myself smile and send shivers down my spine today by recalling Gerrard's header, Smicer's shot, Alonso's penalty and Dudek's saves. That's priceless.

It was also a one-off. I'm pretty sure I won't get to witness anything as miraculous on a football pitch ever again. But could birdwatching provide comparable highs? Can a birdwatching season ever be that exciting? Has Duncton had an ornithological Istanbul?

Watching football for free, on the other hand, is always an excellent and rewarding thing to do. Whether spent supporting your local Sunday league team or, one day, your son's school eleven, that's ninety minutes entirely unwasted. Could this park in Leeds be the birdwatching equivalent?

In the area between car park and birds I found a whiteboard full of the names of the birds seen at the reserve so far in 2006; countless exotic-sounding species, nearly all of which I'd never heard of. I turned away, not wanting to get too scared too early. Stepping out on to a makeshift walkway, I noticed for the first time that it was really quite cold. A grey, wet winter's day, and I was wearing the same shoes and trousers I'd be performing in later that night. I still had a lot to learn.

Nevertheless, without anything resembling a plan, I trudged off in the vague direction of a lake and found myself surrounded by bushes filled with birdsong. I began to understand why it was called a bird reserve. This was a land reserved for birds. No dastardly moggies here. Countless birds flitted and twittered above and in front of me. Unfortunately, I didn't have a clue what any of them were and was too cold and wet to get out my bird guide. I couldn't work out if I was having fun yet. Seeing a sign for the 'Bob Dickens Hide' ahead of me, I put my head down, ignored the UFOs and marched towards shelter.

Some of you may not know what a hide is (I find it hard to know what's common knowledge and what's knowledge you presume everyone has because your dad is a birder), but a hide is a wooden hut where birdwatchers hide.[14] Birdwatching is essentially an enormous game of hide and seek, in which you do the hiding *and* the seeking and the birds have no idea they're involved in a game. I marched towards this particular one with the aim of getting warm and taking stock.

Before I could achieve either, I was joined by four jarringly cheerful Yorkshiremen who bustled noisily onto the uncomfortable stools. At first they ignored me and I ignored them, content instead to gaze out through the slit-like windows at a misty pond. I was embarrassed by my appearance – yellow shoes, jeans, red shirt, my usual stage outfit – compared to their more practical clothes. They had hats! I didn't have a hat. They also had homemade sandwiches wrapped in kitchen foil while I had *pains au chocolat* stolen from the hotel and bound in serviettes. I didn't dare reveal them. I pretended to be utterly absorbed by the view.

Inevitably, though, I found myself far more drawn to their convivial middle-aged chat rather than the birds that may or

---

14 I did meet one non-birder during the year who thought the birds were inside the hut and the birdwatchers were outside looking in through the windows at them. This would make the whole thing a lot easier. It would also be a zoo.

may not have been outside. These men were, essentially, dads. These were the men I wanted to be. At ease in each other's company, they talked, at times competitive, at others kind, often funny and always, surprisingly, interesting.

They discussed their respective New Year's Eve experiences. One announced that he'd gone to bed, grumpy, at 8.30 p.m., only to be woken at midnight by his wife and mother-in-law doing the hokey-cokey in the living room. The others mainly complained about the garish Christmas lights on neighbours' houses. When one of them grumbled that no one knew the words to 'Auld Lang Syne' any more I saw my chance to join in the conversation.

'I'm afraid I don't either,' I said, with what I hoped was an apologetic smile. 'I don't even know what Auld Lang Syne means . . .'

More than happy to share their wisdom, they took it upon themselves to educate me. They argued about the words to the song, each insisting they were right. I told them about my Big Year. Through a combination of showing off and instruction (more fatherly traits) they competed to help me identify as many birds as they could.

'That's a goldeneye,' said one and I dutifully scribbled it down.

'That's a male,' chimed in another. 'You can tell by its black and white chest.'

'And that's a wigeon, over there. Sounds like a pigeon but looks like a painted duck,' said the third. 'And there are some long-tailed tits on the tree to your right. Very nice.'

'Ruddy duck!' shouted the last. I thought at first that he was just sick of the sight of ducks, but that too was another first species for my list.

The highlight of the morning was one of those minuscule goldcrests, the Kylie of the bird world, a bright yellow nugget of petite fun. Unfortunately the loudest of the Yorkshiremen missed it because he was trying to peel an orange all in one go.

He took it well though, just grunting the word 'gutted', before wolfing down his fruit in one go too.

By lunchtime I'd had my fill. I'd enjoyed my first lesson but was now freezing cold and soaking wet. On the way back to my car I passed the first person under the age of fifty I'd seen all day. A boy aged eleven or twelve, with his dad. He too looked damp and just a little bit miserable.

8 January

Despite the four-hour drive back from Leeds on the Saturday night I woke early on the Sunday morning. At first I couldn't work out why I was so excited. I was pleased to be back home with my wife, but this was a different sort of excitement. I was looking forward to something . . . a Liverpool game? No, they'd flukily scraped past Luton 5–3 in the FA Cup the day before. Sleeping in? No, I'd already ruined that for both of us. Birds? Yes! The bird feeders! I was genuinely excited about the bird feeders! Leaping out of bed, I fixed myself a cup of tea, took up my position on the sofa and waited.

Half an hour later a solitary robin dropped silently onto the Defender II for his Sunday breakfast. I blinked, not quite believing what I was seeing; to most people an entirely unimpressive occurrence, to me a major breakthrough in my adult life. A robin in my garden, enticed by my own hand! A brave robin! The bravest of birds. He took his time, plucked three seeds (kibble, I think), then left. And that was the end of the morning rush.

In the triumphant afterglow left by my red-breasted visitor, I decided that garden watching was a very sensible introduction to the hobby. I'd started far too quickly. I'd foolishly tried to run before I could walk. I might easily have hurt myself. Watching birds in your garden is much warmer than leaving the house. You can have the TV on and glance up occasionally when you notice movement out of the corner of your eye. You don't have to trudge around a lake in the rain. And if you do see something, it's nice and easy to reach for your bird guide and see what it is. To anyone contemplating giving birdwatching a go – and I do, of course, heartily recommend it – start by looking in your garden. If you don't have a garden, start by looking out of your window. If you don't have a window, move to somewhere with a window. Most places have windows nowadays.

Ten days into my Big Year I had seen fourteen species. Duncton was on forty, including, he told me, bramblings. Bramblings? This sounded like a bush, not a bird. He was disappointed not to have got a great spotted woodpecker or a golden plover[15] yet. But what he was most thrilled by so far was a rat that had climbed up on to his bird table.

He's like that, Duncton, interested in anything to do with nature, no matter how dull or repulsive it might seem to other, normal people. Since retiring he's been volunteering for the RSPB, helping out at different sites with various projects at least once a week, rebuilding fences, protecting trees, lighting fires. Manly things. Recently he's spent a lot of his time at Pulborough Brooks on the Sussex coast, where the warden set him and his fellow volunteers their toughest challenge yet: to find and count the eggs of the brown hairstreak butterfly. The eggs, they were told, look like tiny white pinheads and are usually found on the underside of blackthorn leaves. So, with three other similarly aged men, Duncton spent several hours studiously tramping round the large reserve in search of miniscule dots on the wrong side of leaves in an extreme version of the traditional Easter egg hunt. The first day they were overjoyed to find thirty-nine of the tiny ova, a record for the reserve. The next day, after a four-hour search, they discov-

---

15 'I haven't even got a golden plover,' he'd said. I thought he meant some sort of yellow jumper. I liked the idea of Duncton birdwatching in a bright gold pullover.

ered just two. So to summarise, Duncton – a man who has now retired from work and could spend all day doing whatever he fancies – spent a whole morning searching for two tiny eggs.

'That's fine,' said Duncton with Zen-like calm. 'It's just as useful to not find something. We now know a lot more about the butterflies.' Adrian Riley would be proud. I was confused. I hoped by the end of the year to get my head round birdwatching but surely insectwatching would always be utterly unfathomable. There are ten times more butterflies and moths than birds in the world, all of which are ten times smaller than their more feathery friends.[16] I have told my mum to beware of any more butterfly-related activities on Duncton's part.

I spent most of the rest of the week at my post, the sofa, and while I do advocate garden watching, I should add that it's probably best suited to those with a fair amount of free time. My rewards were sporadic but cherished, like a couple of wickets on a day's test cricket:

- At 2 p.m. on the Tuesday my robin returned. It was, I decided, my current favourite bird, even if it wasn't yet displaying any signs of increased energy levels.

- Just after noon the following day, something blue landed on the seed shack, only to flit away again as soon as its feet touched down. Clearly this was not as brave a bird as the fearless robin, but still an exhilarating sight. I didn't take my eyes off the feeder for the next half an hour. Nothing. I contemplated setting up a webcam.

- At 3 p.m. on Thursday I noticed *my* robin on next door's bird feeder, which looked to my jealous eyes like a superior model even to my Defender II – surely the Defender III wasn't yet on the streets? I became less trustful of my fickle robin.

---

16 The second half of that statement is a guess.

That evening I noticed Rachel had bought what appeared to be bird food for our breakfast. I was tempted to switch it for the hi-energy energetic energy food.

14 January

Birdwatching in the privacy of one's own home was one thing, openly watching birds with my friends quite another. Up in Yorkshire, I was about 200 miles away from most people I know, but even then it did cross my mind that if I happened to bump into a friend or acquaintance, I'd have rather a lot of explaining to do. I planned to come out at least to my close friends during the spring. But that very weekend, fate conspired to force my hand.

I got married when I was twenty-six years old, an age that seemed young to me but old to most of Duncton's generation. I was the first of my group of friends to wed, but was soon joined by others, including Mark, a fellow comedian, whose wedding was to take place in February, with the stag do a month before.

Most of my friends, inevitably perhaps, are quite like me. Very few of them have much manliness about them. We couldn't even be described as laddish. So instead of a drunken crawl around Bristol, Brighton or Barcelona, twelve of us drove Mark out to a village called Michaelchurch Escley in Herefordshire for a weekend in a rustic cottage. As well as curry and a stew, someone had the presence of mind to cook sprouts and broccoli. It was that sort of stag. Yes, we drank a lot and got up to some mischief – Phill (my friend from Luddington) played table tennis outside wearing only boxer shorts, Lloyd went to bed at dawn, Key threw a trashy romantic novel on the fire – but we didn't get involved in fights with bigger men or have anything to do with naughty women like strippers or prostitutes or hens.

The first item on our sensible stag agenda was a walk up

Skirrid Fawr, a magnificent spur of a hill from whose banks stretch England to the east and Wales to the west. The view was stunning. There must be birds here! I thought. And so, during the silly slippery ascent, I decided I had to tell the group that I was experimenting with birdwatching. I'd brought my binoculars along *just in case* and chose that moment to brandish them, with a flourish, from within my coat.

My admission instantly drove a wedge within the group. Some were fine with it, others even pleased for me, but more than half made their disapproval wholly manifest. Battle lines were drawn up as cries of 'Who brings binoculars on a stag?', 'You're boring me to death' and 'Thanks for taking over the stag weekend and making it all about birds' echoed around the mountain. But just as I'd started defending my decision to bring binoculars rather than drugs or pornography along, Lloyd, one of my allies, spotted a bird of prey hovering just over the Welsh side of the border. Suddenly, my binoculars became a prized possession, as at least three other people showed interest in the bird.

'What is it?' demanded Lloyd.

'I'm not sure,' I replied, confidently. Whatever it was, it was floating impressively a matter of yards away from the group. We all agreed it was blue-ish.

'I think it looks like a woodpigeon,' said the stag.

'No, you mean it looks like a pigeon would,' said Tim. I ignored his joke.

'It's definitely not a woodpigeon,' I grumbled. 'It's some sort of bird of prey.'

'It could be a buzzard,' suggested Owen quietly.

'It's a merlin,'[17] said Tom.

Before settling down to quite a complicated card game that evening, Tom and I sat on one of the cottage's many beds and

---

17 A highly unusual example of a bird's name also being a wizard.

chatted about birds and dads. Tom's childhood had been similarly bird themed ('I once made a cardboard model of a merlin,' he confessed) and it turned out his dad, Jamie (I found it difficult to accept 'Jamie' as a dad's name but did my best to concentrate on the conversation anyway), is also a keen birder. Both glad to have found a kindred spirit (and by now, really quite drunk) we thumbed breathlessly through my bird guide and pored over the picture of a merlin.

'Oh yes, it was definitely a merlin,' I said.

'It's just like my cardboard model,' agreed Tom.

The following morning, hungover and giddy, I sat at the cottage's bucolic kitchen table with Owen and admired the sunrise. Rummaging round the drawers for coffee, we came across all sorts of birding paraphernalia – two pairs of well-worn binoculars, numerous bird guides, a tattered old copy of *A Fieldguide to Wildlife* and Sebastian Faulks' *Birdsong* (not ornithology but to us a sign). Owen even managed to find an old bird feeder (an RSPB Classic Seed Feeder) in a cupboard under the stairs, which he hung up (with aplomb) just outside the window above the sink.

Ten minutes later, as Radio 4 reported a suspected case of human bird flu in Belgium, three great tits gratefully tucked in and we had plenty of time to notice their blackish heads and stocky bodies. I couldn't believe it. In London I'd had to wait a week for even a hint of a robin. As often happens when I'm out of the city (and hungover) I decided that the countryside was definitely the place to live – even the birds are friendlier! (Although this isn't actually the case – there are more birds in the countryside, certainly, but there are also more trees and worms so they don't *need* our bird feeders quite so much. City birds are probably more trusting of people on the whole. Could this be a neat analogy for human city-versus-country dwelling? Maybe, but only if it doesn't offend either party too much.)

Just before the others surfaced, a similarly sized bird with a rounder beak and stripey sides joined the great tits. We found its picture in the bird guide. It was a chaffinch. At the euphoric stage of our morning after, we toasted this beautiful little bird with the first beer of the day. I was tempted to call Duncton and share the sight of what, to me, was the most exotic bird in the world but I refrained, remembering that I was trying to grow up. Having a doctor for a dad means it's all too easy to phone home whenever you've got a sore throat, dodgy tummy or bizarrely swollen ears. Duncton will always be ready with some practical advice – gargle aspirin, drink water, don't worry about it – but at some point I had to start looking after myself. I can't phone Duncton every time I see a chaffinch or feel a bit odd. If I do ever become a dad, I'll be the one taking those phone calls. I don't want to be the middle man again.

16 January

Empowered by the stag successes, I embarked on my next trip with a much more flagrant approach to birdwatching.

You can do stand-up comedy in almost every country in the world nowadays, with successful gigs running in Hong Kong, Amsterdam, Singapore and even Iraq. The often modest fees are made up for by the chance to see the world for free. My first such trip of the year was to the French Alps for three après-ski shows and a couple of days skiing, but I was more excited by the prospect of seeing foreign birds than sliding down a mountain on a pair of long wooden shoes. I'd flicked through my bird guide to see what I might find on the snowy slopes and was looking forward to ticking off some Alpine choughs, a snow goose, an eskimo curlew, a couple of Arctic redpolls, a South Polar skua and, with a bit of luck, a Siberian white crane.

Unfortunately, despite my studious research, the week's *oiseaux*-watching began disappointingly with magpies (and, bizarrely, llamas), the only thing on offer on the way from Geneva to the mountains. Something enormous flew past as we rounded Lake Annecy but once again my ignorance let me down. 'Bird of prey, brown, fan tail, low flight,' I wrote. 'Probably a buzzard.' But the descriptions in the books don't help that much if all you saw was a blur. That's a gap in the market, blurry identification pictures in bird guides, they'd be a lot more useful than conveniently posed models.

Jon and Jason, my fellow comedic travellers, took the news of my birdwatching status in their stride. We discussed the embarrassment value of the hobby and agreed that if I was reading my bird guide on a train I should probably hide it in a *Harry Potter* book jacket to avoid humiliation. Jon came up with the term Hornithology, to my amusement (and envy – how could I not have thought of such an obvious and cheesy pun?). Jason told me about a dye factory in Salford where pigeons go in to nest and emerge in a rainbow of different colours. As I said, everyone's got a bird story.

When we arrived at our chalet I was delighted to find a couple of well-stocked bird feeders in the garden (a fairly straightforward Mayfield Rivendale Premium Oriental Lantern Peanut Feeder), covered with hungry great tits and blackbirds. Trying to sound knowledgeable, I asked the two ladies who owned the place what birds they'd seen recently. They couldn't say for sure.

'I'm afraid I don't know much about birds,' said one. 'We went on a birdwatching trip to some Scottish island once, but we mainly got drunk on Pimms in a hide.'

As we chatted, though, a more unusual bird appeared on one of the feeders, a small, light grey, friendly looking thing. 'That's a nuthatcher!' pronounced the hitherto drunken birdwatching hostess. 'They're new!'

'Oh, a nuthatch,'[18] I corrected, trying but failing not to sound patronising. By now though, the girls were making a lot of jokes about birds and tits and breasts so I did my best to focus on bird number twenty-four of the year.

I'm not great with jokes about sex, especially when it's just me and two women. To be honest, I'm not that good at talking to girls about anything, but discussions involving innuendo make me particularly uncomfortable. Later in the year, I found myself in a particularly awkward situation when asked to identify two birds on a bird feeder owned by the mother of a friend. The birds in question were great tits but I couldn't bring myself to say, 'Those are great tits,' or 'You've got a pair of great tits,' or even just, 'Great tits.' I contemplated scribbling it down on a piece of paper, but decided that handing someone's mum a note with 'great tits' scrawled on it is probably even worse than saying it. In the end I panicked and said, 'I think they're sea eagles ... Yes, you're right, they are small; they're probably juveniles.'[19]

That one nuthatch was the birding highlight of the trip. Out on the slopes I found nothing. What's worse, the shame I thought I'd recovered from returned as I shared chairlifts with some of the coolest people in the world, who stared pointedly at my binoculars and bird guide as if they'd never seen anything so absurd. Unfortunately, the complete lack of any sort of bird on the mountains seemed to justify their prejudice. I felt ridiculous.

---

18 Named not, as I'd hoped, because it hatches out of nuts but because it eats them. What it's particularly good at, however, is climbing head first and vertically down a tree trunk, an excellent talent. A better name would be spidermanbird.

19 Most proper birders have got used to the whole 'tit' business. In fact, birding slang for the 'great' variety is 'Dolly Partons', which I think is a nice way of dealing with the problem.

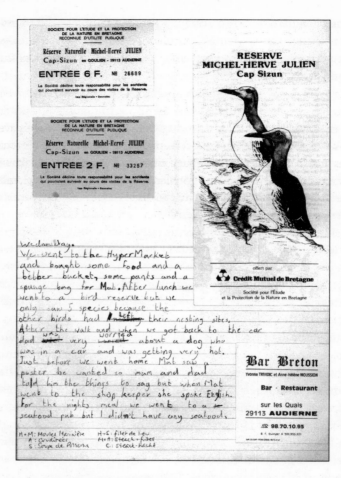

A marginally more successful French birdwatching trip to Brittany, August 1989, as described by Chip.

21 January

For the rest of the month I cowered in Kensal Green. Spending a bizarre amount of my time observing my tiny quadrant of outdoors,

I tried to ignore the steadily rising layer of excrement lying on my beloved tiles and started to appreciate the birds themselves. On one occasion I became engrossed by a spindly worm wriggling its way across the patio. After about ten minutes it had made remarkable progress, nearing the halfway mark. Then, as it took a deserved rest, I noticed a blackbird paying similar attention from a perch on the wall just behind the worm's field of vision. (Do they have eyes? They must have eyes.) A few minutes later, when the flowerbed was just coming into view (they must have eyes) the blackbird nonchalantly flew down and gobbled it up. My reaction? I cheered. Was that right? I don't know, but I realised then that I was starting to enjoy the company of my birds.

Bird lunch in the garden was usually from 1 p.m. to 1.30 p.m., with my robin always the first to arrive, eventually joined by the blackbird and its partner. The female blackbird, by the way, is brown. Again, it seems a silly name for a species only half of whom are black. They may as well be called blackorbrownbirds.

Despite the fact that I'd still not seen a siskin, I enjoyed the return of those same birds each day and started to feel quite protective of my feathery little band. If the robin didn't arrive I'd worry. Sometimes Nemesis Cat would sit smugly on the wall, and we'd have a lazy stand-off, each waiting for the other to leave before the hoped-for birds arrived. From time to time a hefty woodpigeon would saunter along and peck at both the seeds and the blackbirds. Larger than London's famous feral pigeons, fuller breasted and with a distinguished white patch on his neck, he would strut about like Henry VIII before clambering up the wall and bearing down on his next snack. I was pretty sure he was the originator of most of the mess on the floor, but I didn't mind.

One lunchtime two tiny blue and yellow birds hopped onto the Defender II and buzzed around the garden like bees. 'Hi-energy blue tits!' I murmured proudly from behind my binoculars before they were chased away by the robin.

25 January

Two big days marked the end of the month. The first was my TKDay. If you're unfamiliar with this apparently modern concept, this was my ten-thousandth day on earth. I was about twenty-seven-and-a-third years old, but *exactly* ten thousand days. I had reached the five-figure mark and that was it. I would now be five figures for ever. My first, tenth, hundredth, thousandth and now ten-thousandth day landmarks were all behind me.

Traditionally, of course, you're considered an adult at the age of twenty-one (when you can become an MP, fly a helicopter and supervise a learner driver), eighteen (when you can donate blood, change your name and take your top off for a tabloid) or even sixteen (when you can sell scrap metal), but I know I didn't feel anything like a grown-up on each of these birthdays. Yes, in the eyes of the law I could do anything I wanted when I was twenty-one, but in practice I couldn't. On your TKDay, however, you should be able to do anything. At that age you should know how to change a tyre, a fuse or a mortgage. You should be able to name the birds in your garden. And you shouldn't be terrified at what wasn't even an imminent prospect of fatherhood.

I celebrated this landmark in a pub called The Paradise By Way of Kensal Green with a few friends. Having been steeped in birds for the last four weeks, I could talk about little else. I told anyone who cared to listen that there were about 10,000[20] species

---

20 That figure comes from the veteran biologist Edward Wilson. It does sound conveniently round but give or take some hotly debated sub-species, a few that have recently become extinct and others that are yet to be discovered, it seems to be accepted as about the right number. Whatever the exact total, considering you would then have to times it by two, it would be a lot of birds to fit on one Ark.

of birds in the world, one for every day I'd been alive. Imagine seeing a different species of bird every day of your life!

A lady called Phoebe Snetsinger had just such a thought. According to the *Guinness Book of Records* she saw more species than anyone else in the world.[21] This is remarkable partly because she was a woman and birdwatching is a generally male hobby (which, since I can't really talk to women who aren't my wife, comes as a massive relief) while bird *chasing* in particular, especially on this scale, seems to be exclusively a masculine urge. Not one of the other top twenty all-time world bird listers are female.

But what's even more amazing is that Phoebe Snetsinger didn't start seriously birdwatching until 1981, when she was diagnosed with a terminal melanoma at the age of fifty. Given eighteen months to live, she resolved to spend her life doing something she loved – following birds. Staving off the disease by birding with remarkable determination and focus (she even missed her daughter's wedding), she spent the next twenty years hurtling round the world, surviving shipwrecks and earthquakes as well as the cancer. She died in 1999 in a mini-bus crash in Madagascar, after becoming one of just a handful of people to have ever seen a red-shouldered vanga, a species which had only been discovered two years earlier. In total, Snetsinger saw more than 8,500 species of birds. No one has yet seen all 10,000.

---

21 Since my Big Year, Phoebe Snetsinger's record has been broken by two men, one of whom has a brilliant name: Tom Gullick and Jon Hornbuckle. But her story is so good I'm going to leave it in. So there.

I used to know all the birds

> This is a super piece of work, Alex. GREAT!

> I brought in my bird book and it had kestrels and pheasants and lots of other birds are in there and I have seen all of the birds and there was some eagles and there was some golden eagles and they are the king of the birds and they glyd and some times they hover and coloured doves and then it was lunchtime we had fish and chips and then it was pudding and after that we went birdwatching and then I went to bed and then I woke up and I was going to a football match and it was man utd v Liverpool and man utd won 10-3 and I supported Man Utd and when we got home it was lunchtime sausages baked beans and then we went birdwatching and when we got home we went to bed

* At the age of five and three quarters I think I would have described myself as a birdwatcher.

* This should really be collared doves, but coloured is more socially acceptable.

* As I've explained, I am now a Liverpool supporter. A slightly ashamed glory-hunting Liverpool supporter from the south coast (I do support Sussex in the cricket – does that help?), but a passionate Liverpool supporter all the same. I blame the facts that my dad was a Spurs fan, we lived exactly halfway between Portsmouth and Brighton and Liverpool were really really good when I was getting into football. This elegant piece of prose was read out by my Man Utd-supporting brother at my wedding and shall always be a source of embarrassment for me.

28 January

I hadn't until now been aware of an event called the Big Garden Birdwatch. For one day, each January, the RSPB urge people all over the country to spend an hour spotting and counting the different birds in their garden in a bid to harness the collective power of the nation's bird lovers. It's an excellent way to gather data that would otherwise be impossible to collect. And now that birds were on my radar, the Big Garden Birdwatch 2006 seemed to be everywhere: Radio 4, *The Times*, BBC Breakfast – OK, fairly middle class, respectable media, but all banging on about birds.

Choosing what I thought was the most popular time of day for birds to visit my garden, I sat down at 12.30 p.m., feeling nervous. I'd already seen my robin and the blue tits earlier that morning and was afraid they wouldn't return. What if I saw nothing during my allotted hour? Trying to be positive, I also turned on the BBC's live FA Cup 4th round match featuring Newcastle (the magpies) versus Cheltenham (whose central midfielder was called David Bird). Here's how the hour panned out:

- 12.36 p.m.: Ray Stubbs makes a bird joke. David Bird's wife is due to give birth today. 'If she does, she should call it Robin!' he says, and laughs. I don't completely understand why. He may have been referring to the fact that it's still winter and the player's surname is 'Bird' or he could be implying that Cheltenham would be 'robbing' Newcastle if they win. Either way, I don't think it quite works.

- 12.52 p.m.: 0–0 in the football. My fat robin arrives. Phew.

- 12.57 p.m.: Two starlings land on next door's fancy bird feeder. Frustrating.

- 1.11 p.m.: Still no goals and no more birds. Are the two star-lings the other side of the wall scaring off the other birds? They're certainly not helping.

- 1.12 p.m.: A magpie! Next door, but tantalisingly close to my side of the wall.

- 1.16 p.m.: My male blackbird arrives. The fat robin joins him. I'm now drawing with the Anglo-Italians next door.

- 1.17 p.m.: Another, thinner, robin arrives. Not another species but a welcome arrival.

There then followed a flurry of activity.

- 1.24 p.m.: Chopra scores for Newcastle in the forty-first minute of the game.

- 1.25 p.m.: Scott Parker makes it 2–0 just as the female black-bird and a blue tit arrive.

- 1.30 p.m.: They think it's all over. It is for me. It is for Cheltenham too. The score remains 2–0. Newcastle will go on to lose in the quarter-final against Chelsea while Liverpool will batter Birmingham 7–0 away.

The hour flew past. I surprised myself by watching the birds more than the football, the highlight being my fat robin messily eating out of the Defender II while the blackbird couple ate the spilt seeds from the ground. This, I felt, was my first real test and I'd passed. I had no trouble recognising any of the (three) species that came my way. I did wish there'd been a few more, but it felt good to be part of a birdwatching movement. About 500,000 people took part, spotting over six million birds in total. (This was, according to the RSPB website, 'a mind-boggling response' – how's your mind now you know those figures? Boggled? They're right then.) I hadn't seen a carrion crow, a chaffinch, a coal tit, a collared dove, a dunnock, a feral pigeon, a goldfinch, a great tit, a greenfinch, a house sparrow, a jackdaw, a long-tailed tit, a rook, a woodpigeon or a wren, all birds that made it onto the RSPB's subsequent 'most common' list. But, as Duncton says, seeing no birds is just as useful for the data. After all, he'd spent four hours searching for two tiny eggs.

31 January

My Granny phones her son Duncton every Sunday evening. When the phone rings around 7 p.m., he'll say, 'That'll be Granny.' He then spends the next thirty minutes gossiping away about the week's events in Sussex, Kent (where she and he used to live) and Norfolk (where she lives now). The top three topics are family, friends and politics, although since Tony Blair stepped down she doesn't get quite as worked up as she used to about the latter.

I'm fairly sure such a timetabled phone call is not unusual, but I've often wondered how or when it was first implemented. Did something happen to make Duncton decide an allotted time was necessary? Maybe it was Granny who became too busy for unscheduled calls? I suppose things are different now with mobile phones and emails, but I can't quite imagine sitting my own parents down and informing them that from now on I'll be ringing them on Thursdays afternoons at the end of *Countdown*. I might just try it one day soon – it'd be fun to see how they react.

During our Big Year, I decided a monthly bird update, rather than a weekly call, would be sufficient. Fifty-two phone calls about birds seemed ridiculous, especially if they were all to be as disheartening as the first.

I was proud of my first month's haul of twenty-eight species. Before the year began I'd tried to name as many birds as I could off the top of my head (species, not types – so barn owl, not owl) and had only managed fifteen before becoming desperate and saying Thunderbird. With winter still very much upon us, I'd already seen almost twice as many species as I previously knew existed. I was even getting quite good at telling some of these species apart. I could differentiate the two main tits with ease, was pretty confident on robins and had a vague acquaintance with a number of ducks.

Duncton, however, was already on eighty-five. Eighty-five species in one month! And he hadn't even left Sussex. I'd driven 3,145 miles around the UK and flown to the French Alps. He'd barely left his front room.

To put this in a broader context, Adrian Riley, the birdwatcher whose record I was trying to emulate, ended his first month with the words: 'My score for the month was a poor 164. I *was* "the weakest link".'

I was way behind Duncton, who only had about half the score of a proper competitive birdwatcher. And that proper competitive birdwatcher was disappointed with what I thought was an incredible tally. But, as he explains, '. . . for the first time, I was aware that I was playing with the big, bad boys. No more hiding behind the bike sheds with a crafty fag; no more lunchtime beers; it was "game on".'

The 'big, bad boy' mentioned here is a certain Lee G R Evans, perhaps the most famous twitcher this country has ever produced, with whom Adrian had once been friends, and against whom he was now competing.

Like nearly all non-birders, I'd never heard of Lee G R Evans[22] before reading Adrian Riley's book, but a quick bit of research showed that his reputation stretches far and wide within the birding community. Duncton may be a birder, but Lee G R Evans *is* birds. Born in Luton, he got hooked on birds after seeing a green woodpecker at the age of eight. They now provide his livelihood, through books published and birdwatching tours. His fascination with them is absolute, and in the course of his single-minded and colourful birdwatching career he's been at the heart of so many adventures and scrapes that he has become almost legendary. While his dogged tactics are sometimes questioned, his dedication is not. Looking at his own, very popular website, I saw that Lee found 221 species in the first month of 2001. He was also the UK record holder for year listing (spotting as many species as possible in twelve months, just as Duncton and I were trying to do), achieving 386 species during 1996. He was, indeed, a 'big, bad boy'.

As I listed my sightings during our first phone call, Duncton told me that merlins don't hover and kestrels do also have a blue, silvery sheen. I'd seen a kestrel on the stag, not a merlin. This was

---

22 I'd heard of Lee Evans, the hugely popular physical comedian and actor, but not Lee G R Evans. They're definitely different people.

disappointing news. And to make matters worse, Duncton had seen a merlin in the last week of January. He didn't break this news with any hint of malice. But as he described his various successes ('My rarest was probably the cattle egret. And I've had three sightings of hen harriers.') and future plans ('I'm off to Minsmere with Peter[23] tomorrow so I should tick a few more off there.'), I started to wonder if all I'd done was to fan the embers of his birding desire, rather than absorb any of his passion myself. Up till now he'd seemed happy to trundle along, noticing whatever birds came his way whenever that happened. Now, he had a focus. He was making lists. Perhaps these urges were always there, bubbling beneath the surface, and I'd simply turned on the tap. Either way, I had another eleven months of potential humiliation ahead of me.

As we wound up our conversation, Duncton noted the despondency in my voice. I told him I worried his lead was already insurmountable. 'No, no, no,' he chuckled. 'It's like the tortoise and the hare. You'll be fine!'

For a brief second, I was consoled. That's right, I thought, I'm the tortoise – and the tortoise always wins. But the more I thought about it, the less that sentence rang true.

Surely on most occasions the tortoise doesn't get anywhere near winning? Surely in more than ninety-nine per cent of races between hares and tortoises the lithe, long-legged mammal thrashes the lugubrious, long-living reptile? Surely the only reason that particular tortoise's victory is still celebrated today is because it was so unusual? Could it ever happen again?

I would certainly need a lot of luck, possibly even a birdwatching miracle. But at least, if it did happen, it'd be a memorable, if scarcely believable tale.

---

23 Another ex-GP and recently converted birder. 'It's odd how some people come to the hobby later on,' Duncton once told me. 'I'd always thought people like me suffered from our affliction from a very early age, but apparently you can catch it late too . . .'

CHAPTER 2

Home and Away

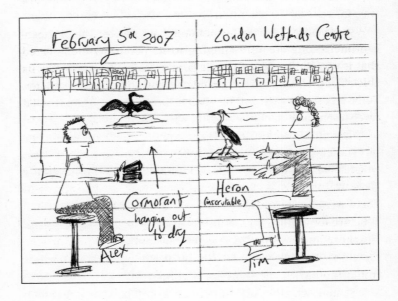

February 5th 2007   London Wetlands Centre

Cormorant hanging out to dry

Alex

Heron (inscrutable)

Tim

'My honesty, integrity, ability and physical and mental stamina were all up for public and self-examination, and I could simply not afford to fail in any department. It was only February, and already there was a dawning of this realisation.'

– Adrian M Riley

Alex: 27 species
Duncton: 85 species

3 February

At exactly midday on 3 February, a dashing great tit dared set foot in my garden for the first time. While not necessarily a miraculous occurrence, I was excited. This was a sign. I'd seen great tits on the stag in Herefordshire but to have one in my backyard was, for that one moment on that one day, tremendous.

A year before, I'd probably not even have noticed the fourteen-centimetre-long creature clinging to its perch, let alone cared that it was the largest of the tit family, easily identifiable by its thick black neck-tie markings and cheerful chirrups. A year later, I'd be so used to them, so blasé about my birdwatching, that I'd rarely even raise my binoculars in their direction. So the arrival of this small but great bird represented a magical time in my birdwatching career, a short-lived period of innocence and wonder, a childlike time. And while 'childlike' wasn't the quality I was aiming for when I set off on this quest, I was briefly content. There were birds out there and I could find them.

Before long, this ingenuousness would morph into cynicism, treachery and frustration, but for now I was happy to devote myself to my garden birds. The great tit himself seemed less comfortable with the situation, flitting in nervously, grabbing a seed and scuttling off, almost as if he knew he was being watched. The blue tits were just as hurried, always in pairs and always in a rush. 'Come on, darling,' one seemed to say to the other. 'We've got so much on today. You can't just dawdle round the kibble.' And while the blackbird couple hopped clumsily below, pecking at worms and each other with equal abandon, the now fattened robin watched on with an expression that suggested he was cross, full, bored or all three. One afternoon he even stared down Nemesis Cat from his perch on the wall as his potential killer sauntered across the paving stones towards him. I was worried his newly acquired heft might hinder a sudden take-off, but the cat eventually turned away from the robin's death stare and the little bird burst into triumphant song.

4 February

Keen that my renewed enthusiasm did not wane, Duncton sent me what in other circumstances might seem a bizarre gift: a cutting from *The Times* with the headline 'Get Your Lard out for the Tits' and half a coconut stuffed with fat and raisins, a sort of homemade bounty bar. Miraculously, within twenty-four hours this mystical object had worked its magic. As I drew back the curtains the following morning I saw the large hairy nut being savaged by the two starlings I'd seen on next door's Mighty Bird Attractor Tower 2000 the week before. I smiled in disbelief. The next day not one, not two, but three woodpigeons were marching round the garden, pecking at the coconut scraps left by the blackbirds, tits and magpies that had now joined the starlings on the husks above. My garden had become a veritable Ark, an aviary, filled with feathers, squawks and, I had to admit, shit.

But the mess didn't bother me. I was so pleased to have created this bird-friendly environment in my own backyard that I didn't care about the dirty side effects. My theoretical kids will love this, I thought, they'll be proud of their dad. I loved the fact that Duncton knew the secrets of the starlings and could summon them at will with his secret recipe. He might not have the faintest idea about texting or celebrities or anything relevant to modern life, but his was a more fundamental knowledge. He was the keeper of forgotten formulas and it was my duty to pass them on to the next generation of Hornes.[24]

---

24 I think I may have been a little carried away with my new hobby at this point.

5 February

On Duncton's advice, I tore myself away from my beloved bird
fun park of a garden and headed south of the river to the London
Wetland Centre, the capital's capital bird reserve where, he told
me, I could continue my training. Wanting to share the experience with someone else and eager for the hobby not to swallow
my entire social life just yet, I invited my friend Tim along.

I've got quite a few friends called Tim. Scrolling through the
contacts list on my phone[25] I discovered that Tim is my fifth
most popular name after John, Chris, David and Steve. I know
twelve Johns! But only two Jameses. Over eighty per cent of my
contacts are male.

Two of these five Tims I see fairly often, one almost daily, the
other roughly monthly. They're not strictly regulated meetings;
that's just the way it seems to happen. I work *and* play with Tim
Key (called simply Key elsewhere, in a dismissive but practical
manner) so spend what is probably an unhealthy amount of
time in his company. Being self-employed at something that isn't
really a job means that my work and social lives tend to blur
together.

After performing three consecutive shows at the Edinburgh
Festival together (on the sciences of laughter, body language and
Latin), Key decided not to join me on my birdwatching mission.
When I suggested he join me in exploring my dad's hobby for
a year, he told me I was on my own.

The other Tim, meanwhile, would become my birdwatching
soul mate as the year progressed, earning the title of Tim both
here and in my notebooks in the process. Without a birdwatching
dad, he was even less knowledgeable of the pastime than me,

---

25 I superstitiously never delete anyone from my phone and tend to add the
details of anyone I've ever met, and so the word 'contacts' is an accurately
broad description.

but far more naturally curious, enthusiastic and open to new things. He's a teacher, and a fine one at that. If my prospective children were to be taught by someone like him, it would take a great deal of pressure off me.

So, after getting over the shock of having to pay £6.75 to enter the centre ('London prices,' we were told when we queried the cost), the two of us strolled into the reserve. By now, I should say, I was flushed with the first fruits of my labour, and so assumed the role of wise old guide. A little knowledge may be a dangerous thing, but it's also quite annoying.

Unfortunately, I was completely unprepared for the sights and sounds that we discovered within. Having spent a month carefully noting down the particulars of my handful of garden birds, I suddenly found myself confronted by the most extraordinary looking freaks, some tall and bulky, others weighed down by ridiculously outlandish plumage, all jabbering away in a clearly foreign tongue. I felt lost and confused, like a first-time visitor to the capital.

I didn't have a clue what any of these birds were. Well, I did have clues – quite big clues, really, because not too far from each of these exotic creatures was a convenient sign identifying them and explaining where they were from. This was no ordinary bird reserve, this was no Fairburn Ings. Here there were no walking boots, few binoculars and hardly anyone who looked like Duncton. There was neither mud nor rain, instead there were young people, couples, tourists, all noisily chatting away, not skulking in the shadows. People were having fun!

Not me though. I soon realised that none of these birds would count on my list. These were captives in what was basically a zoo. Their wings, I later found out, were pinioned – an apparently painless procedure by which crucial feathers are removed rendering flight an impossibility – so they weren't going anywhere. Sure, it was interesting and informative to see such spectacular species close-up, but I was fifty birds behind Duncton. Fifty birds! And not one of these would make that gap any smaller! I didn't have time for the interesting and informative.

Thankfully, Tim's enthusiasm overcame my impatience. I began grudgingly to have a nice day out, enjoying Tim's company, making slanderous comments about fellow visitors and admiring the birds like pictures in a gallery. And what birds they were, all shapes and sizes from all over the world, including a black-necked swan (think normal swan but with a black neck, 'compla-cent', according to Tim), an oldsquaw (basically a duck with a long tail, 'low key' said Tim), magpie geese (yes, pretty much a cross between the two, 'angry') and my favourite, an East Indian wandering whistling duck. Now that's a classy name for a duck. And this was a duck that could carry it off. It was wandering (within its enforced boundaries), it was whistling (sort of) and it was, apparently, from East India. Very much the Bob Dylan of the duck world. We decided this species alone was worth the honk we'd had to shell out.

The reserve was divided into geographical zones and as we walked from 'Iceland' straight into 'Hawaii' we admired more eccentric birds, some with heads that were clearly too big, others with haunted expressions that looked like they'd seen things birds should never see. We both said 'boo' to some geese in a bid to prove our manliness and were on the verge of nicking a duck when we spotted a tree house structure called the Wild Side Hide. We liked the sound of that. What's more, tucked away inside the hut were several bona fide birders, with binoculars and even telescopes trained out through the windows towards the Thames beyond. So despite the fact that there were no more East Indian wandering whistling ducks and rather a lot of mallards, this really was the wild side. At last, birds that would count on my list – and some comfy seats. Tim and I shuffled on to padded stools next to a suitably camouflaged married couple and looked out, taking turns with my binoculars. Now I was keyed up. Now I could show off to my friend.

'That's a moorhen,' I exclaimed right away.

'No, I don't think so,' countered Tim. 'Moorhens are just black with a little white bit.'

'How about we look it up in the book,' I said.

'But how do you look them up if you don't know what they are?' A sensible question, the paradox of the novice birder.

'What I tend to do,' I said knowingly, 'is think, well, it's some sort of waterbird, so I go to the waterbird section and look at all the pictures. So, it's one of these . . . there. It looks like that one. And then you look at the description: "Stout blackish bird on pond margins, pigeon-sized, long green legs with long toes. Bill red with yellow tip." There, that's a moorhen.'

'Oh yes, well done. I guess that *is* pretty much a moorhen.'

Further scanning of the river in what I hoped was a professional manner revealed several birds that I hadn't seen before this year, their shapes and colours unfamiliar. This was both good and bad news. Good for my total, but no chance for me to display my hard-earned bird knowledge. But I recognised a few of them, and was able to impress Tim by pointing out one grey heron and two cormorants in a quite Zen-like fashion. Again, Duncton's subliminal training was paying off. I knew these distinctive, distinguished-looking birds. The herons were graceful and surprisingly large; the cormorants dark and brooding but occasionally letting themselves down by striking ridiculous poses, arms outstretched, like scarecrows, to dry their feathers in the breeze.

We went on to tick off tufted duck ('I like that because it looks like what it says it is,' said Tim) and a great crested grebe,[26]

---

26 Great crested grebe is clearly a triumphant title. I'd like to read a comic book about a superhero called the Great Crested Grebe. Other dashing characters could include 'The Masked Gull', 'The Whiskered Tern' and 'The Magnificent Frigate Bird'.

Tim's favourite of the day (although when he first saw it dive beneath the surface he was sure it had drowned). Only by looking at the grebe through binoculars can you truly appreciate the crest itself, displayed proudly on the summit of its slender neck. There's a medical complaint birdwatchers are particularly prone to, like tennis elbow and jogger's nipple, called 'warbler neck'. After years of looking up, binoculars raised, at tree tops, clouds and occasionally birds, a birder will often experience a swelling of the neck area and pain in the upper back. Even after a single year's birding, my neck size increased to a slightly manlier fifteen-and-a-half inches. Duncton's, of course, is enormous, a huge eighteen inches, a size barely catered for by the short-sighted collar industry. From a distance he looks like the opposite of a great crested grebe. Instead of an oversized flower balanced precariously on a willowy stalk, Duncton's head and neck look more like an apple perched on the trunk of a mighty oak (a bearded apple, with glasses and greying hair, but size-wise, definitely an apple).

What most appealed to first-timer Tim was the process of spotting a bird, noticing its features then trying to work out what it was. He enjoyed the detective work, piecing together the evidence, poring over pictures of potential suspects and the eventual Columbo-like revelation.

We sat on our stools for a good couple of hours, vaguely trying to identify the birds, but mostly enjoying the peaceful view back across the Thames. Apart from Tim's occasional outbursts, the tranquillity was broken only by a commotion at the other end of the hide where the shout of 'parrot' suddenly went up, followed by much scrambling of children and me to see if this could indeed be the case. A parrot? I thought, I bet Duncton hasn't seen a parrot!

To my surprise it was indeed a parrot, and no, Duncton hadn't seen one yet. Even more remarkably, this one wasn't a captive.

It would count on my list. For as I admired its lurid green feathers, a ridiculous outfit to be wearing on a winter's day in London, a man with a very long camera next to me grumbled, 'Bloody nuisance.' For the benefit of the bird novices around him he went on to explain that having been brought over in the 1960s these ring-necked parakeets had settled and thrived and could now be seen in their thousands all over the city.

When we'd finally had our fill of birds, we spent the rest of the afternoon in a pub watching Liverpool lose 2–0 to Chelsea in the Premiership. We always lose to Chelsea in the League. On my wedding day, some of the first words my fellow Liverpool supporter and now father-in-law, Terry, said to me after the service were, 'We lost one nil.' Bloody Chelsea.

After the game I tried to work out which experience I had enjoyed more, the birdwatching or the football. I was certainly happier with the bird score (eight new species in one afternoon), but if I was honest I'd have to say I cared more about the football. I was getting quite excited about new birds, but I wouldn't have missed the game for them. Then again, ninety minutes of football had left me feeling depressed. And drunk. I could already see which was the healthier of the two pursuits, and perhaps with time would start to redress the current imbalance.

10 February

Determined to sharpen my identification skills, I followed the Wetland adventure with trips south and then north.

It seemed like a logical decision to spend a day at my parents' house in Midhurst. Duncton had been cultivating his own bird haven for the last twenty-five years, and I was keen to see just how many of the ninety-odd species he'd already counted were literally on his doorstep. On the side of a cupboard in the kitchen an elderly piece of paper entitled 'Birds Seen On or Over Silvertrees' (the once accurate but now misleading name of our house) had been gathering dust for as long as I can remember.[27] The moisture from its blue tack had years since seeped through on to the page itself, and while the words, typed on a typewriter, had begun to fade, the list was still legible and the forty or so original species had been joined by an appendix of more recently spotted birds, neatly handwritten beneath. In total a remarkable fifty-nine species were listed, plus 'teal', but teal was written in brackets and when I asked him, Duncton couldn't remember why.

The day I dropped by my parents had gone out. This was not unusual; they're always out. I find it quite frustrating. I guess about ten years ago it was me who was always out, and they who didn't know what I was up to. Now I'm the one who's meant to be working and they've got all the free time. As I say, I find it quite frustrating.

Tiptoeing round like a burglar (I don't know why I tiptoed, it wasn't necessary), I headed for the place with the best view of the various bird contraptions strategically positioned around the garden, in a chair by the window of a room currently known as The Study. Originally The Playroom, this was a place where the Horne children once played with their LEGO, progressed to fighting over table football, then graduated to hours and hours of Kick Off 2 on the Amiga.[28] When we all flew the nest, Duncton reclaimed the space for himself, filling the shelves with his

---

27 Along with various witty bird postcards, several pictures of particularly exotic birds and a Motherwell poster from 1989. We thought it would be pretty funny if Mum supported Motherwell. Her second team was Queen of the South. Those were our sorts of family jokes. When I was ten, I decided to learn the French Horn because my name was Horne. That's the sort of thing we find quite funny.

28 An Amiga was a fairly basic but at the time quite reputable games console. If a friend phoned any of us while we were using it, one of Duncton's favourite jokes was to reply, 'He's just playing with his girlfriend,' having found out that *Amiga* is the Spanish word for one. This was particularly funny because none of us ever had girlfriends.

stereotypical stethoscopes, spooky sample jars (empty) and piles (not a pun) of medical journals. These in particular were a source of grim fascination for me. They'd flop through the letterbox like any normal monthly publication only to surprise you with a graphic front cover featuring gaping wounds or mangled kidneys. One of my proudest moments as a child came when I was featured in an article in the *British Medical Journal*. I'd had my appendix removed, and during the operation the surgeon discovered a dog hair had pierced and infected the ineffectual organ. I had got appendicitis by swallowing dog hair, a medical curiosity that was deemed worthy of the great periodical.

For a while then, this room became The Doctor's Sanctum. When Duncton retired the gory magazines were replaced by birdwatching journals, photography guides and binocular brochures. The Amiga was superseded by a chunky PC before which Duncton would sit for hours, obsessively tinkering with his snaps, glancing up now and then at the birds. In many ways it's become a playroom once more.

Just a few yards from his window, his mighty bird table, the timeless Large Ashford Bird Table, formed the centre of his private reserve. Strong but elegant, it would have taken up most of my Kensal Green garden. From its six beams hung six bird feeders of varying shapes and sizes, cylindrical peanut dispensers (Avian Bird Feeder Thistles), rectangular fat holders (Suet Selective Squirrel-proof Bird Feeders) and the trademark coconuts (Duncton's Dangling Coconuts), all swinging temptingly in the breeze. Since Horace, our bird-molesting cat,[29] passed away at

---

29 One of two twin black cats, Horace died soon after Hamish, the black labrador whose coat gave me appendicitis. Horace's brother Boris would celebrate his nineteenth birthday in May, but was a very lazy sort of a cat and rarely a threat to birds. All our pets were male, obviously. Like everyone else we knew, we also had several goldfish – Jaws I, Jaws II, Jaws III etc., and some unnamed stick insects that were dead for quite a while before anyone noticed.

the end of 2002, Duncton had been able to make this a bird-friendly zone. I don't think I've ever seen an empty bird feeder or a soiled bird bath in Duncton's garden.

Within sixty minutes of sitting in his swively chair, I had seen no less than sixteen species dining at the table. All my usual north London suspects had appeared, looking decidedly healthier here in the country, alongside several new species for my list. First, a cuddly collared dove almost over-balanced the weighty structure as it tried to prise a peanut from its container. As he banged away at the bars, a diminutive dunnock hopped around beneath. An entirely unimpressive brown bird, which I think I'd mistaken for wrens my entire life. Looking at the book then looking back at the bird again, I tested the word 'dunnock' a few times out loud. 'Dunnock. Dunnock. Dunnock . . .' No, I'd never heard of a dunnock. Still, I'd seen one now and that was all that mattered.

A little later, my maiden coal tit arrived, casually knocking back a seed or two before diving for cover. Two black-headed gulls then landed in the middle of the lawn and chased each other round like albino puppies. I'm always confused by these seabirds. Why are they so often seen away from the sea? Do they not know their own name? I didn't have the answers.

Finally, I managed to make out a bullfinch, gnawing away at one of the two coconuts swinging from a tree by the garage. For me, bullfinch is another not entirely fair name, partly because it sounds a tiny bit too close to bullshit for comfort (if you're sitting in a hide, listening to a fellow birdwatcher witter on, a sudden cry of 'Bullfinch!' could easily be misinterpreted) but mainly because they don't look anything like bulls. They may well be 'A rather big and very compact finch' as the *Collins* explains, but they're not really bullish enough to justify that comparison. They look to me more like a robin who's really let himself go – like my Kensal Green one might in a couple of years. The male boasts a plump red stomach, puffed out like a retired rugby player who's been enjoying the post-match hospitality a bit too often, the female paler and grey, understandably, but equally rotund.

17 February

A week later it was time to visit my new parents. For the first time since our wedding the two of us, all four parents, Rachel's brother and sister and both their partners were all getting together for a weekend in the hotel where our reception had taken place, just south of the border in County Cavan. The trip got off to an excellent start, when the pilot welcomed us on to the plane with the words: 'Welcome to Easyjet Flight 216, my name is Captain Bird.'[30]

I love visiting Ireland. That might sound trite but it's true. We go to see Rachel's family every couple of months and I always look forward to the drive from Belfast to County Fermanagh, the hills rolling along beside us, and the roads gradually narrowing down to the final single track that leads to their house. I like the feeling that gently takes over as you head out towards the middle of nowhere. Not that Lisnaskea, the nearest town, is nowhere. It's definitely somewhere. And it's quite like Midhurst, just a bit smaller and much harder to spell.

What I haven't always loved is working in Ireland. One of the

---

30 Now, I don't know whether this is an example of nominative determinism – a phrase coined by the *New Scientist* to describe the phenomenon of one's name determining one's career – or aptonymy, the more coincidental occurrence of one's name being particularly fitting for one's personality, but I came across several such examples in the birding world. See how many you can spot during my year. In fact, see how many names with any bird associations at all you can spot – I'll put my answers at the back of the book.

most notoriously tough gigs on the stand-up comedy circuit is the Empire in Belfast where countless comics have come 'all the way from London' (as the compères often revel in announcing) to be greeted 'enthusiastically' by a packed and well-oiled crowd. Now, I've watched several shows here from the point of view of the audience and can safely say that it's a brilliant night for anyone that side of the stage. There's nothing nasty about the treatment English comics receive. Let's just call it thorough. The crowd is simply keen to stress that the comics are not in England now. They're in Ireland. So they should probably talk about Ireland. Ideally the current political situation in Ireland. But they better be funny too. If these criteria aren't met, they're not interested. Jokes about 'the Tube' and 'London's pigeons' don't go down well.

When I was starting out as a stand-up, I had a couple of tough nights at the Empire. What usually happened was I'd come on, look nervous, the audience would sense that nervousness and grow confident. I'd sense their confidence and grow more nervous. This would go on until both of us reached our elastic limits and I fell silent while they did a bit of shouting. After about ten more minutes I'd admit defeat. People would then come up to me at the bar and say, 'Well done, mate. You were shit but you did it. I wouldn't have had the balls. What are you having?' I'd then have to drink more Guinness than I can handle and try not to embarrass myself for the second time in one night.

Even trickier was a gig in Bangor, County Down, in 2003. Fresh and full of confidence from my first Edinburgh Festival, I was due to perform my one-hour show about the science of laughter called *Making Fish Laugh*. Unfortunately for me, everyone at the theatre thought they were simply getting an evening of blokey jokes. When Key and I arrived on the fateful night we were greeted by a sign outside the theatre that read *Adult Comedy*

Night with Alex Horne. Inside, 200 drunken men in suits were laughing loudly. The staff had cleverly managed to save some honk by showing an old, adult, Billy Connolly video instead of employing a warm-up act.

At exactly 9 p.m., the technician pressed pause on Billy (who remained on screen looking appropriately shocked) and I walked out to deliver my hour-long lecture on the perfect conditions for laughter. Ten minutes later the technician pressed pause once again and we slipped quietly out through a back door.

Over the years, you gradually learn that dying is just a part of comedy. It's not the end of the world. You get used to it. If you think you're never going to die you're either the best stand-up in the world or far too sensitive for the job. After the 'Bangor Fiasco' Key and I locked ourselves in our tiny twin hotel room, ate a dodgy Chinese takeaway and left early the next day before we could make eye contact with anyone who had witnessed the 'performance'. As soon as we were on our way back to the airport the incident was forgotten.

But the most challenging performance I've given in Ireland was my wedding speech. This time the 'audience' was almost too mixed. People of all ages, half from England, half from Ireland, all keen to hear what this 'comedian' had to say. Some wanted rude jokes, others had made it clear that rude jokes wouldn't be tolerated. It was a difficult line to tread.

Thankfully, and a tiny bit luckily, tread it I did. Back then my father-in-law Terry was a cigar smoker of some repute. He's since given up but I do like to picture him with a fine Cuban cigar in his hand, much like Duncton and his binoculars. Back in December 2004, the smoking ban was already in place in the forward-thinking Republic of Ireland, well before the UK caught up. Due to our hotel's otherwise convenient location in the southern counties, this meant Terry would be deprived of his beloved cigars on the day of his youngest daughter's wedding. I therefore wrote the following letter to Paul Murphy, then Secretary of State for Northern Ireland in the House of Commons, and read it out during my speech:

17 December 2004

Dear Paul,

Happy Christmas. I know you're probably fairly busy at this festive time of year but I have one very quick question. I'm getting married to a lovely, pretty girl from Fermanagh on New Year's Day – two weeks tomorrow! – and we're having our reception just over the border in Ballyconnell. The thing is, my fiancée's dad Terry really likes smoking cigars and he's going to have to go outside in the cold to smoke them on this very special day. Because, as I'm sure you know all too well, you're not allowed to smoke inside hotels in the Republic of Ireland.

'So how can I help?' I hear you ask. Well, Paul, I was just wondering if you'd be able to lower the Northern Irish border by just a couple of miles for just a couple of hours on New Year's Day in two weeks' time. That way Terry could smoke his cigars to his heart's content without breaking the law and without getting arrested. It would mean a lot to him and it might just put his new son-in-law in his good books.

I'd be really grateful if you could let me know as soon as possible as I have to tell him either way in my speech in fifteen days' time. Thank you so much for taking the time to read this. If you do not write back I shall assume it's a yes.

Yours sincerely,
The Groom

This went down surprisingly well at the wedding. I was congratulated on my cheeky but well-informed reference to Irish politics. I smiled and nodded. To be honest, I hadn't even thought about anything political. I just thought it might be funny to see what the man said. It hadn't crossed my mind that the idea of moving the border now so that a man could smoke his cigar on the occasion of his daughter's wedding, after so many years of fighting about that very same boundary, might be a funny one. I've still never cracked the Empire, by the way.

So it was with happy memories that we were to revisit the hotel. But before my parents arrived, Rachel and I spent a night at her parents' stunning house on the shore of Lough Erne. It's quite like Midhurst's South Pond, just a hundred times bigger and you can jet-ski on it. When Rachel and I first got to know each other she told me she loved living near water. I told her I did too. It turned out I'd exaggerated my 'water' and she hadn't. And when I say 'exaggerated', I think I probably mean 'lied about'. There's a fine line between embellishment and dishonesty, whose whereabouts I would learn more about as the year progressed.

Settling down for a welcoming cup of coffee in the kitchen, my eyes were drawn to the window and a splendid-looking bird feeder on the balcony. It had always been there, I was told, but I'd never noticed it.[31] In fact, I could barely see the bird feeder beneath the crawling mass of frenzied birds clinging to its bars. Oblivious to the parallel activity going on in the kitchen (we had biscuits with our coffee), all sorts of gaudy birds were buzzing round the nuts, flapping and squawking like market traders in the morning.

The scandalous news that I was now 'doing birdwatching'

---

31 In case you're wondering, it was the classic Bob Martin Fat Snax: Garden Guests Edition.

had, of course, reached Lisnaskea, so when asked to identify these individual species I was relieved to be able to confidently point out blue tits, great tits and coal tits. A couple of the other birds I glossed over. These were slightly bigger, even more colourful, like classy canaries, gold, green, red and yellow – again, I couldn't understand why I'd never paid them any attention before. But after a good few minutes staring I thought I'd worked it out and returned my verdict to the jury. 'What you have there,' I said, as formally as is appropriate in such a situation, 'are greenfinches, goldfinches and – I don't say this lightly – a siskin.'

Thus, very early in my first birdwatching year for two decades, I'd laid my reputation on the line. Duncton was to arrive the next day and would either confirm or reject my opinion in an instant – for him, of course, the shape and faces of these common birds are as ingrained as mine, Mat and Chip's. But I was almost certain I was right. The greenfinch – a green*ish* bird, with bright yellow splashes and the tell-tale stout beak of the finch shaped to maximise nut-cracking potential; the goldfinch – a gold*ish* bird, mostly white and brown with yellow sparks, jet-black wings and a bizarre red face holding a similar but slightly slimmer beak; and then, of course, this alleged siskin. Yearning as I had for a sighting of this bird since I'd embedded the Defender II back in Kensal Green, I was now so familiar with its picture in the guide it was quite an odd sensation to see it in real life, rather like setting eyes on a famous person in the flesh after gazing at their face in the tabloids every day for a month. At first I couldn't quite make sense of what I was seeing. It was only when I stopped and stared that it sunk in. That's not what I think it is, is it? I thought. Yes, I think it is, I thought. Well, well, I thought. I had convinced myself at least.

Of course no one in Rachel's family had any reason to doubt my conclusion. Why would they? They had every faith in their young birdwatching son-in-law, for which I was, as always, grateful, and I liked to think that Rachel was even a little bit proud of her newly knowledgeable husband. But the next day, when Duncton did indeed confirm that this was a siskin ('Yes, they're siskins, they particularly like the nuts in red bags, people think they remind them of pinecones. They're winter visiting finches from Northern Scandinavia.'), I was nearly overwhelmed with relief and satisfaction. I was definitely whelmed. I felt proud of myself. I felt like I'd passed another test. I was on my way.

Later, walking around the hotel's golf course, I correctly pinpointed cormorants and Canada geese on a water hazard and a bunch of long-tailed tits that darted along the branches beside us. I was on a roll. Duncton taught me how to tell the jackdaws from the rooks in the trees above us ('The rooks have a lot of white on their beaks and are a bit bigger, and they've got really evil-looking white rings around their eyes, like little gangsters.'). Even Rachel got in on the act, pointing out a pair of 'wee willie wagtails' on the grass by the carpark. These mini magpies are a funny sort of bird. Once you've seen one you'll notice them everywhere.[32]

Back at Belfast Airport at the end of a triumphant weekend (Liverpool had knocked Man Utd out of the FA Cup on Saturday, really sealing the deal on the cherry on the icing on the cake), a typically dry security officer couldn't help but comment on my birdwatching equipment. Carefully swabbing my binoculars for traces of something treacherous, he looked me in the eye and said, 'Been over here looking at our birds have you? Seen any nice tits?'

'Well, sort of, something like that,' I stuttered, still unable to cope with a Belfast heckle.

---

32 They're officially called pied wagtails, the pie, as in magpie, referring to their black and white colouring, not an actual pie.

20 February

Confidence, in bird terms, at an all time high, I decided to explore the Kensal Green that lay beyond our constricting garden walls. Between the canal and the first row of houses lies Kensal Green Cemetery, one of the best graveyards in London. I don't think cemeteries are actually rated in top ten terms, but Kensal Green is the oldest of the 'Magnificent Seven' nineteenth-century graveyards still in operation, and the only one with an Act of Parliament that prevents its bodies being disturbed or the land itself being sold for development. This means that large areas have grown over into sprawling wilderness, and you can walk for hours between the crumbling obelisks and mausoleums. Among the 500 people listed in the *Oxford Dictionary of National Biography* who are buried here are Marigold Frances Churchill, daughter of Sir Winston, Princess Sophia, the mathematician Charles Babbage, Isambard Kingdom Brunel and the writers William Makepeace Thackeray and Anthony Trollope.

When I'm working on comedy material I like to say it out loud, preferably while pacing around. Because our garden wasn't more than five or six strides long, and not wanting to look too much like a nutter on the streets surrounding our home, I would often retreat to the cemetery and wander aimlessly and noisily for hours, in the hope of squeezing a joke out of something I'd noticed that day. I can imagine that the sight of me, roaming up and down the aisles (aisles? Sounds rather supermarketty), talking to myself and occasionally chuckling may well have been an alarming one. But throw binoculars into that mix and you've got a genuine and potentially dangerous eccentric on the loose. Luckily there was rarely anyone else there (except for the 250,000 souls tucked away in their earthy beds) so for the rest of the month, indeed for the rest of the year, I made regular trips to the cemetery, clocking up what must have been an enormous graveside mileage as the shrubs blossomed then shrunk back around me and the graves sank further into the earth.

On my first such trip of my Big Year, I brought along a list of birds I hoped to spot and a list of the top twenty graves I thought I might also stumble across. I wondered which would be harder to locate. Unfortunately it was freezing cold and my fingers couldn't turn pages or hold binoculars steady, so after finding my first song thrush and the grave of Ernest Augustus, son of King George III, I gave up. Trying to find twenty grave-stones in a sea of 250,000 was never going to be easy. That's the equivalent of six full Anfields pouring out on to the street and me wandering amongst them trying to spot someone I recog-nise – while shivering a lot.

Steadily, though, as the year marched on, I grew to know the limitless alleyways (better than aisles? Maybe, but a little too seedy), and the birds and graves they accommodated. The para-keets tended to flock in the western section, near the Anglican Chapel, robins often guarded the triumphal Entrance Gateway and magpies liked to stand symbolically along the Central Avenue. As far as I know I'm the only person who has ever 'birded' the graveyard. That was probably my main patch for the year. I never saw anything particularly out of the ordinary, but I loved searching for life amongst the death. It was, to me, the most peaceful place in London.

24 February

My life was ridiculously bird-orientated by now. I'll end this month with three quotes that typified my days. The first, a line or two from a lunchtime edition of Radio 1's *Newsbeat*:

Top vets from around Europe will decide today whether the EU should allow poultry to be vaccinated against bird flu. The British Government isn't convinced it will help, but virus expert Professor John Oxford disagrees: 'The Vietnamese, of all countries the least you'd expect to eradicate the disease, seem to have done it. And they've done it not just by culling – for every animal they've culled they've vaccinated ten.'

If the people at Radio 1 thought such a bizarre quote worthy of their listenership, you can see how all-pervasive the story was at that time. Nevertheless, Duncton's RSPB newsletter for February (more bird reading matter sent up to London from Midhurst) concentrated more on things like their Big Garden Birdwatch and 'How to Give Your Old Binoculars a New Lease of Life' than the apparently surprising fact that Vietnam was managing to cope with the apocalyptic disease. My favourite story was sent in by a man called Les, and was entitled 'Trial and Error':

A few sparrows were feeding on my lawn when a young sparrowhawk hurtled towards them. The sparrows saw it coming a mile off and scattered while the sparrowhawk, too late to pull off its headlong dive, crashed at high speed into a rhododendron bush. It struggled to free itself from a tangle of twigs then hopped to the top of the bush where it sat for several minutes, straightening its feathers, frequently shaking its head as if to say 'It looked much easier than that when mum did it.' Highly amusing to watch but it showed what a steep learning curve this young bird was on; the crash could easily have resulted in an injury which would have meant certain death, many more failed hunts and possible starvation.

That's the sort of tender interest all the birdwatchers I'd met so far took in their birds. Duncton in particular seemed fairly indifferent to the listing element of our competition and was concerned instead that I'd actually get to know the birds and remember them when the year was over. Then again, in one typically lengthy and digressive phone message he did reveal that he was also going out of his way to see extra birds this year. This is an exact transcription of his message:

> Hi Als, it's dad speaking, erm, hope all's well with you and that Milton – not Milton, *New* Milton went well – I used to live in a place called Little Milton near Oxford – and that your meetings with Key were OK and that all goes well tonight in Norwich . . . Sorry, I'm a bit out of breath, just walking along the South Downs Way, desperately searching for additions to my number ninety-four on the list. Erm, but I should be gardening really. So I'll break the news to Mum when I'm back, that I snuck out for a walk and some birdwatching . . . And I hope to speak to you soon. We're off out to supper tonight with David and Rosemary who came to one of your shows on Saturday. And anyway, hope to see you soon – well, hope to *speak* to you soon – and looking forward to seeing you Wednesday evening . . . Ah, I'm being shot at here . . . and [*laughs*] speak to you soon anyway, bye for now.

During the course of this three-minute-long message he'd managed to wander unwittingly into a field used more for hunting birds than watching them. I should never have doubted his commitment.

CHAPTER 3

Big Brother

'March is the first anticlimax of the year. At least it usually is. The frenetic activities of January and February are over, and all the winter birds are safely gathered in.'

– Adrian M Riley

Alex: 51 species
Duncton: 95 species

2 March

By the third month of his Big Year, Adrian Riley had already seen 217 species of birds, considerably more than Duncton's and my combined totals at the same point in ours. 'Less than creditable,' was how he described this already extraordinary number. 'Still not even level with Lee's score for January.'

I suppose I was in the same boat. Not necessarily exactly the same boat, but a similar boat at least – maybe a scale model of his boat. After all, I still hadn't seen as many birds as Duncton had in his first month. But although I knew I had some catching up to do, I was still prepared to give myself some credit for the fifty-one species I'd seen so far.

I didn't know quite what to think about his notion that March might 'usually' be the 'first anticlimax of the year'. In footballing terms, the quarter-final of a major tournament is generally pretty anticlimactic for England. But in this, my first birdwatching year, I wasn't even nearly at such an advanced stage. An anticlimax now would be like England failing in their very first qualifier.

And while all Adrian's winter birds were 'safely gathered in', nearly all of mine were still recklessly tearing round the countryside. Spring was approaching, the year was gathering pace; I couldn't afford an anticlimactic month. So it was perhaps quite an eccentric decision to start March with trips to see birds I knew I couldn't count on my list.

Norfolk is arguably the best county in Britain for birdwatching. The Isles of Scilly may be the most popular place for particularly rare visitors[33] and over 350 species have been spotted on

---

33 In the autumn these islands are such a target for serious twitchers that during one particular month – the Scilly Season – the whole area turns into a bizarre birding holiday camp. An annual Birders versus Islanders football match takes place in front of a fairly sizeable crowd, expert birders present

the Scottish island of Fair Isle, but these places are expensive and troublesome to get to, playgrounds reserved for the most dedicated of birders. Norfolk is the spiritual home for 'normal' birders. (An oxymoron? I wasn't sure yet.)

Cley Next The Sea is a village perched on the shoulder blade of the Norfolk coast. I don't know if the name is ungrammatical, or simply points out what happens if you drive through the village, but Cley (as most people sensibly call it) is where serious twitching began. It may have a population of less than 400 people, but during the 1970s that number included a certain Nancy Gull who with her husband Jack ran a commune-like café at which the burgeoning birdwatching community could eat cheaply and grow. In his book *Birders: Tales of a Tribe*, Mark Cocker describes how the café's phone was the heart of the young birdwatching scene:

> I don't ever remember hearing the phone ring at Nancy's and it being a call for the residents of the house. It was always other birders on the line and whenever birders were in the café they themselves answered it. We usually took it in turns. That way everyone got to eat while maintaining the news service. But it was essential to do so. It was part of the unspoken protocol of Nancy's and, indeed, of being a birder.

Nowadays the village is still dominated by birds, although its unofficial status as the birding capital of the UK has slipped. During the 1980s that single phone was replaced by Birdline, set up by the birders Richard Millington, Steve Gantlett, Roy Robinson and Adrian Riley's rival, Lee G R Evans, and which

---

slide shows, hold quizzes and sell bird products, and the whole shebang culminates in a Birders' Disco where, according to Mark Cocker, twitchers have been known to dance with binoculars still dangling from their necks if a particularly rare bird (like the blue rock thrush of 1999) has been sighted.

people could call from anywhere in the country to hear what birds were where. Although Richard Millington runs Birdline from the village, as well as publishing *Birding World* magazine, it is no longer quite such a crucial place for birders to visit.

When Duncton goes to visit his mother and sister in Norwich, he usually finds an excuse to nip up the coast and check out the birds that he'd rarely get to see in Sussex. When I paid a visit to my grandmother and aunt at the beginning of March, however, this world was still unknown to me and I had to be content with the sight of a few garden birds I'd already seen on their respective bird tables. I didn't know that just a few miles away lay a coastline teeming with birds and birders.

What I also didn't know was that my aunt's family actually have their own birds, three Japanese chickens to be precise, one male, two female. They were born the Christmas before and are called Noel, Holly and Snowdrop. The downside of having chickens, my aunt told me, is that they make quite a lot of chicken mess and chicken mess is difficult to clear up. Luckily, my aunt and uncle also have two dogs which enjoy the taste of chicken mess. With faeces consumption being one of the easiest ways to catch dastardly bird flu, this was a worry, but their garden was kept relatively clean.

I knew that, being pets, the chickens wouldn't count on my year list but I was excited to see these exotic, eastern birds up close. They may 'only' have been chickens, but they were from Japan! And my aunt was keeping them as pets! That was quite a hard concept to get my head around, not helped by her comment that she'd got a pair of females 'So they wouldn't get too knackered by all the raping the male does.' That's an odd sentence at the best of times.

Each holding a cup of tea, Polly and I watched the birds parade around the garden, partly, I suppose, in the hope that we might witness some of this raping. Unfortunately (probably not the right adverb to use here) we saw only some chasing and a bit of pecking, but this was entertaining enough. Puffed up and jet black, they looked like they were trying to pretend they were some other, much more important species. This wasn't bird-watching in the traditional sense, but I came away with just a little more knowledge about the world of birds, as well as two perfect Japanese eggs.

5 March

This slightly fraudulent form of education continued with a trip to London Zoo with my friend Lloyd (a pro-bird campaigner on the stag back in January). I was hoping to pick up a few tricks of the trade and swat up on the birds I'd meet in Israel later in the year.

I've never really known what to think about zoos. On the rare occasions that I do 'have an opinion' about something, it's usually after I've listened to the views of other, cleverer people. Whatever Stephen Fry says, for example, I usually believe. So for a good many years I held the view that zoos were one of the worst examples of human brutality, after I read Fry's essay on the subject in *Paperweight*:

What then will our grandchildren wonder at in our world? What practices that we indulge in will turn their stomachs and make them amazed that we could ever have called ourselves civilised? I have a strong feeling that zoos will figure high on the list. Is it possible, they will ask, that we actually stole polar bears away from the arctic and set them in concrete-floored cages in southern climes to be gawped at? No! *My* grandfather would never have countenanced that, he would have demonstrated, or lobbied Parliament or written to the newspapers; he, kindly old grandpa, would have been ashamed to live in a country which imprisoned animals for show. Wouldn't he?

Fry's right! I thought. Even at that young age I feared that my grandchildren would be disappointed in me and so I adopted a strictly anti-zoo stance. 'Zoos are like prisons,' I would tell anyone who had the misfortune to stray within range. 'But the animals are innocent! Sure, put them away if they start stealing cars or embezzling funds (I thought this quite funny and didn't then know about the rapist chickens), but until then, release the blameless creatures!' I think I even contemplated setting them free myself, sneaking into zoos at night with some metal cutters and releasing tigers back into the wild (well, the suburbs).

As time went by and my idealism faded, I conveniently forgot these views. Nowadays it's a bit like vegetarianism: I still like animals and don't particularly think they should be locked away (or eaten) but then again I do like looking at them (and eating them). As a kid (before being corrupted by Fry) I loved trips to Windsor Safari Park and barbecues. My childhood wouldn't have been complete without them. Obviously any zoo should be as humane (or the equivalent word for animals) as possible, but how else can kids in this country see rhinos, snakes and brightly coloured, fun birds?[34]

London Zoo, I told myself, must treat its animals well. It's *London Zoo*! And although I was no longer a kid, it was time for me to once again explore the alien animals. I needed to have a close look at birds I wouldn't otherwise see.

On previous visits I'd have first sought out the rhinos and snakes, but now we aimed straight for the aviaries, ignoring anything with tusks, fur or scales. Just the week before a new

---

34 One answer to this deliberately rhetorical question would be 'On nature programmes on TV with Attenborough.' I don't yet have a comeback to that excellent point.

wing (it's hard not to make some puns in a book about birds) had opened right at the heart of the zoo, entirely devoted to African birds and while I only found a couple of the birds I thought I might later come across in Israel (the fantastically named Arabian babblers and brown boobies, as well as a pristine flock of eastern white pelicans), I was happy to admire what really were brightly coloured, fun birds.

The African enclosure was very different to the birdcage prisons I'd once railed against. The different species were free to mingle in a gauze marquee-type structure about the same size as a big top (a circus tent, not a large pullover). Even better, this free range accommodation was open to human visitors like me. Entering through a sort of one-way cat-flap, we could wander round the Africanesque landscape, just feet from the most spectacular birds I had ever seen, more dazzling even than the toucans of Costa Rica.

The appropriately named superb starling was among the most impressive. As far removed from our own common starling (which is a beautiful bird in its own right) as their adjectival first name suggests, they were an electric blue, so bright, in fact, that I thought at first they must be fake. Clashing nicely with these cobalt creatures was the brilliant red ibis, tall, gangly and again, ludicrously bright. I should mention that it was pouring with rain at this point, so while their feathers dazzled, their expressions did tell a slightly different story. The red-tailed Abyssinian ground hornbills looked particularly irate, outraged, it seemed, by this unwanted holiday destination. 'This isn't what it looked like in the brochure,' they seemed to say. I tried not to worry too much about them and instead appreciated the magnificent names and plumes of the village weaver, hammerkop, hyacinth macaw, king vulture, purple-tailed imperial pigeon and tawny frogmouth (the bird with the biggest mouth in the world). If I could only have counted these colourful captives on my list, I'd have taken an unexpected lead over Duncton.

Eventually emerging from this tiny corner of Africa, we raced round the rest of the zoo, admiring the majestic birds of prey, spotting sleepy owls dozing in their nooks, and smiling at the antics of the rockhopper penguins ('Now that's the Hollywood side of birds,' marvelled Lloyd). Their pool, by the way, was as open as the African exhibit, but without the gauze roof. Like ostriches, emus and kiwis, penguins can't fly, so there's no need to hem them in from above. What this does mean, of course, is that other birds that can fly find their way into the penguins' water park. One of the many perks of flight, of course, is that you have greater access to places like this and don't need to worry about ticket barriers.[35] While we watched the ever-popular penguins dive and swim, a solitary heron swooped down onto the bank and, like us, stood and stared. His expression wasn't easy to read – herons have pretty good poker faces – but he seemed interested in his distant relatives. I couldn't quite tell if he was more interested in their agility under the water or their lack of it on firmer ground, but he was engrossed for a good few minutes and I enjoyed this brief spot of birdbirdwatchingwatching.

7 March

Before leaving the zoo, I returned for a second stroll around the African enclosure. The rain had eased and I sat for a while beneath a bare Saharan tree covered in sunbirds.

---

35 Thanks to its location either side of the canal, there are areas of London Zoo that even us flightless humans can experience without having to pay. From the towpath you get an excellent view of the Snowdon aviary on one side and some warthogs on the other. Indeed, from Regent's Park itself you can often see the heads of the giraffes peeking back at you over their fences. If you're a particular fan of giraffe faces and not all that worried about the rest of them you never need pay to visit.

A couple of days later I met up with my older brother Mat for our first ever joint birdwatching trip. He was about to head off to Africa himself for a year with his girlfriend Morri, the first six months of which would be spent working on a nature reserve, researching animals just like the ones I'd seen in their actual African home.

Mat was also, of course, taken on innumerable birdwatching outings as a child. But while I shunned the trips as soon as I reached the age of any sort of independence, Mat remained loyal to Duncton's hobby throughout his youth and while only a part-time birdwatcher today, he's a veritable expert compared with me. He still got into the other things boys get into as they grow up – football, mainly, of course – but he'd caught the bird-watching bug while I was, apparently, immune.

During our respective childhoods, Duncton organised various father-son bonding events in the form of one-off, one-on-one trips to a destination of our choice. When we were each thirteen years old and moving from one school to the next, he decided he'd take us off to wherever we wanted to go, to do whatever we wanted to do. We were more than happy with the idea.

Being the eldest, Mat became a teenager first. That's how age works. So in the summer of 1989, soon after Liverpool had beaten Everton in the FA Cup in the wake of the Hillsborough disaster, he and Duncton made the laborious but exhilarating trip up to Fair Isle, that bird-magnet of a Scottish Island mentioned earlier. Having driven from Midhurst to Gatwick, they caught a plane to Aberdeen, another plane to Shetland, then a boat to the island itself. It would have been cheaper and quicker to fly to New York. Once there, they spent a merry week working for free on the island's bird observatory, trapping birds for research purposes, attaching rings to the legs of gulls and being mobbed by vicious auks (this story may well have been exaggerated around the dinner table in the adrenaline-fuelled weeks that followed their return – I know I thought they meant 'orcs'). It was, I've always imagined, a perfect father-son bonding event. You couldn't get a much tighter bonding experience than a week on a remote Scottish island grappling with furious Scottish beasts. Duncton still gardens in his Fair Isle Bird Observatory sweater.

When it finally came to my turn (three years that felt like decades later), I decided not to go quite as far north, requesting instead to spend a weekend in Liverpool on something called a 'Soccer City Weekend'. I have no idea where I'd heard about the scheme, but over the course of a couple of days we were taken on a tour of both the Liverpool and Everton football grounds (there was no option to omit the latter from the schedule), given the opportunity to walk out onto the sacred Anfield turf and admire Liverpool's trophy hall and the corresponding cupboard at Goodison. On top of those treats, we were promised a trip round the city itself, a visit to the Beatles Museum, meals at both club restaurants and, of course, the chance to watch whatever game was on that weekend. On our weekend, Liverpool were playing host to the mighty Coventry.

I was immensely excited by the whole thing and it passed in a blur. I remember being peculiarly enchanted by our guide Lorraine who spoke with the first live Scouse accent I'd ever heard, almost fainting at the sight of Jan Mølby in the hotel's reception on match-day morning and getting a little bit bored in the Cathedral. I remember more about our grown-up meal in Est Est Est on The Albert Dock than Liverpool's scrappy 1–0 win. I do recall Lorraine, a Blue, smiling and saying 'You were lucky!' when we got back on the magnificent coach. But then, all too quickly, it was over. The trip I'd been looking forward to my whole life was already a memory. Surely any serious bonding would take more time than that?

Four years later and Chip's time arrived. I guess this is as good a time as ever to explain why he's called Chip. He's not really called Chip. Well, he wasn't originally. My parents didn't go on a mental safari after Mat and Alex and name their third child after a potato-based snack. Chip used to be called Christopher. But at the age of two (or whenever babies start talking) he struggled with the hefty consonants in his Jesus-bearing name and referred to himself simply as Chip. Chip stuck. Teachers called him Chip. Chip continued to call himself Chip. After leaving university he actually changed his name by deed poll to Chip. Outwardly, Mat and I have always derided our little brother's American-sounding moniker, but I think we're both secretly a tiny bit proud. Saying your brother is called Chip is a little like saying your dad is a birdwatcher. It's not particularly odd or interesting but it is intriguing. There's a hint of 'isn't he wacky' about it that we hope might rub off on us.

Then again, when I ordered some mother's day flowers from the three of us last year I was asked what message I'd like on the card.

'Lots of love from Mat, Alex and Chip,' I said.

'Fine,' she said. 'Mat, Alex and Chip. Chip's the dog is he?'

Influenced partly, I like to think, by me, Chip also made the pilgrimage to Liverpool after his thirteenth birthday, this time with the focus on the Blue half of the city. He's an Everton fan. Our football allegiances are shamefully glory-based. But by now the father-son thing was even more diluted. Chip brought his friend Seth along, due to some administrative mix-up they and Duncton were the only three people on that week's tour so went round in a taxi rather than a coach and Everton ended up losing to a Shearer-led Blackburn. I'm sure he had a brilliant weekend but it didn't sound quite as memorable as Mat's (or mine, for that matter).

Being boys, the three of us have obviously never discussed our respective trips in more detail than what food we ate and what souvenirs we brought back, but for some time now I've wondered what Mat's expedition was actually like. Was it the experience that set him on his birdwatching course? Or was his interest already there, the trip merely a manifestation of his inner bird-watching self? This is a classic nature versus nurture debate. We hold the key to one of science's great riddles! Would I be a birder now if Duncton had whisked me off for a week on a wet and windy island? Or would I have turned my back even more emphat-ically on all things winged and wild?

I had plenty of time to ask Mat all about Fair Isle on this, our maiden brotherly birdwatching outing, but I never quite got round to it. I guess I didn't want to make things awkward just before he left for a year in Africa by talking about anything remotely personal. Instead we pottered along, amiably discussing this and that (prob-ably football and Africa), content to spend a rare day in each other's company doing something a little out of the ordinary.

Ready to explore the next frontier beyond my back garden and the graveyard, I'd found out about a place called Brent Reservoir on the internet. Located just inside the North Circular, this seemed to be the main birdwatching spot in my particular borough of London. The grim journey up the Edgware Road through Kilburn and Brondesbury wasn't all that encouraging, but turning left by a pub called The Welsh Harp, we suddenly saw the water stretching out before us, like a mirage in some barren tract. I found out later the pub was named after the reser-voir, which was in turn given the musical nickname on account of its shape. Whether or not it actually looks anything like a harp from Wales, The Welsh Harp certainly sounds more romantic than the Brent Reservoir.

After reluctantly leaving my car all alone in the carpark of some disused playing fields nearby, Mat and I walked over to the lake then followed a path into the woods and around the water's edge towards a couple of hides he'd seen on the far bank as we drove in. I hadn't noticed them, and was already worried that my observational skills would come up a little short as the day progressed. I was relieved, therefore, to point out a group of long-tailed tits as we skirted the reservoir. I wanted Mat to see that I was finally taking this bird business seriously.

The London Birders[36] website on which I'd read about the lake showed pictures of a still, clean and scenic sanctuary. Unfortunately, the page had last been updated in 2002. While the website remained pristine, the birdsite was strewn with litter, walls covered in graffiti and the water itself dotted with several requisite shopping trolleys. Hurdling fallen trees and squelching through a mud bath that was once a footpath, the first hide we came to bore a plaque reading: 'Opened by Bill Oddie in 1991'. Unfortunately someone, who didn't get a plaque, had since closed it. The door was firmly bolted shut. In fact we couldn't even find a handle with which to try to open it. Neither of us had Bill Oddie's phone number, so we decided to move on.

Thankfully the second hide was open, although that was because the door had been smashed in by, it appeared, an axe. As we approached, we noticed the shattered door swinging eerily on its hinges, allowing us brief glimpses of wood splinters scattered around the floor inside and the remains of the lock, torn in two as if by some frenzied metal-shearing werewolf. Feeling a little bit like characters from *The Blair Witch Project* we cautiously entered the battered hut, where, aside from the fractured wood, there was no evidence of criminal activity. If there had been an axe-wielding murderer or man-eating beast, they'd been very careful not to leave any traces of blood. Deciding that we were probably not in any immediate danger we perched ourselves on the two stools that had survived the attack and concentrated on the view outside. Quite a view it was too. A bigger expanse of water than you'd expect to find in northwest London, but also, looming up above the streets and houses, the arch of the new Wembley stadium,

---

36 www.londonbirders.com

recently raised and straddling Brent like a rainbow. We sat serenely for a couple of hours, occasionally munching on some Mr Kipling Lemon Slices, two brothers in a shed by a lake.

The whole adventure was a lot of fun. The hides may have been a disappointment (and when I got home I did leave a sanctimonious comment on the London Birders website saying how sad I was they'd been so badly maintained), but exploring a place we felt we weren't allowed to be made us feel like kids again. As Mat taught me the difference between teal and tufted ducks or common, black-headed and lesser black-backed gulls, our status of older and younger brothers was restored. I was slightly in awe of his instant knowledge, he seemed happy to share it. The highlights for me were two birds we saw on the walk back to our car (which happily also escaped any sort of axe attack). First, a large magpie-like bird, perched in a tree a good fifty yards away that I would never have spotted. More colourful than their more common cousins, with a stripe of blue on one side, these are the subject of more confused phonecalls to the RSPB than any other. 'It's a jay,' the patient person at the other end will tell you when you phone to say you've discovered something exotic. You'd have been right though. They are exotic, glamorous birds, and while not really rare, they are well worth a closer look.

As soon as we lowered our binoculars and turned back to the path, a fast-moving green smudge swooped past in front of us. 'Green woodpecker,' said Mat without even raising his glasses. 'You see how it bobbed up and down as it flew along, that's what they do.'

Tremendous. I never knew that. But he was absolutely right. If you see a greenish bird with a swoopy sort of flight it'll almost certainly be a green woodpecker. And if you can follow its flight to where it lands you'll also see it has a brilliant red, punk-like cap and a Sherwood Forest outfit that befits such a quirky creature. Thank you Mat.

9 March

We've never quite figured out how to say goodbye, Mat and I. We've both now got other halves who are really very good at reaching out for a peck on the cheek and a hug, but that's normal protocol for those relationships. There's no norm for brothers. A handshake would be far too formal and really quite odd, a hug just a bit over the top for people as typically English as us. We see each other a couple of times a week; we can't cuddle each other every forty-eight hours! So I dropped Mat back home with a slightly hesitant wave and wished him all the best for his year in a different continent.

Duncton, on the other hand, has got his familial salutation ritual sorted. I can't remember exactly when it started, but some time after I left school and before I finished university, he adopted a full back-slapping embrace as his way of marking the moment a son leaves or arrives. It took a little while to bed in, the first few awkward attempts were accompanied by a slightly embarrassed laugh and an involuntary intake of breath, but I think we're all glad he initiated more physical contact amongst the Hornes. Being a four-males-to-one-female family, all hugs had previously been directed to Mum, so I guess Duncton felt it was time for him to get his fair share.

When I drove to Midhurst for the second time in the year, it was with such a clinch that Duncton greeted me. I'd actually driven down in the evening so we could head out birdwatching early the next morning, meaning I wouldn't get to watch Liverpool play Benfica in the Champions League so I think he wanted to express his appreciation at my commitment. As it was, Liverpool were beaten 2–0 and so had to bid farewell to the cup they'd won so magnificently the year before. I wasn't as gutted as I might have been in previous years. Perhaps this was a sign that birdwatching is more important than football. No, that's too strong, I'm not sure even Duncton would agree with that – a sign that birdwatching is *as* important as football.

We rose with the sun the next morning and drove out to Pulborough Brooks, where Duncton did most of his RSPB volunteering, including the tiny egg chase. Stopping off at Burton Mill Pond, one of Duncton's favourite spots, I felt an unexpected sense of pride that I was on a proper birdwatching outing with my dad. Duncton had his best pair of binoculars round his neck and his telescope slung over his shoulder. I had only the mini pair of binoculars he'd given me for my honeymoon, but I was wearing a pair of his Wellington boots and his second best hard-wearing outdoor coat, so I looked the part. People even stopped and asked us bird-related questions, like whether or not we'd seen the bittern on the pond. I scrunched up my face knowledgeably and gestured to Duncton as if the question was beneath me. 'Oooh, they're so hard to see,' he explained. 'A couple were spotted out by those trees last week, but they're more likely to be found in the early evening. Somebody reported them at about 8.30 a.m. a few days ago, but I've never heard of them being around in the morning.'

'Yes,' I murmured in confirmation, 'it was by those trees but only in the evening usually.'

Unfortunately, when we returned to the carpark my car alarm went off and refused to stop going off, thus ruining my short-lived birdwatching cred.

At the reserve itself, Duncton led me to his preferred hide and pointed out yet more waterbirds on the marshes. There really are a lot of different types of duck. The mallard has done very well to steal so much of the limelight. As well as nearly all the species I'd already seen, I added pochard, gadwall and pintail, all ducks (dabbling ducks to be precise) and all with uniquely attractive characteristics. Pochard and Gadwall I thought were particularly gallant names, as suited to Arthurian knights as these wildfowl.

I saw my first wader in the form of a lapwing which instantly shot to number one on my favourite bird chart, mostly due to its catwalk-fashion-style wispy crest. The sound they made as they flew aerobatically in front of us was similarly outlandish. It's hard to do it justice on the page, but Mat's *Collins Bird Guide* described it as 'Heartbreakingly shrill' which is pretty close. Considering it's a technical, almost scientific book, that's some pretty emotive language. Much to Duncton's disappointment, we managed to dip a snipe, a phrase I wouldn't have come close to recognising just a couple of months earlier.[37] As we scanned the water's edge in vain I asked Duncton what a snipe looked like. 'Oh, it's a light brown, speckled bird,' he said. I nodded. Great.

'Is it particularly light brown, or particularly speckled?' I asked, conscious that quite a few birds might fit that description.

'No, it's about average,' he said.

Exasperated, I looked the bird up in my bird guide and was amazed to find a picture of a bird average in every way except for the most disproportionately long beak I'd ever seen. Compared to any other bird I'd set eyes on this was a remarkable sight, much more remarkable than its light brown speckledness. To me this was like describing Cyrano de Bergerac as having distinctively mousy hair.

'Why didn't you mention its incredibly long beak?' I protested.

'Oh yes, sorry,' said Duncton, 'I thought you'd know that. But no, you don't know anything do you. Right, sorry.'

There really can be a huge gulf between birdwatchers and non-birdwatchers at times.

As thoughts of lunch began to crowd any others from my head, a thunderclap sounded and thick rain began to dollop onto the

---

37 'To dip' is birding parlance for 'to miss out on a bird that was, at some stage, within reach'. The opposite is 'to connect with'. Dipping is generally followed by a sighing and swearing. Connecting is generally followed by cheering and swearing.

roof of the hide. A couple of minutes later, a noisy crowd of school children was herded into the hide. Weighing up these new conditions, Duncton and I decided we weren't going to get a lot more meaningful birdwatching done, so braved the rain and scuttled back to the cafeteria for sausages, beans and a baked potato. Duncton was disappointed not to have seen anything more spectacular during the morning, and I tried to reassure him by saying that for me everything was novel, and, in a way, spectacular. In truth I was slightly relieved we hadn't seen a particularly impressive bird, lest I had failed to recognise it. I've watched football games with people who've never seen the sport before and know how irritating it can be when they cheer at a throw-in or look nonplussed by a thirty-yard screamer. But could I ever get excited by the birding equivalent? I would have to wait and see.

17 March

I was well aware that with spring approaching, any lapse in my birdwatching education could be fatal, and so I took the opportunity of a gig in Manchester to explore what I hoped was a good local bird spot. I saw its name on one of those brown signs you usually ignore on the way in to a city, and on impulse stopped for a look.

My first impression of Etherow Country Park was that it wasn't nearly as nice as Pulborough Brooks, partly because it seemed to consist only of a pond and some unremarkable buildings, but mostly because I didn't have Duncton to show me round. At reception, however, I was spoken to at length by a loud couple who seemed both overjoyed and alarmed by a visitor and who took it upon themselves to guide me.

'What do you want to know, dear?' asked the lady.

'Well, do you know what that colourful goose is out there?'

I enquired, timidly. I'd seen a colourful goose out on the pond.

'Have you been here before?' the man demanded, refusing to answer my question just yet.

'No, I'm not from here. I've come up from . . . London,' I replied, more nervously.

'The one with red eyes, do you mean?' asked the lady, a little more benignly.

'Yes, that's the one.'

'It's an Egyptian orphan.'

'Does he mean Popeye?' bellowed the man, refusing to look at me.

'Yes,' said the woman. She wouldn't stop looking at me. 'He's been here for years. I think he's the last one left. He makes a lot of noise when he's hungry.'

By now the three of us had wandered out to the pond and the unfortunate bird.

'Now this one here,' said the man, suddenly bursting into life and thrusting an arm out towards a different goose, 'is Chinese. There was a pair but the other one got foxed. About twenty years ago. We've been trying to find him a partner, but no luck.'

'Regulations,' agreed the woman, gloomily.

'And these are Aylesbury ducks!' announced the man with some pride.

'They're not!' countered the lady, 'they're a type of muscovy. Aylesburys walk upright and are slimmer than that.'

'But we have got two Aylesburys here – Josie and Gertrude.'

'What have you called them?' shrieked the lady.

'Josie and Gertrude.'

'After me?'

'Maybe.'

'And is there a bird hide here anywhere?' I interrupted, keen to move on now.

'Yes,' said the man with a sigh, 'if you walk right down to the weir – we don't advertise it mind – but go down those steps, follow the path, down the road, round to the right, go over to the bridge where they're doing all the work, bear left and that's the start of White Bottom Farm, but if you follow up the road, on the right side there's a footpath that says Cheshire Wildlife Trust, follow that and it'll take you round to the river.'

'Brilliant, and how long might that take?'

'Oh, about three-quarters of an hour,' said either Josie or Gertrude.

'No! No! No!' scowled the man. 'No way. Five minutes. Takes me five minutes.'

Fifty minutes later, I still hadn't seen any sign of a hide and I had to start at least thinking about getting back if I wanted to get to my show on time. Suddenly though, a particularly eye-catching bird bobbed down the river towards me, a brightly coloured jester of a duck. If he was a student he would have been one of those amazingly cool ones who dress so trendily they very nearly look like idiots. With orange whiskers and matching tails at the back, white spectacles and a lurid coat, the duck was trying hard, maybe just a bit too hard. I was very pleased to see him, especially because I instinctively knew what it was – my first shelduck. Thanks Dad, I thought.

Making my way back to the car, I passed the bickering couple again, thanked them for their truly awful directions and told them about the duck. 'Oh yes, the Mandarin duck,' they said. 'Yes, there are lots of them around.' Oh dear. It wasn't a shelduck. Still, I'd not seen a Mandarin yet either.[38]

I don't think it would be spoiling anything now to say that even after birdwatching for the entire year, I was still rubbish

---

[38] I had no idea, by the way, why it was called a Mandarin duck or what it was doing in Manchester. And I couldn't face asking these two 'characters'.

at birdwatching. If you commit yourself to having a go at most hobbies a few times a week, you'd usually be quite good at them at the end of twelve months. If I decided to take up fencing, I'm sure I could hold my own in a sword fight the following year. If I took up running (as I tell myself I will at the start of every month), I'd probably be able to run quite far without wanting to cry after a year. But birdwatching is different. There's so much to learn with birdwatching. Even people like Duncton who've been studying birds all their lives say they're not really up to scratch, and that's not just because most birders are modest. Simon Barnes has written a book called *How to be a Bad Birdwatcher*, entirely based on the fact that he's not very good at it. Of course his knowledge and instincts are far superior to mine, far superior to most, but even he feels ignorant compared to the true ornithologists of the world (who in turn, I'm sure, would say they don't know anything, either).

You're probably aware of a television programme on Channel 4 called *Faking It*. Even Duncton's heard of it, and he only really watches programmes featuring David Attenborough or Tottenham. If you haven't, it's like a shortened version of my Big Year. As the pithy pitch on the show's website explains, 'Our faker is plucked from their natural habitat and given four weeks to master a skill well enough to fool a group of expert judges.' So in just a month a chess player must become a football manager, a management consultant has to master dog training, a choir girl is asked to morph into a rock chick. It's good TV.

But I don't think Channel 4 could ever do a *Faking It* on birdwatching. There's too much to learn. Even after my first ten weeks of birding, there was absolutely no way I could have persuaded some genuine bird experts that I knew what I was doing. There are too many nuances, too many calls, too many brown, speckled birds. A *Faking It* on birdwatching would be like doing a *Faking It* on Being a Mouse. It would be that pointless.

You'd have four weeks of training on How to Walk Like a Mouse, How to Squeak Correctly and Which Cheeses to Eat. Then the day of the test would arrive and you'd have to line up next to three actual mice and the judges would take one look at the line-up, point at you and say, 'Well he's not a mouse, clearly, he's far too big.' After ten weeks I was nowhere near to being a mouse.

18 March

But knowing I had the whole world at my disposal, and the Israel trip on the horizon, I did think I still had a chance of winning the competition and pulling off what would be a remarkable upset. So back in London I knuckled down and tried to make sure I at least knew the basics. I may not ever become a mouse, but at least I might learn to do a better impression of a mouse than most people.

I therefore joined the RSPB. I'd never joined a society before, so this was a fairly big decision, but when I read on their website that I'd get a free fourteen-inch feeder on joining, I was sold.

19 March

Every gig was now an opportunity to grab more birds, but one show down in Exeter provided a chance to grab a birdwatcher too. The parents of Tom, the merlin man, had moved to Dawlish in Devon the year before. Like Duncton, they'd retired at a sensible, youngish age, and had chosen to escape to the seaside for at least some of the rest of their lives. Dawlish wasn't far from Exeter, so they suggested I drop in.

Unfortunately, I was doing one of my Edinburgh shows that night, and had Key with me. Key liked Janet and Jamie, Janet and Jamie were really quite fond of Key, but Key was staunchly anti-birdwatching. I wanted to go birdwatching, I'd heard Jamie liked to go birdwatching, but Key was doing me a favour by doing the gig for very little money, on the condition that I wouldn't make him go birdwatching. This was tricky.

'Well, we're here early, and it's a nice day, why don't we all go for a walk!' I suggested ingeniously when we arrived.

'Good idea,' said Jamie and Janet.

'Mmm,' said Key suspiciously. I discreetly tucked my binoculars down the front of my coat.

The four of us piled into Janet's car and headed down to the beach, me and Key like kids in the back with our surrogate parents in the front, occasionally spinning round to stop us squabbling. As we drove through Dawlish town centre, Jamie pointed out a black swan minding its own business on the pond.

'There it is,' he said. 'The black swan.'

'Great,' I said, making a mental note of this bonus species. Key shook his head and tutted.

At the seafront we bought ice creams, sticking closely to our assumed roles, and wandered along Dawlish Warren, a seashore boasting gravelly beaches, sand dunes, grassland and scrub, and therefore perfect for avian activity. I managed to engineer a situation where Jamie and I were alone, with Key and Janet chatting away further ahead.

'A lot of birds out there,' I said, gesturing to the sea.

'Yes,' said Jamie.

'Tom tells me you're into birdwatching,' I continued hopefully.

'I do like to feed them in the garden. I find them relaxing.'

He's an amateur! I thought. What am I doing here?

'Hang on,' – Jamie was still talking – 'what are they out there? . . . Oh look, oystercatchers! They're always nice.'

I looked up to where he was pointing and squinted. Nothing. I reached into my coat and brought out my binoculars. 'Oh yes, great! Well spotted!' Terrific. Red legs, red beaks, these were good new birds, and Jamie was clearly a fine, if laid-back, birdwatcher.

Unfortunately, just then Key looked round and caught me with my binocs out.

'No birds,' he cried, 'you promised!'

So that was it. The four of us carried on walking, with me occasionally looking helplessly out to sea.

'I'm sure you'll be back,' whispered Jamie reassuringly.

'I doubt it,' I grumbled.

We turned back for the car about a hundred yards short of the only hide. As a kid this would have been a great result. Now, I was gutted.

26 March

My RSPB welcome pack arrived, including the complimentary seed dispenser, so I went straight out to buy some luxury Bob Martin Bird Food from Sainsbury's. I hadn't known that Sainsbury's sold bird food, but I was gradually realising I'd been mysteriously blinkered to all things birdy for many years now.

31 March

Deciding not to revisit the axe-addled Welsh Harp Reservoir just yet, I paid a visit to a comparatively tiny nature reserve just yards from King's Cross Station called Camley Street Natural Park on the last day of the month. In complete contrast to The Welsh Harp, this miniature oasis was perfectly kept, a tiny haven for all things natural, wedged between the gasworks and the new Eurostar station. Unfortunately, it really was very small and after an hour I'd circled the pond three times, examined all fifteen trees and become personally acquainted with all ten birds on the site, so headed off again. But it did hearten me to think that a place like this could exist in the most urban of landscapes. As a resource for inner-city kids that wasn't a zoo, this was an unexpected treat.

As worthy as that sounds though, it didn't do any good to my numbers. I saw that I needed help; I needed someone to tell me where I could see rare birds. I needed a guide. So, with Mat leaving for Africa and Duncton my adversary, I went back on the web that evening and for the second time that month, joined something I'd never joined before. This time, a forum! The forum connected to the London Birders website in fact. If you're not familiar with internet forums, they're not all that similar to the forums of Ancient Rome. They're more like notice boards in a community centre. People post messages about their interests, other people reply. Sometimes they get graffitied. With the bird phone at Cley now a little outdated, birdwatchers use the London Birders forum to alert people to the arrival of particularly rare birds in the area, ask questions about troublesome birds and, in my case, beg for help.

The message I left on the site read 'Hey guys' – the correct way of addressing members of a forum, I hoped – 'I'm a novice birdwatcher, and also a comedian,' – and then I thought I should do a little joke to justify the claim – 'would anyone like to take me under their wing!!!' Not a great joke, obviously, but I wanted them to see I was fun, so added three exclamation marks at the end of the sentence.[39] Taking a deep breath and hitting send I then went one step further and logged on to Lee G R Evans' website[40] (which is, by the way, well worth a look. Not only can

---

39 I've never been a fan of single exclamation marks as they can warn both of humour and danger. This, I feel, is confusing. It's only really relevant in McDonald's when someone spills something and they bring out a yellow sign with a picture of someone falling over and an exclamation mark – because that is potentially both hazardous *and* quite funny.

40 www.uk400clubonline.co.uk

you read his story in his own words, but you can also book him to run a mobile disco for you[41]), found his contact details and sent him a message too. With less exclamation marks this time, I explained my situation, the challenge with Duncton and the fact that I was going to Israel later in the year. Since he was an expert on birds all around the world and an experienced bird-watching tour guide around the Western Palaearctic[42] and North America, I was hoping Lee might be my Israel instructor.

Having sent two emails to people I'd never met, I went to bed.

Earlier that day, while on my final lap round the Camley Street Natural Park pond, Duncton had sent a text to his children saying:

**IM UP IN LONDON HE (sic) ANY OF YOU ARE
AROUND FOR COFFEE.**

I walked straight over to Great Portland Street where he was sitting in a café, and was soon joined by Mat for one last chat about football and family before he migrated south for the summer. Just before we all parted company, Mat noticed a heron high above Regent Street, the same heron, I liked to think, that had dropped into the zoo at the beginning of the month. For about thirty seconds we fell silent, standing in the middle of London, gazing up as the graceful creature coasted past, still poker-faced. I don't know what it meant to the others, but I took it as a very positive sign, and after Mat and I had hugged Duncton goodbye, the three of us went our separate ways with spring in the air and our steps.

---

41 Although, since finishing my year, Lee G R Evans seems to be now concentrating solely on birds. Only recently have people other than Oddie been able to make a living entirely out of birdwatching. For someone like Evans, this must be a dream come true.

42 A zoogeographical region comprising Europe, North Africa and the temperate part of the Arabian peninsula.

CHAPTER 4

Wingman

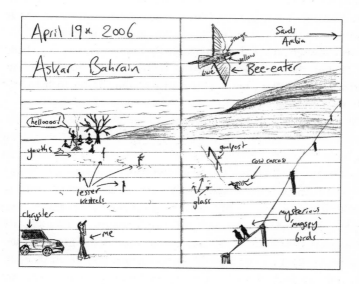

'By the end of March my total had increased to 243 species, and I was beginning to feel on top of my game ... In my days as a football coach, I would always tell my players to concentrate fully on their own performance and forget about that of their rival teams. The most important competition is that which you have with yourself. It was time for me to practise what I had been preaching.'

– Adrian M Riley

Alex: 63 species
Duncton: 104 species

1 April

Once or twice a year a bird will turn up in Britain that is so rare even the national press get excited. Usually the unfortunate vagrant will have got lost on the way somewhere fairly exotic and ended up in an incongruously mundane British location. At the end of March, an American robin in south London ticked all those boxes and, for a brief while at least, shunted bird flu scare stories out of the papers.

'Peckham welcomes American Cousin' announced *The Times* proudly, with the hack's subtitle: 'Don't tell Del-Boy. A new bird has flown into his manor and it's got some of the neighbours twitching.' 'You don't have to spend long with a bunch of birdwatchers to realise what it's all about,' said Harry Fawcett on Channel 4 news. 'Waiting! And this morning, we're waiting in a street in Peckham in the drizzly cold.'[43]

Frustratingly, while birdwatchers from all over the country were flocking down to this drizzly cold street in SE15 to see the poor little lost bird, I'd had to travel to Swindon, Ipswich and Caernarfon for gigs, locations so far apart I didn't even have time to stop for a quick stroll around a bird reserve on the way, let alone a jaunt down to Peckham beforehand. I knew Duncton wouldn't be making the pilgrimage to southeast London either, but this was exactly the sort of bird needed if I was to get anywhere near his total.

To my wife's well-hidden disappointment, Saturday morning was the first time since news of its arrival broke that I could actually try to see it, so after spending twelve hours in the car

---

43 The London Birders forum was predictably excited by this TV coverage of one of *their* birds. 'Can't believe they interviewed Mad Franko!' wrote one member. Watching the piece a couple of times I tried to work out which of the interviewees this madman could be. I concluded that it was probably a bloke with a moustache, a vaguely Russian hat and a glint in his eye.

the previous day driving to and from the furthest corner of Wales, it took me another two hours to crawl the six miles down to Denham Road where, according to the London Birders forum, the robin had last been seen.

But that last sighting was now two days old. Since then, there'd been silence. So when I arrived at what was a completely deserted street, my heart sank. Where were the birders I'd seen on the news? Where, more to the point, was the robin? I felt like I'd been given the wrong date for a party. I felt like an April Fool.

I did go for a wander round the streets, peering discreetly into gardens and listening out for any hint of an American accent. I did chat for quite some time with a very nice elderly resident, who told me cheerfully that I should have been there two days ago. Had she seen the bird? I asked her. 'Oh yes,' she grinned, 'everyone saw the bird. It wasn't very good though. It was just a bird.'

I even sat clutching my binoculars in the car for an hour, looking like the most inept private detective in the world, when actually I was the most inept birdwatcher in the world. I was certain the bird had flown, but I also knew that even if it hadn't, I wouldn't be able to recognise it by myself. It would look to me, and most of the residents of Peckham, like any other little brown bird. I was counting on being able to follow the gaze of a crowd of dedicated birders and find it that way.

On my dejected drive home I got stuck in another horrendous traffic jam and only had about ten minutes to spare before having to drive to Derby for another gig. It's not always the most relaxing hobby, birdwatching.

2 April

If missing the American robin was something of a false start to the month, the next day I left the blocks a little later than I'd have liked but went on to run a fantastic race.

Just before leaving for Derby I'd checked my emails to find two bird-related messages in my inbox. The first was from Lee G R Evans. In a brief but helpful note he got my hopes up by explaining that 'Israel is the top birding destination in the Western P.' then dashed them with the clause, 'but only in spring I'm afraid.' To underline how bad my timing was he went on to say that 'By August the heat will be in the 40s and birds will be scarce apart from a few returning warblers in the wadis and larks at K40 and flamingos at K20 Reservoir.'[44] Of course I appreciated him taking the time to advise me and was thrilled to receive any sort of communication featuring the words, 'All the very best, Lee G R Evans', but Israel suddenly looked less like the promised land.

The other message, however, was more hopeful. It came from the London Birders Forum and, to be precise, a man called David. 'Yes,' he wrote, 'I'd be happy to take you under my wing (ha ha). I've got kids so am pretty busy but could do Sunday (tomorrow) morning. How about you meet me at Ferry Lane in Tottenham Hale at about 7 a.m.? If we have a good walk round the reservoirs there we should be able get you quite a few more species – maybe even rock pipit, red-breasted merganser and ring ouzel?'

Nearly all this was music to my ears. I'd never even heard of these mythical sounding birds. But 7 a.m. in east London? After a late night in Derby? Is that ever wise? I emailed back to say I was incredibly grateful but couldn't really make it before 8 a.m., if that was OK. David agreed and I managed to race back from the Midlands and slip into bed by 2 a.m.

My alarm went off at 6.45 a.m. I didn't even stir. Being a comedian (and naturally lazy), I'm not used to getting up much before 9 a.m. Being a journalist (and naturally far more hard working) Rachel is, and so even at the weekends her body clock

---

44 Two ironically dry sounding bodies of Israeli water, famous for their birds.

will often wake her ridiculously early. So, at 7.30 a.m. she dug me in the ribs, I looked at my watch, swore very quietly and ran out to the car. Thankfully at that time on a Sunday morning most other people aren't rushing out to their nearest bird reserve, so the roads were quiet and I arrived just two minutes late, setting off only one speed camera on the way.

I'd never met a stranger from the internet at 8 a.m. by a reservoir in east London before. And if I do happen to again, I doubt they'd be as good company as David. He was instantly disarming, intelligent, funny, calm, self-deprecating ('It's a stupid hobby really,' he said within the first hour. 'You spend a lot of time standing still and looking at bushes!'). But above all, he was extremely knowledgeable on the subject of birds.[45] After a hearty handshake and the briefest of acknowledgements that this was a little odd, his first words were, 'Have you got a redstart yet?' Of course I hadn't, but I did recognise that he was referring to a species of bird, and so looked as excited as I could at that time of day.

'Come on then, there's one over here.'

Sure enough, after ten minutes of patient waiting on a path just down from the carpark, we heard a few sharp whistles from a bush, then saw a small black and red thrush burst up and out into the open. I'd decided to say, 'Yes, I saw it', whether or not I set eyes on the thing, but it sat obligingly on a branch for at least ten seconds. 'Brilliant,' I said. One new bird in the first few minutes, this could be quite a trip.

David had given me no hint as to how long we'd be out. Rachel was meeting friends for lunch, so I had no particular deadline, but I assumed I'd be back in time for the lunchtime kick-off in the Premiership. None of my outings with Duncton or Mat had lasted more than a couple of hours. So when I looked at my

---

45 We're still in touch now so when I say 'was' I should really say 'is'.

watch on our eventual return to the carpark I couldn't believe that we'd spent more than six hours walking round the urban waterscape.

The birds had performed well: dinosaur-like cormorants resting on dead trees with the skeleton of a waterworks looming up behind them, meadow pipits, chiffchaffs and wheatears dancing round just yards away from us, and several green woodpeckers swooping and diving as we crossed bridges, ducked under tunnels and circumnavigated endless pools of water. My personal favourite was a grey wagtail, pottering about by the water's edge. Another bird with a name that doesn't really do it justice, it had a yellow chest brighter than anything I'd seen in the zoo and seemed entirely out of place in this metropolitan environment.

David tried to teach me about the birdsongs we (well, he) could hear. 'That's a little grebe singing there,' he whispered, 'they always have that on the soundtrack to jungle films. I hear it and say, "That's a little grebe! What's that doing in the jungle?" It really annoys me!'

And this was the most amazing thing about the trip for me. There wasn't one awkward moment during the entire morning. I'm normally fairly bad in social situations, even with people I've known for years or am related to. The whole business of interaction, whether it be looking someone in the eye, shaking their hand or delivering a baby, I just find difficult. I suppose I'm too self-conscious. But with David leading the way, I was more than happy to walk at his side, chatting sometimes, silent at others, just birdwatching.

After reading my message on the forum David had Googled me to see if I was who I said I was and was intrigued at the idea of a comedian observing his hobby. He wondered how I'd make it funny. I did too. He apologised for not being the geeky caricature people might expect and which would, of course, be an easier target for comedy. But I was glad to have discovered a different sort of birdwatcher. After all, Duncton may be a typical dad in many ways, but he's not the stereotypical twitcher lazily alluded to in the media during the American robin furore the week before. Birdwatchers aren't all the same, they don't all wear anoraks and they're not all loners. In fact, I'd say I was definitely more socially awkward than any of the bird lovers I had the pleasure to spend time with over the year, and I've probably got a similar amount of waterproof clothing.

Having been interested in birds as a boy, David was in bands most of his adult life, releasing seven albums before calling it quits and heading off in a different direction.

This desolate collection of manmade lakes was David's patch. He came here three times a week to do a couple of circuits and keep an eye on what was coming and going. Today he couldn't believe we'd missed common sandpiper, stock dove and willow warbler. 'Well, I'll just have to come back for them,' I said.

Although exhausted by the end of the trip, I was also exhilarated. To me, walking almost non-stop for that long represents an expedition, a hike, a dedicated ramble. To David, this was a normal birding outing – except it started a bit later than usual. By the time we'd reached my car I'd learned a lot and seen eight new species, a modest but welcome haul. More than anything, though, I felt considerably closer to the birdwatcher breed than ever before.

And just to turn it into the perfect internet date, we found the nearest watering hole and carried on nattering away. I asked naive questions about birds, David gave me answers.

'So why are there so many seagulls so far from the sea?' I asked.

'Good question,' he replied patiently. 'Seagull is a misleading name. Gulls can live near any sort of water, a lake, a river, an estuary or the sea. But they're also scavengers and can survive just as easily by a rubbish tip as on the beach. Black-headed gulls are often found on farms, following farmers as they plough their fields and churn up worms.'

'And what's the best way to find all these birds?'

'I'd say you should join something called Birdguides. They'll text you with rare sightings. So next time there's an American robin around you can get there in time. You'll be on call twenty-four hours a day.'

'Like a doctor or a fireman.'[46]

'A bit like that, yes.'

'And where do Mandarin ducks come from?'

'Good question. Birders tend to be quite snobbish about them as a species because they were introduced from China, so they're not native birds. But a fossilised Mandarin duck from about 40,000 years ago was recently dug up here in Britain so they were actually here first.'

'Good answer.'

That's the sort of trivia that could grace any pub.

It was probably only the fact that I was driving which prevented us staying in the pub all day. As we said goodbye I thanked him a little too profusely. I didn't want to say, 'Do you want to see me again?' Thankfully another warm handshake and a 'That was a good morning,' from David reassured me that this might not just be a one-off.

5 April

One thing the trip round Tottenham Hale taught me was that birds can thrive even in the bleakest of landscapes. I still hadn't learned that getting up early is the best way to see them though, so at 10 a.m., with a newspaper, a cup of coffee and a bacon

---

46 More manly occupations.

sandwich on the passenger seat beside me, I pulled up for the second time beside The Welsh Harp.

Marching round the reservoir more purposefully this time, I passed the first hide, still locked, only to be denied access to the second one too. The axed door had been bolted shut with some basic plank and nail carpentry and when I squeezed my head through a hole in the wall to have a closer look I saw that everything, splinters, bolts, even the two stools, had been removed. Not to be thwarted, I perched on a log at the water's edge and tucked into my breakfast, still not quite able to shake off the feeling that something bad was going to leap out at me from either the water or the woods.

Watching the coots and swans float serenely by, I relaxed. After thirty minutes I'd finished my supplies and hadn't seen any new birds. I began to get restless. I was pleased to be able to identify everything out on the water, but was, frankly, a bit bored. I thought I'd seen some sort of bird of prey out on the horizon but without David to identify it, it could have been anything. I had a look at the newspaper, but since a dead swan apparently carrying the deadly avian flu virus had been discovered in the village of Cellardyke in Scotland the day before, there wasn't much to cheer a jaded novice birdwatcher.[47] Over in east London we'd kept moving and the hours had flown by, so I resolved to circumnavigate the lake.

Walking round The Welsh Harp wasn't easy. After twenty minutes my path came to a dead end and I had to decide whether to climb a fence into unmarked territory, cross a bridge into what

---

47 This bird became the key player in the whole bird flu saga. *Drivetime* on BBC Radio 5 Live reported: 'It's thought this bird was a mute swan, probably of local origin, which suggests that it caught the virus from another bird, bringing it into the area . . . Officials in London held a high-level meeting of COBRA, that's the Government's crisis management committee, today . . .' That's a relief, I thought, COBRA are on to it! COBRA! How could the virus not be scared off by COBRA!

was clearly private industrial property or turn back. Twenty minutes, I reasoned, is too long a time to walk in one direction to then just turn back at the first obstacle, so I clumsily hurdled the fence (no one was watching but I was embarrassed at how ineptly I got over it) and found myself in a boggy forest. With the lake to my right, I waded ankle-deep in mud, clambering over sloping trees. For the first hour, I thoroughly enjoyed my ramble. I remembered how we would explore for whole days as kids, not caring about dirt or the time. When I finally emerged from this municipal Narnia, I was even closer to Wembley, and again I felt a childlike excitement as I looked up at the steep walls of the stadium and could almost hear the rumbling of a match day within.

A couple of hours later, as I staggered along the final stretch back to my car, I passed a sign that told me I was now on part of the 'Capital Ring', a walking route which circles the whole of London. With the end now in sight, a mere three hours after setting off from my log, doing the 'Capital Ring' seemed like a very good idea. As soon as I got home I looked it up online and saw that I'd been on the section between Greenford, the most westerly point, and South Kenton. If I'd kept going I'd have walked through Highgate, Finsbury Park and Hackney, before crossing the river at Woolwich, turning back east again at Grove Park, stomping through Crystal Palace, Streatham Common and Wimbledon Park before crossing back north of the river at Richmond and heading round through Southall, back to where I started. It was only seventy-five miles long. How satisfying would it be to circumnavigate London on foot? Once I've done this bird-watching year, I thought, I'll do that.

6 April

As well as binoculars and a coconut, Duncton had given me a book called *The Birdwatcher's Yearbook and Diary 2006* in a gesture of support. Not, as you can tell by the positioning of the apostrophe, a homemade album featuring the faces of all that year's birdwatchers with wacky comments like 'Most likely to mistake a buzzard for a bustard', but an all-purpose log book for the everyday birder. According to the blurb on the back of the book, it's an 'indispensable companion', 'the essential work of reference for birdwatchers' and is 'now in its 26th great year.' I couldn't help thinking that the book was better than me. A good friend, crucial for birders and a year younger, it had everything! Including a huge section on all the nature reserves around the UK, which I could use to pick spots near my gigs. I used it to locate the nearest reserve to a forthcoming gig in Nottingham, settling upon Wollaton Park, located five miles west of Nottingham and home, apparently, to spotted flycatchers, the occasional smew[48] and all three species of woodpecker: lesser spotted, great spotted and green.

The park is attached to Wollaton Hall, one of the finest Elizabethan houses in England. I'd arrived a good few hours before the gig so parked up and wandered off aimlessly into the woods. I'd love to have a garden with woods.

Instantly there was birdsong all around me. Whenever one sounded close I stopped, waited, then had a look through my binoculars to see . . . a great tit. Every time. There were hundreds of them, teasing me with their cheerful calls and flashing wings. I soon got frustrated and headed over to a lake (I'd also love to have a garden with a lake) only to find a load of mallards, some Canada geese and a goldeneye – not my first, but always nice to see a duck that is also a James Bond film.[49]

Where were these flycatchers and woodpeckers? Where was

---

48 A lovely phrase. 'Smew' always sounds to me more like some sort of bodily noise than a bird – as do 'scaup', 'shrike', 'quail' and 'chough'.

49 The carrion crow is the only bird that could also be a smutty British film.

the occasional smew? How occasional was it? Just at Christmas? There were no helpful signs or hides; I really was just moseying around the grounds. I need focus, I thought, had a look at the lake, and decided I should probably walk round it.

Having successfully avoided interaction with a handful of youths at the far end of the water, I began to enjoy myself. Yet again I hadn't seen any new birds, but I was out and about in Nottinghamshire, strolling round a country house instead of leaving late and getting stuck on the M1. Then, about four-fifths of the way round the lake, I heard a click in the trees beside me, definitely different to the 'ping ping' of the great tits and too high to be my own feet stepping on a twig. I looked up, raised my binoculars and immediately clapped eyes on a spotted woodpecker – my first for the year! I was inordinately excited. I had found one of the key birds for this site. It started drizzling as I watched the bird obligingly peck away at the tree then hop to a different part of the trunk, but I barely noticed. It was like the end of *Four Weddings and a Funeral*, only without an American woman. This was just me and my woodpecker.

Leafing through the guide, I was slightly taken aback to see that there were three types of spotted woodpecker: the great, the middle and the lesser varieties. The middle spotted woodpecker, it said, is never found in the UK, so was this the lesser or the great? They both looked pretty similar except, unsurprisingly, there is less of the lesser than the great. But from where I was standing I couldn't really say for sure if this one was twelve or twenty-two centimetres. Without a ruler, I just couldn't tell for sure. Maybe nature reserves should hang rulers from the branches, I thought to myself.

I looked closer at the book and the bird, as if playing some sort of outdoors spot-the-difference competition. I noticed that my one didn't have any red on its belly. Ha! I thought, just as the birders among you will have, It's a lesser spotted woodpecker! For as well as the red crown that both birds share, the more common great spotted woodpecker has a bright red tinge to what the guide calls its 'vent'. This one didn't. I scribbled down these details in my now soggy notebook and raced back to the car. I'd got a very hard woodpecker – a lesser spotted woodpecker!

At least I had managed to convince myself that I'd seen a lesser spotted woodpecker. Later that week I told both Duncton and David the good news and on each occasion was greeted with guarded congratulations. 'Well done,' they each said. 'You know they really are quite hard to find.' Neither of them had seen a lesser spotted woodpecker so far that year. In fact Duncton wouldn't see one at any stage of his Big Year. I began to doubt myself. Had it been smaller than a great spotted woodpecker? Maybe, but I couldn't say for sure. Was there definitely no red on its belly? Well, it was raining and my binoculars aren't great; again, I couldn't say without a doubt. But at the time I was certain it was a lesser. I just didn't know then quite how hard to find they are. Could I include it in my total? Well, I thought, I'll stick it on my list but won't tell the recorder.[50] That way if I am wrong I'm only lying to myself. And Duncton. I could cope with that.

Perhaps lying is too strong a word anyway. 'Lying' implies deliberate deceit and duplicity; I might simply have made a mistake. The British Birds Rarities Committee, to give it its full name (it's also known as the Rare Men) currently has sixteen members, all male, including statisticians, an archivist and a museum consultant who work together to combat bird fraud.

---

50 Every county has a recorder who keeps track of who has seen what where, which in turn helps to support species and site conservation. Like the RSPB's Big Garden Birdwatch, this is a typical example of the birdwatching community striving to work together for the interests of the bird.

They examine the evidence of an unusual sighting with forensic attention to detail, a thoroughness that might seem like neurosis if it weren't for the numerous scams they've exposed. Sometimes charmingly ill-thought out, occasionally worryingly complex, these shady schemes have included people taking photos of birds in zoos, of models of birds they've made themselves, or of birds shot and killed overseas then 'found' in the British countryside. On each occasion, the con artist has claimed them as genuine British birds and the Rare Men have been forced to prove them wrong.

But my claim, I told myself, was a far more innocent one. To this day I can't be sure what I saw. Deep down I can't help thinking I may have cheated just a tiny bit by including it without confirmation by an actual birdwatcher but I was convinced at the time and anyway, it was a much better story to say I saw a lesser spotted woodpecker.

Going through my material on the way to the gig I worked out that about ninety per cent of what I say to an audience is untrue. I tell them I'm from Swindon, but only because I first say I'm from Sweden then dash their hopes with the more mundane location. I say I saw a cowboy outside the venue driving a small German car, but only so I can pretend I waved and said 'Audi'. I even say I hate football to help paint a picture of myself as weak and scrawny in comparison to some manly man in the front row. But then if I did come on and say I'm from Midhurst, nothing happened on the way here and I support Liverpool, it wouldn't be all that entertaining.

Having said that, sometimes making stuff up isn't all that entertaining either. The show in Nottingham was what comedians might call 'an awful gig'. As the compère, my job was to warm up the crowd, get them settled, tell a few jokes and introduce the acts. Before I'd even got to the stage, however, drunken women were bellowing 'say something funny' in an angry way.

It's hard to know what to say to that sort of heckle. I could have pointed out that I had always intended to 'say something funny' but appreciated the advice nevertheless, but as the volume of their yells increased I realised it didn't really matter what I said. The audience was almost totally made up of stags and hens, both groups as raucous as each other. Not for the first time I wondered why the male equivalents of a hen party weren't called cocks. I spent most of the evening doing my best to find different ways of telling adults to shut up and wishing there was a law stopping people from disturbing comedians (just as there is for birds).

As I said earlier, I know dying on stage is not the end of the world. But you still feel quite low after it's happened. On this occasion though, I drove home with a smile on my face, thinking not about the wasted hordes I'd failed to amuse but the wood-pecker, whichever type it was, that I'd succeeded in finding. I'd decided not to mention my birdwatching outing on stage (which would itself have been a birdwatching 'outing') but that was definitely the most interesting thing that happened to me on the way to the show.

7 April

It always amazes me how you can say the same words in the same order on two separate nights and get completely contrasting reactions. After the grim grind of Nottingham, my job was a pleasure once again in Sevenoaks the following evening, where the audience was just the right side of 'up for a laugh'. I've always liked the Kent town, perhaps partly because my grandparents, Duncton's parents, lived in the nearby village of Kemsing throughout my childhood, and indeed, throughout Duncton's. I had decided to hedge my bets once more by leaving for the local Kent birdwatching hotspot nice and early before the Sevenoaks gig. If I'm going to have a bad time on stage again, I thought, I'd better make sure I get something out of the trip. The M25, however, had other ideas. It took me four hours to crawl the forty miles anticlockwise round London. I would have been better doing my walk. Alone in the car I shouted things like, 'This is ridiculous!', 'No wonder nothing gets done in this country!' and 'Bloody Tony Blair!' Granny would have been proud.

I eventually reached the Sevenoaks Wildlife Reserve an hour before it closed its gates, by which time the several remarkable birds chalked up on the notice board outside had headed home, as had the birdwatchers who'd spotted them.

Independently, though, I managed to find two things that would have made up for any 'awful gig' later in the evening. First, from the landing of my first split-level hide of the year, a frisky flock of swallows, dynamic birds, dipping and flitting over the water, gratefully plucking flies from the air like miniature Mr Miyagis. They must have arrived from Africa in the last few days, probably passing my brother Mat on the way. While the light slowly faded I watched them as though in a trance, trying to imagine their journey over here and Mat's over there. It's always hard to picture friends or family when they're abroad, easier to look forward to their return. Now I thought of Mat and the swallows on some sort of interspecies exchange programme and hoped that my brother was having as much fun as these birds clearly were in their new environment.[51]

---

51 One further note on 'swallow', the bird and verb. One of the world's leading palindromists, an enigmatic American called J A Lindon, wrote the following sentence, using words rather than letters as his symmetrical building blocks: 'You can cage a swallow, can't you, but you can't swallow a cage, can you.' Like nearly all palindromes, it doesn't have a particularly profound meaning, but that's not necessarily a bad thing.

I went bird Wathing and I saw a robin and a kestrel and two herons and then We went home and then we played With our mardles and our cars as well then after that We went down the stairs. Statues but when we were going birdwatch we saw a swolw Mathew won the first games and I won the second games

As I climbed back down the steps, I noticed a brass sign on the wall reading, 'The Jeffery Harrison Hide'. Just as I had with the swallows before, I stopped and stared as if under a spell. 'The Jeffery Harrison Hide,' I whispered. 'I know that name.'

Later that evening I phoned Duncton and told him I'd spent the evening in Sevenoaks. I often complain that since I began birdwatching, I can't get him off the phone, although he may easily say the same thing about me.

'Ah,' he said with as much nostalgia as you can squeeze into a single sound. 'How was it looking?'

'Yes, nice,' I said. 'A bit dark.'

'You know I once met Prince Philip there?'

'No, I didn't know that,' I said, excited to hear a brand new anecdote, rare after twenty-seven years of being his son.

'Yes, it was the opening of the reserve and Prince Philip arrived by helicopter to host the ceremony. But he had a broken wrist. So did Jeffery actually. Anyway, Peter Scott was there too and we all planted alders together. I remember I was assigned to Lord Beeching. This must have been 1970. Of course I was at university with Prince Charles too. You know I once saw him on stage in a *Footlights* sketch. He was in a dustbin . . .'

'Yes I do know that, Duncton. You've told me that story a couple of times before . . .'

I never knew he'd planted trees at the reserve though. As I was walking along the path to and from the car I would have passed saplings sown by Duncton's young hand. These were actual family trees. Both they and I had sprung from his seed (I scrumpled up my face a bit at that thought).

'And did you go in the Jeffery Harrison Hide?' he asked, inter-rupting my uncomfortable train of thought.

'Yes, yes, I did. Now, I know that name. Why do I know that name?'

'Well, it's your name,' said Duncton matter-of-factly. 'You were named after Jeffery Harrison, you know that.'

Of course I knew that. My middle name was indeed Jeffery, chosen in honour of Duncton's own birding tutor, this Jeffery Harrison character. Himself the son of a great naturalist, Jeffery had grown up in a house stuffed full of stuffed birds. That was what great naturalists still did in those days. As well as becoming a GP, Jeffery grew into a big birdwatcher (both in size and ability) and devoted much of his free time to converting a disused gravel pit, once owned by the Redlands Cement Company, into the bird reserve I'd been wandering around and where Duncton had honed his own birding skills.

I'd conveniently forgotten that for the last twenty years. I was so embarrassed by the name as a schoolboy that I told my class-mates my second J stood for John. 'Yes, Alex James John Horne,' I would say and the moment would pass without anyone laughing at me. 'Just a white lie,' I would tell myself, 'they needn't know the truth.'

But Alexander James Jeffery Horne is who I am. And just to add another twist, up until very recently the whole Sevenoaks sanctuary had actually been called The Jeffery Harrison Bird Reserve. So for a brief moment I was sitting in a hide in a reserve and all three of us had been named after the same man. In Venn diagram terms this was terribly exciting. It was like Queen doing a gig on the QE2 with Her Majesty the Queen in the audience. Except that I actually enjoyed my experience, while I heard Queen Elizabeth II thought Brian May's guitar playing (and hair) a little too loud when he played on her roof in 2002.

On my way home that night I caught myself thinking about what I'd call our children. What would I pass on to my offspring? Who would I want to name my kids after? How would Rachel react if I suggested Oddie – even just as a middle name?

I'd barely given it a thought before – except for childishly thinking that names like Sean, Ivor and especially, Dawn, would be quite funny. Without realising it, I was starting to take the idea of fatherhood just a little more seriously. I was making progress.

8 April

Already, April had been a big month. I'd been out in the field almost every day and was starting to use phrases like 'out in the field'. I was beginning to feel like a birdwatcher.

David, my guide and surrogate father, had emailed me after our trip with some advice as to how I might see which birds, and where, without him. He gave me the Birdguides[52] number so I could get regular updates texted to my mobile, and he also suggested I subscribed to a birdwatching magazine. The first

---

52 www.birdguides.com

suggestions were fine. I looked up some of the bird reserves he'd recommended and worked out which ones I could visit on the way to gigs. Keen to have my very own Batphone, I happily signed up for the birding emails and text messages.[53] Birdguides is a well-oiled machine. You can define your own settings and choose which birding areas you want to hear about and which birds you're interested in, so I chose to receive texts and emails about any interesting birds in London and its surrounding counties, and any 'mega-rarities' elsewhere.

But subscribing to a bird magazine felt more serious, even more of a commitment; there would be no turning back from this direct debit. Only people with a deep devotion to their hobbies subscribe to magazines on the subject.

When I was a kid I used to buy the footy mags *Shoot* and *Match* every week. *FourFourTwo* didn't start till later,[54] but if it had been around I'd have snapped that up too. As an adolescent I quite often copied my friends by buying *Kerrang!* and *Metal Hammer*, two heavy metal magazines whose names sound a little bit silly nowadays.[55] I knew which day the new editions hit the shelves, and would rush out to see if they had a free poster (featuring Liverpool, England, Metallica or Iron Maiden; never Man Utd, Everton, Guns'n'Roses or Def Leppard).

The shop of choice was, of course, W H Smith, the idiosyncratic British high-street chain famous for its board games,

---

53 It's not a matter of huge importance, but it has struck me that if Batman ever decided to acquire a mobile phone *in addition* to his flashing red telephone, the name might be a problem. With his Batphone and Batcave, 'Batmobile' would be the obvious title, but that's already taken and parked in the Batgarage. He could go for 'Bathandphone' but that might be read as 'Bath-and-phone', a dangerous combination. It can't be easy being a superhero.

54 While *Shoot* was first published in 1969 and *Match* in 1979, the first issue of *FourFourTwo* didn't come out till 1994 – a magazine statistic for you there.

55 First published in 1981 and 1986 respectively. Another mag stat!

horrible carpets and oh-so-tempting-to-children-who-wouldn't-normally-think-of-stealing-anything pic 'n' mix. Their magazine section was and is bigger than anything normal newsagents could dream of providing.

Perusing the titles now, over a decade since last buying a magazine (I'm afraid I'm happy not to be laddish enough to buy the likes of Loaded[56]), I felt seedy. I couldn't quite put my finger on why, but as I scanned the garish front pages for anything featuring a bird of prey or the latest Bob Martin Bird Feeder I felt that I looked like a pervert.

The trouble was, there were so many magazines on display. I was there for what seemed like hours. First the brash women's titles that read like a conversation shouted across a street: 'Elle!' 'Hello!' 'Look!' 'Now!' 'Closer!' 'Your Hair!' 'Red!' 'Heat!' 'OK!'; then the educational puzzles section, featuring 'Brain Trainer' and 'Sudoko Special'; followed by the drudgery of Investors' Chronicle, Scientific American, The Economist and Spectator, names that filled me with as much excitement as a bowl of All Bran might. Still nothing about birds.

Moving on to the special interests section, I ignored headlines like 'Tiger Woods Laid Bare', 'Spring Clean Your PC' and 'Ferrari Sets Scorching Test Pace' and was surprised by the sheer quantity of fishing-related publications – Anglers' Mate, Trout and Salmon, Carp Talk and my favourite, The Crafty Carper – but still couldn't locate anything about anything with wings. Land Rover Monthly, Yachting Monthly, Athletics Weekly, all helpful names, but not what I was looking for. What Hi-Fi, Sci Fi Now – what about the birds?

Convinced the security guard thought I was trying to pluck up the courage to reach for one of the 'gentlemen's interests' mags on the top shelf, I asked a red-shirted employee to help

---

56 1994. That'll do, I think.

me. 'I'm looking for a magazine about birdwatching,' I mumbled. 'It's not for me! It's for my dad, he's one of them . . .'

Nodding sympathetically, the girl, who looked about twelve years old, led me to the home and lifestyles section, where, at last, I found the bird mags, nestled coyly behind *Gardeners' World, Heritage Railway* and the *Hornby Magazine*. Finding it impossible to decide between *Bird Watching, Birdwatch* and *Birding World*, I grabbed all three, paid without looking the cashier in the eye and hurried home.

11 April

There can't be many situations in which birdwatching skills can save lives. Unlike hobbies such as mountaineering, skydiving or lion-taming, being good at birdwatching is not usually a matter of life or death. An inability to correctly identify a redshank from a hundred yards will rarely prove fatal. But thanks to a spot of basic bird identification, the whole country was saved from an unspeakable pandemic, for now at least anyway.

The scientists examining the bird-flu infected swan in Cellardyke last week had presumed it was a mute swan. After all, most swans in Britain are mute swans. And since they thought it was a mute swan, they leapt to the conclusion that it was a native British bird and that we were therefore all going to die.

Regrettably, the bird in question didn't have a head and was heavily decomposed. The main way of definitively identifying a mute swan is by its orange beak and the odd black lump between its eyes. Apart from these distinctive facial features, a mute swan is pretty much identical to a migratory whooper swan in terms of size and plumage, especially when it's in an advanced state of decay.

Several days after the initial panic caused by the most famous dead swan ever, scientists revealed that after looking at its DNA, they could now say that it was in fact a whooper,[57] not a mute. This was good news for everyone (except the swan, for whom it was irrelevant in every way). Whooper swans are migratory birds that flock to Scotland from Iceland and northern Europe every year. This meant that it was much more likely the bird represented an isolated case of bird flu, rather than an outbreak here in the UK. Instead of a native bird being infected by a new arrival, the swan had probably been infected elsewhere, died during its migration over the North Sea (had its head bitten off by some evil fish) and was then washed up at Cellardyke.

Arguably, it shouldn't have taken the scientists so long to ID the bird. The bodies of the two species do of course look very similar – that's why I'm finding this whole birdwatching thing so tricky – but you might have hoped scientists would get these things right, or at least remain silent until they were certain. In this instance, several newspapers immediately ran alarming headlines about the swan, as well as outlining government contingency plans to deal with the thousands of deaths that would occur when this pandemic hit. Unsurprisingly, some people got scared. They started to fear birds. Bird reserves and wetland centres in turn started to worry about people staying away. For them, the interests of the birds come first. For others, avoiding this plague was more of a priority.

Reports of this misidentification and its significance were far less shouty than the original stories. Good news, and especially good news that involves quite a subtle piece of ornithological analysis, doesn't sell so many papers. But a few journalists did

---

57 In their weighty tome (one of the only weighty tomes I've ever read) *Birds Britannica*, Mark Cocker and Richard Mabey write that according to Scottish folklore these swans were 'viewed historically as good omens. Even today their arrival in northern Scotland or the outer isles evokes a sense of reassurance in autumn, and of loss with their going in spring' – rarely has folklore been so accurate.

take time to explain the events, question the apparent mistake and even decry the plight of the poor whooper. In the *Guardian*, Matthew Weaver wrote that whoopers are, 'believed to be the origin of the phrase "swan song", after the call they make as they die. It is unclear whether they make the same noise if they are dying from bird flu.' That's quite poetic. He also added that, 'Last year the composer Sir Peter Maxwell Davies got in trouble with the law when he tried to eat a dead whooper swan. He wouldn't try that now.' That's not so poetic.

12 April

Later that week, as I was sitting on the sofa trying to generate any sort of interest in an article about wing markings, David sent me a text asking if I was going to get the Alpine swift that had dropped in to Hampstead Heath. While my Birdguides account was being processed, David had taken it upon himself to make sure I wasn't going to miss anything good. And an Alpine swift, he insisted, was good.

The birdwatching magazines had left me a little cold. I liked the pictures, but they bore little resemblance to my own blurry views of birds. This was a rare chance to rectify that imbalance.

After my disappointing skiing trip it seemed fateful that this Alpine bird would come to me, and the next morning I was up at 6.15 a.m., the earliest time that year and, with the exception of the beginning of holidays, pretty much ever. It was so early I didn't even feel tired, just excited by this unusual nocturnal activity. By 7 a.m. I'd driven over to the heath, eaten my peanut butter on toast and was standing on Parliament Hill looking out across London. The sun was up, the city looked resplendent and I was extremely cold. In my early morning mania I'd made some basic clothing errors and my arms were bare.

According to the London Birders website, the bird had last

been spotted the previous evening at this end of the heath. I was surprised, and a little affronted, not to have found it straight away. In my naivety I had assumed I'd turn up and immediately bump into the exotic visitor. In fact, all I could see were two blue tits and a dunnock, not even nearly an Alpine swift.

Further down the hill, I made out the unmistakeable shape of two birdwatchers and decided to ask them for help. This was potentially one of the most awkward social situations I've ever been involved in; it was very early in the morning and I was approaching two strange men on a heath. My best tactic, I thought, would be to get straight to the point, so after a brief bark of 'Morning,' I plumped for: 'Have you seen the swift?' By omitting 'Alpine', I hoped I sounded like less of an amateur than I felt.

The men weren't impressed. 'Oh no,' one said, shaking his head. 'He's a late riser.'

Such a short, simple sentence, but spoken with so much authority. There was the immediate comprehension of the subject, of course, the 'he' implying both familiarity and knowledge of the bird's sex, then 'late riser' – relaxed, colloquial, almost humorous anthropomorphic language.

'Is he?' I said. 'Well, well, well.' My early morning energy instantly dissipated, and I felt very tired.

Reluctant to shuffle away just yet, I lingered, trying to elicit a little more information about this lazy creature. It was all a bit stilted, but they said they were sure he'd turn up at about 10 a.m. and one of them gave me a mint before they made their excuses ('Right, so we're off to work the bushes . . .'). I sucked on the sweet, wished it was a bacon sandwich, and sat down on a bench. Was this fun? I could be in a nice warm bed with my wife rather than on a cold heath being rejected by strange men.

I wallowed in my chilly gloom for as long as I could bear it, then realised I should try to stay warm if I was going to survive the morning. I walked briskly towards the woods, swinging my arms as I went. By now the heath was filling up with dog walkers and joggers and I could just about appreciate being outside on what was still a bright morning. Emerging from the swiftless trees, just beyond the male swimming area (where the sight of wet men in pants shivering by the edge of the water did make me feel a little bit better), I found about half-a-dozen more bird-watchers, standing in a line and looking out over the water (away from the swimmers). This was more like it. Here I would surely find camaraderie, warmth and maybe even the swift.

I joined the group much like one might join a queue. At first I kept myself to myself, having a look through my binoculars at the ducks taking their own morning swim and playing it pretty cool. After about five minutes of this, the tall, dapper gentleman in front of me initiated a conversation by saying something like, 'Bit chilly, isn't it?' I nodded and we happily exchanged similar comments for the next thirty minutes, not looking at each other, but constantly scanning the horizon.

'Here for the swift?' I asked.

'Oh yes,' he replied.

'Been here long?'

'Not really.'

'Well, he's a late riser, isn't he?'

'That he is.'

This was going immeasurably better.

After about an hour I discovered that my neighbour's name was Martin.

'I'm Alex, by the way,' I blurted out.

'Oh, Martin,' he said, coping well.

'Hello Martin.'

'Nice to meet you, Alex.'

'Nice to meet you too . . . I'm still quite new to the whole birding thing, so don't know the etiquette.'

'Oh,' said Martin, who had clearly never thought about the

etiquette of this situation, 'you can talk to anybody. Always happy to engage in conversation. Just to pass the time as much as anything.'

That's right, I thought, these are all normal people. Like Duncton.

We started to have a good chat, occasionally even making eye contact. He must have been in his fifties, a softly-spoken, gentle man. I'm sure he could tell I was a beginner but when pointing out a green woodpecker on the grass beneath the trees to our right he did so as if we were equals: 'Green woody over there,' he noted quietly, remarking, not boasting. I jotted down 'one green woody' in my book.

'Ah,' he said, 'indispensable tool, the notebook! Always keep one myself. Always worth keeping some kind of record, and handing it in to your county recorder. It all helps.'

By now I was no longer last in the queue. Another handful of hopefuls had joined and I was in the middle of the gang. I had been accepted by the tribe. Being a fairly large group, passers-by started stopping[58] to ask what we were looking for. Someone would mutter 'Alpine swift' and the rest of us would nod seriously. Martin was more patient, explaining why this bird meant that so many men had gathered together on this particular morning, but it was definitely a case of 'us and them', and I felt honoured to be in the 'us' group.

Then, at around 9.25 a.m., it happened. Lawrence, an unusually trendy birder with long hair, goatee and bike, had given up for the day and was reluctantly cycling off for work, when he suddenly shrieked, leapt off his bicycle and pointed up to the sky. We ran towards him as one. If he'd been looking at us rather than the bird, we would have made a terrifying sight. Following Lawrence's finger, we each caught sight of the bird wheeling around in the blue sky above us. I was about the fifth to locate

---

58 Can a passer-by stop? If he does he is no longer a passer-by. Potential passer-by? Failed passer-by? I guess it doesn't really matter.

it and was even able to point it out to an elderly birdwatcher beside me. He was overjoyed.

More than anything, I was simply relieved to have seen the bird. Unlike everyone else there, I hadn't even seen a common swift, but as I looked at their smiling faces, I couldn't help but share a little of their delight. 'Well done Lawrence!' shouted someone. One man wolf-whistled; another whispered 'Lovely' under his breath. 'Who'd have thought it?' said another. Even unruffled Martin got quite excited: 'First the American robin, now this. It's been a good fortnight.'

Once I'd seen the bird, I didn't know how long I ought to stay looking at it. After five minutes everyone else was still rooted to the spot, so I continued to watch it circle above us, wondering if I could slip away without anyone noticing. The swift itself, by the way, was quite big, with a white underbelly. These were the things that meant it wasn't a common swift. This one was also a bit of a show off and seemed to be performing for its fans, twisting and turning, rising and falling, also showing no signs of leaving. At one point it was joined by a sparrowhawk (another first for me) and genuine tension spread throughout the group as a skirmish ensued. Would the arrival of the Alpine swift be followed by its vicious murder? How would birdwatchers react to such an event? Surely it would still count on my list?

But it was only a minor kerfuffle. After a couple of flappy punches the sparrowhawk gave up and flew down towards south London. Soon the swift got bored too, banked sharply to the left and shot off north over the hill. Like an audience united by a feel-good film, the watching crowd gradually dispersed, occasionally acknowledging the event with a shy smile and the odd, 'Well, that was very nice.' Martin was now late for work, so I gave him a lift to Kentish Town tube station, where we said goodbye and vaguely agreed to probably see each other at the Wetland Centre (his convenient but expensive local patch) one of these days. My first twitch was over. I'd done it. I'd seen a bird Duncton almost certainly wouldn't. When I got home I went back to bed but was too excited to sleep.

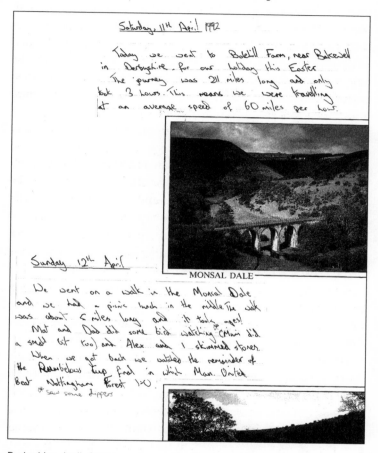

Saturday, 11th April 1992

Today we went to Bolehill Farm, near Bakewell in Derbyshire for our holiday this Easter. The journey was 211 miles long and only took 3 hours. This means we were travelling at an average speed of 60 miles per hour.

— MONSAL DALE —

Sunday 12th April

We went on a walk in the Monsal Dale and we had a picnic lunch in the middle. The walk was about 5 miles long and it took ages! Mat and Dad did some bird watching (Mum did a small bit too) and Alex and I skimmed stones. When we got back we watched the remainder of the Rumbelows cup final in which Man. United beat Nottingham Forest 1-0.
* saw some dippers

Derbyshire, April, fourteen years earlier. These are Chip's words (although Mat did subtly add the phrase 'saw some dippers') – note the good use of statistics and the two camps of birders and non-birders with Mum somewhere in between. The Rumbelows Cup, of course, was the what the Milk Cup was called for a couple of years – after it had already changed to the Littlewoods Challenge Cup and before reverting back to drinks, with Coca-Cola, Worthington and now Carling.

14 April

Being retired means Duncton can spend his time doing whatever he fancies. If he wanted, he could sit inside and watch
snooker all day, drinking Stella and getting fat. Luckily for both
him and Mum, he's a man with many interests, so easily fills
his days with photography courses, Italian lessons, trips to
Goodwood racecourse, and, of course, birdwatching. For the last
month or so he'd been attending a course on birdsong, so when
I suggested a birdwatching trip somewhere in Sussex on Good
Friday, he agreed immediately, keen to put his new knowledge
to the test.

Being a comedian, I can also do whatever I fancy, during the
daytime at least, and was enjoying adding a sense of purpose
to what can be long, occasionally lonely days filled with snooker-
beer-and-fast-food temptation. I'm not complaining, obviously –
being a comedian is a ridiculous, luxurious job – but you can't
spend the whole day at home writing jokes. One decent new
gag a week is a pretty good strike rate.

About twenty miles southwest of Pulborough, on the coast
between Chichester and Bognor Regis, lies a village called
Pagham whose harbour has been designated a Site of Special
Scientific Interest thanks to its salt marshes, mudflats, lagoons,
reed-beds and shingle beaches that frequently attract rare migratory birds and Duncton in the spring. It was to this bird Mecca
that we were heading, and it was these visitors we were hoping
to see or, in Duncton's case, hear. But when we asked one of the
wardens what was around that morning, it was a local breeding
bird that he was most excited about.

'Well, the highlight at the moment is a long-eared owl,' he
said. 'It's down at the second severals. If you're walking from
this side it's on the first hedge when you get to the second
severals . . .'

For Duncton, a long-eared owl represented something of a holy grail. In all his many years of watching birds he'd never seen this crepuscular[59] species. The long-eared owl would be for him what birdwatchers call a 'lifer'. And while nearly every new bird was a lifer for a novice like me, Duncton rarely had the chance to see something for the first time any more. So as soon as the words were out of the warden's mouth, we were off, striding towards the place where it was apparently dozing. As long as we arrived before dusk, the bird should be there. For me, the Great Owl Chase that followed neatly encapsulates the whole practice of birdwatching, as well as offering an insight as to how both a birder and a father should behave.

The 'severals' in question were, according to Duncton, 'a good walk' away. We had to be patient. Like the Alpine swift, I couldn't expect to see the bird straight away. I had to put the hours in. And as we marched purposefully along the edges of fields and down towards the shore, the tension rose. Every birder we passed corroborated the story with comments like, 'Yes, we saw it, it's in the second severals' and 'Oh yes, it's right there on the first hedge in the second severals – you can't miss it.' But what if we do miss it? thought Duncton. And what is a severals? thought I.

Of course, as we were walking, we were also watching – a birding trip with Duncton is never about just one bird, no matter how rare that bird might be – and at the end of the day (literally, not footballistically) the waders I had seen for the first time, prowling as if with their hands behind their back in the marshy, watery, brambly fields around us were, for me, at least as exciting as the solitary owl. There were plenty of redshanks showing off their bright orange legs; spotted redshanks, bigger

---

59 Yes, a tremendous word. It's from my *Collins Bird Guide* and means 'being active at twilight or before sunrise'. Lovely.

and scruffier, a first also for Duncton that year; black-tailed godwits, whose name sounds like an insult;[60] beaky curlews, petite common sandpipers, entertaining oystercatchers and finally, the crafty snipe that had evaded me every month so far. Following Duncton's instructions and using his telescope, I could only just make it out, camouflaged brilliantly against the bank, but there it was, another lifer for me and another species for my list.

In the bushes on the side of the path we also saw some minute rouge-chested finches that Duncton told me were called linnets, and a little brown job called a Cetti's warbler. As the year progressed, I would grow to dislike all warblers. They all look pretty much identical and can only be distinguished by the warbling after which they are named. That's no fun. On this occasion, however, I was glad Duncton had the chance to show off his birdsong studies with the pronouncement: 'Loud metallic cry – that must be a Cetti's!'

'Well done Duncton!' I said, 'very impressive.' He could, of course, have been making the whole thing up. But that's not what dads do.

Or at least that's what I thought. As we neared the beach and Duncton's first long-eared owl I finally asked him about the mysterious 'severals'. 'Exactly what are they?' I said casually.

'Oh, you know,' replied Duncton, 'just fields really.'

'Right,' I said, and we carried on walking, looking for the first hedge in the second field.

'Well it can't be either of those,' said Duncton as we passed a couple of meadows on our right, the sea to the left. 'There are no hedges, birdwatchers or owls. I guess it's further on.' He did take time to point out some of my first seabirds – stocky knots,

---

60 Other birds whose names you can use as taunts include 'little bustard', 'Kentish dotterel' and 'twite'.

bright white little egrets and turnstones turning stones – but I sensed he was beginning to worry. The sun was definitely thinking about setting and, as we all know, long-eared owls are famously crepuscular.

We passed another group of people, including three small children, all of whom had seen the bird and who gave us yet more detailed descriptions ('If you look down from the horizon, it's in line with a church, about chest high, above the reeds, in a tree, you can see it from the edge of the severals . . .'). Suddenly concerned that Duncton didn't in fact know what he was doing, I decided to take control, using my novice status to our advantage. 'I'm dreadfully sorry for my ignorance, but what *is* a severals?' I asked.

'Oh, it's that reed-bed over there,' they replied, pointing a few hundred yards down the beach.

'Yes, it's a reed-bed,' confirmed Duncton. 'We'll be there soon.'

Bluffing, it seems, is one of the secrets of good fatherhood. From the kestrels of my youth to the Cetti's warbler that afternoon, Duncton had always appeared omniscient. If I wanted to know anything – about birds, illnesses, anything – I would call him and he would tell me. But here, for perhaps the first time, he'd been caught out. He hadn't known what a severals was, he told me, but he hadn't thought it mattered. A couple of minutes later we found the owl and he was proved right; it hadn't mattered. So to be a dad you don't need to know everything. It just helps to look like you do.

As for the bird itself, for me it was a perfect example of something that looks to an outsider like nothing much at all, but which means absolutely everything to the enthusiast. It was the apparent anticlimax that marks all proper hobbies. It was a penny black, an expensive bottle of wine, a scrappy scoreless draw away from home.

It was Duncton, of course, who spotted the bird through his

scope. I think I may have seen it a couple of seconds before through my battered binoculars, but had dismissed it as a woody lump. Because that was what it looked like – a small woody lump on a tree a long way off. It didn't move once during the twenty minutes we were in its presence. From where we stood, I could just make out its wise, solemn face, but couldn't even see its ears.[61] How the first person spotted it, let alone identified it as a long-eared owl, I had no idea. It didn't call, annoyingly for me. I was looking forward to hearing 'twit-twoo' and saying, 'That's an owl,' without having attended a single birdsong class. It just sat there and, to my disappointment, did nothing for me. I wasn't yet at the point where I could appreciate a birder's bird.

But Duncton was overjoyed. 'That is wonderful,' he kept saying, 'gorgeous.' I'd never seen him so ecstatic. He even phoned up Mum to tell her the good news and I could tell just from his side of the conversation that she knew how much it meant to him. While they were chatting away like only people who've been married for thirty years can, my friend Tim sent me a text:

Horne – I've seen a moorhen. It's in front of me in Regent's Canal. There's also a large goose. Tim x.

This made me almost as happy as the owl had Duncton. Tim had started birdwatching. This was great. I had a partner! A protégé even! And that same selfish part of me was proud too that I had suggested the trip to Duncton. It was because of me that we'd come to Pagham. It was thanks to me, really, that he'd seen his first long-eared owl.

---

61 As everyone knows, they aren't actual ears. Just feathery tufts on the top of their heads. Yet another bad bird name. What you might not know, however, is the expression 'Like an owl in an ivy bush.' It comes from Francis Grose's *A Dictionary of the Vulgar Tongue*, first published in 1785 and is 'said of a person with a large frizzled wig, or a woman whose hair is dressed *á-la-blouze*'. Think Elton John in his prime.

17 April

I still wasn't getting myself up and out of bed as early as a proper birdwatcher but it was Bank Holiday Monday and I did manage to make it over to The Welsh Harp by 9.45 a.m., so I was doing OK. I'd checked my various Batphones first thing and since there was nothing unusual about, thought I should give my local lake another chance. David had passed on the phone number of the area's top birder who had very kindly agreed to show me round. Unfortunately I'd only had time to eat a Cadbury Crème Egg for breakfast, so I started feeling hungry as soon as I parked the car.

A pattern was already emerging among the birdwatchers I'd met that year: calm, patient, rugged, practical, healthy and erudite; all qualities befitting a good dad. They were also all male, another useful quality for fatherhood.

Andrew didn't break that mould. In fact, he fitted so neatly into the mould it was almost as if the mould had originally been made around him. As a birder committed to Brent Reservoir he voluntarily looks after the place and generously guides newcomers like me around the different birdwatching spots. Today two other birdwatchers had also phoned for his help and he was more than happy to spend his day off leading us by the hand around the place he clearly loved. He told me to meet him in the Heron Hide, which, I found out, was that same Bill Oddie hide I'd tried and failed twice to enter earlier in the year.

As soon as I arrived at the now familiar closed door, I felt a sinking feeling in the pit of my stomach, that dreaded feeling of embarrassment when you know you've been a complete prat and that someone now thinks you're a prat and they're absolutely right to think you're a prat. Taking a deep breath, I walked up to the door. There was still no obvious handle so I scrabbled round, trying to get a grip on the wooden frame, managing to girlishly break a nail in the process. Just as a third splinter pierced my right hand I heard muffled voices from within shouting 'push'. I pushed. The door swung open and I entered the grotto to find three fully fledged and grinning birdwatchers.

My humiliation wasn't yet complete. I shuffled onto the nearest bench, and discovered the softest, warmest seat beneath what in most other hides would be my chilly posterior. 'This is lovely,' I said involuntarily, and a bit too loudly.

'Thank you,' said Andrew. 'I'm Andrew. Are you Alex?'

'Yes,' I said, and immediately regretted it.

'Yes, well I read your note on the website, I'm sorry you had such a difficult time here with your brother. The thing is we've had so many problems with vandalism that this hide is often locked. But just give me a call any time and you can come and pick up the key. Now then, about your challenge, how can we help you?'

I couldn't believe I'd been so rash and haughty the first time round. This was the typical novice behaviour I'd been hoping to avoid. I'd become that person watching a football match and saying all the wrong things. But Andrew was so nice that I still felt completely welcome in the small wooden hut he spent his free time overseeing, and which I'd slagged off on the website he also maintained. I was an awful person.

I soon underlined my utter ignorance by failing to recognise some ruddy ducks as we looked out at the reservoir; 'So those out there with the black and white heads, those are shelducks aren't they?' I said, expecting a nod of confirmation and approval.

'No, those are ruddies,' came the tolerant reply. I shrank a bit more into my cushioned bench. This was stuff Mat and Duncton had already tried to teach me, but which hadn't sunk in. This was my *Faking It* failure.

After he'd patiently explained to me what every bird out on the water was, Andrew suggested a walk round the north side of the reservoir. By now the two other followers had arrived (another first time year lister and an Australian birdwatcher on his first trip to the UK) and the four of us made slow but cheerful progress round the water's edge. Every few steps Andrew would stop and tell us why that rattling call on the left was a wren or why that shrill laugh above us was a green woodpecker. We all frantically scribbled down notes like students on their first day at university. As with Duncton and David before, I was impressed by his expertise, in awe of his nous and just a little bit worried about how much I still had to learn. Luckily, as we roamed through playing fields, hedgerows, pathways and marshland he managed to find us a great spotted woodpecker,[62] common terns, two whitethroats and a mistle thrush, so while my confidence was shrinking, my list was swelling.

At the northern end of the reservoir we sat down in a sort of half-hide structure and looked out at a smaller pool. This particular shelter consisted of a long bench in front of a high narrow table surrounded on three sides by low wooden walls. There was no roof or door. Unfortunately this more open arrangement meant it had been mercilessly daubed by gleeful graffiti artists, who'd painted the words SEX HUT on the outside. Each letter was bright yellow, at least a foot high and positioned in such a way that from a distance an observer would read the words and see our four heads at about the same time. Oblivious to this regrettable subtitle, it was here that we spotted our best bird of the morning. Just as we thought we'd noted down everything on offer, a blue flash streaked across the water.

'Kingfisher,' said two voices at once. Andrew looked at me.

---

62 One of the few birds whose name you might shout anyway when seeing it: 'Great! (I) spotted woodpecker!' Other examples include 'Ruddy ducks' or 'Moorhen' if you've seen a lot of ducks or hens, 'Little Bustard' if you missed one and 'Bittern' if you got too close.

'You saw it then?' he asked.

'That was brilliant!' I grinned.

Back in Midhurst a couple of decades before, Mat and Duncton had spotted the same bird at the pond near our house. I'd missed it – it was just too quick – and the two of them went on about it for what felt like years afterwards. Every time I passed the spot from then on, I'd stop to see if I could find one too. I felt like I'd missed out on something special. But I never did see one by myself. I didn't really know what I was looking for. 'A blue flash,' is what they kept saying. How can you look for a blue flash?

But now, at last, I'd got my kingfisher, and I could finally understand why Mat and Duncton had gone on about that bloody blue flashy bird for so long.

Pathetically weak with hunger, I left the other three to their own devices soon after midday, but only after one final burst of excitement. On the way back round to the Heron Hide Andrew stopped still for even longer than usual then became quite animated.

'There it is,' he cried, 'the first cuckoo of the year!'

As he was looking down at the ground at the time, the three of us followed his gaze, expecting to see a baby cuckoo crawling through the grass. In fact, of course, he was listening out for its familiar eponymous call and before long we all heard it, loud and clear, and tore off through the woods in a valiant attempt to pin it down.

Unsurprisingly, we scared it off. But thirty minutes later, as I sank my teeth into a well-deserved sausage sandwich at the nearby Railway Café, I was already looking forward to returning to the reservoir, and 'working it' by myself. I was sure I now had at least some of the skills needed to find these birds on my own.

18 April

With increasing regularity, I was finding excuses not to spend my free time writing comedy but instead delving deeper into Duncton's hobby. By now I'd decided to tell his story in one way or another at some point, and told myself that any time spent 'researching' birdwatching was therefore valuable work. The delivery of Bill Oddie's book *Gripping Yarns: Tales of Birds and Birding*, meant this particular morning passed with me greedily gobbling up his stories, most of which were taken from a column he wrote for *Birdwatch* magazine. David had recommended I read it to see how Britain's most famous bird-watching comedian (well, most famous birdwatcher, really) talks about his hobby. It was immediately obvious just how dedicated a birdman he is. Like Duncton, he'd grown up a bird-watcher. His life has been about birds. The radio and TV programmes he made were partly opportunities to go birding. It dawned on me once more just how deep the birdwatching well is; how much birdwatchers know and how much time they quietly spend for the good of their hobby. I now worried that any sort of comedy show, or indeed book, on the subject might do them and Duncton a disservice. I was also worried that I wouldn't even scratch the surface of the world of the birdwatcher in one year.

Just as I was about to drive off to a gig up in Coventry, Duncton phoned in a particularly excitable state:

'You know that golden oriole I was telling you about,' he began. No 'Hello,' 'Are you there?' or 'How are you?' for me any more.

'Yes Duncton,' I replied, conscious that I was already running late. The day before, in the latest of what were fast becoming daily phone calls, he'd told me that a magnificent golden oriole had been spotted in Pulborough.

'Well, Peter (his occasional birdwatching and former medical partner mentioned in January[63]) and I headed over to Coldwaltham Brooks this morning. It was a beautiful morning – how was it with you?'

'Fine, Duncton. Carry on.'

'Right. Well, we'd walked a few steps along the path when I saw it, perched at the top of a tree. Brilliant! A couple of minutes later it flew off. A couple of minutes after that Bernie and Dave came along and missed it altogether!'

'Bernie and Dave?'

'You know, Bernie and Dave – two of Sussex's top birders! They did get it later that day but for a while there we were the only ones who'd seen it!'

I'd rarely heard him so worked up by anything other than Tottenham before. Of course I felt a little jealous that he'd got another rare bird, without, it appeared, even trying. But I liked being in on the joke and being able to share his Schadenfreude.

19 April

In case you hadn't already noticed, the stand-up comedy circuit is really no such thing. The word 'circuit' comes from the Latin *circuitus*, meaning 'a going around', from where we also get the word 'circumference'. I did a circuit round Brent Reservoir. David and I did a circuit of Walthamstow Reservoirs.

Travelling on the stand-up comedy circuit, however, involves jagged trips criss-crossing the country, back and forth. I would say it's an entirely random route, but the gigs often seem to be

---

63 Sorry, brackets *and* footnotes here. I think it's worth noting that Peter's hearing and Duncton's eyesight are both about the same: below average. Together, therefore, they are greater than the sum of their parts. Often Duncton alone will hear a bird which Peter alone will then see. Like doubles partners in tennis, one will set the other up for a smash. They are a formidable team. I think they should high-five more.

placed in such an awkward fashion that it almost looks planned. It's as if the comedy lords want to maximise the 'a funny thing happened to me on the way to the theatre' potential.

The way it works is that until a comedian reaches a certain critical mass, when his or her name alone can command an audience, you go wherever they will have you. If you're lucky you can plan a few gigs in a row in the northeast, or a weekend of shows in the west, but it's not usually possible to pick and choose where you play. Almost every town hosts a comedy night at least once a month nowadays, and you have to not mind travelling sideways if you want to climb the comedy ladder.

At the beginning of the month my agent phoned to let me know what gigs I had coming up. Revealing this particular week's treats with his customary indifference, he said, 'So, you've got Luton on Tuesday, Bahrain Wednesday and Gloucester on Thursday.'

I was scribbling down the details.

'So, Luton, fine, that's not too far. Erm, Bar Rain – is that in London?' I asked, assuming it was some new trendy, weather-themed pub.

'No, Bahrain, in the Middle East,' he barked.

'Jolly good,' I said. 'Then Gloucester Town Hall on the Thursday – that's not too bad then.'

As mentioned earlier, you can do a comedy show in almost every country as well as every county. Normally you'd get to stay at least forty-eight hours in the place before heading on to the next location, but this time I was meant to fly into Bahrain on the morning of the gig, have an afternoon seeing the sights, then do the show and head straight back to the airport to catch a plane home that night.

'Actually, that's ridiculous,' I said, in a rare show of defiance. 'That's so bad for the environment, I just can't do it.'

Instead, I cancelled the Gloucester show and booked myself

into the Bahraini hotel for an extra couple of nights with the aim of hiring a car and exploring. It might not have been any better for the environment (in fact, it was definitely worse for the environment as I was now flying and hiring a car) but on some strange level it felt slightly more ethical.

One of the great things about birdwatching, Duncton once told me, is that you can do it anywhere and everywhere. On every trip abroad you'll see different things. No matter how long the history or how great the culture of the country you are visiting, there will be birds. For me this was particularly relevant, because despite the occasional accusation that I am 'cultured' and 'intelligent', I'm actually very bad at going to museums and art galleries. I prefer to wander about a bit and perhaps have a drink in a café. So I was looking forward to wandering about a bit in Bahrain with extra justification.

After almost a third of the year spent thinking about birds every day, it was they that first struck me when disembarking the plane at Bahrain International Airport. Not the dry heat or austere landscape, but the little brown jobs, buzzing around the tarmac. What are they? I thought, immediately panicking. Is that still a chaffinch? Do they have wrens over here? Why isn't anyone manning the information desk?

Before leaving I'd managed to find the name and number of a British ex-pat birdwatcher, Howard, whom I hoped would be able to answer these questions, but as he wasn't answering his phone when we reached the hotel, I headed out instead to the local souk with Barry, one of my fellow comedians. I can deal with markets on trips abroad. I like seeing what other people buy and sell, I enjoy the hustle and bustle, it's often those sights and smells that stay with me long after I've gone home. But here in downtown Manama, I couldn't quite throw myself into the experience. I didn't feel like bartering with a bloke over a magnet. I wasn't tempted by the misspelt T-shirts or trick packets of chewing gum. I just couldn't stop thinking about birds.

Perhaps partly because the pavements were littered with scraps of takeaway food, there were birds everywhere. Hundreds of what I presumed were the same feral pigeons as in London hopped in and out of the traffic, miraculously cheating death every time; tiny dunnocks bounced up and down from the bare trees that lined the pavements; and two ominous magpie-type birds seemed to follow us wherever we went. Emerging from a twisted alleyway, they'd be there, on a roof, staring down at us. Doubling back on ourselves, returning to a stall so that Barry could buy a mosque-shaped alarm clock, we'd catch sight of them again, poking about in the overflowing bins.

I had brought with me *A Photographic Guide to the Birds of Israel and the Middle East* that I'd got for the Israel trip later in the year, but it was nowhere near as full or as detailed as Mat's trusty *Collins*. What were these spy-like birds?

I tried calling Howard again. Still no luck. I went into the hotel bookshop[64] and asked if they stocked any books on birds. The bookseller said no. I asked if he knew where I could watch birds.

'*Watch* birds?' he asked me right back.

'Yes,' I said.

'No,' he said. 'I know where you can buy them from though. There's a stall in the middle of the souk, if you go now they should still be open . . .'

I thanked him for his advice and tried reception instead. 'Do you know if anyone offers birdwatching trips?' I enquired.

'Yes,' she said.

'Great!' I shouted.

---

64 Do most hotels have bookshops? I've only had a limited experience of hotel life but this did strike me as odd.

'I know that no one offers birdwatching trips round here,' she continued. 'I think you should go to the zoo.'

I thanked her for her advice and went for a swim. While struggling with the backstroke I saw the two sneaky magpie-type birds watching me again. 'Who are you?' I mouthed. 'Mag-spies' would have to do for now.

The gig itself was unremarkable. About fifty people had turned up to the hotel's penthouse bar, not really enough to justify the 3,000-mile, seven-hour flight, but they were nice enough. It was an average sort of a gig, but I did meet a man who called himself Krazy Ken (yes, with both those Ks) who suggested I drive as far south as possible if I wanted to see the best birds. That was all I needed to know.

After the show, the other comics went straight back to the airport as planned and I very nearly had a sensible early night. Unfortunately, Ken lived up to his name and insisted we go out for 'a drink or two'.

'I thought you couldn't drink here,' I protested.

'You can't,' he winked, 'but I do.'

But despite what turned out to be an expensive and quite shouty pub crawl, I was still the first guest at breakfast the next morning. I felt extremely proud of myself and ate pretty much everything on offer at the enormous buffet, including typical British fry-up fare, a lot of white cheese and a bowl of meat soup made from boiled sheep heads. I was even canny enough to stuff my pockets with bananas, bottles of water, cakes and doughnuts before staggering out. I was going birding!

Amazingly, the hotel's car hire company were more than happy for me to borrow one of their vehicles, despite the fact that I'd forgotten to pack my driver's licence.

'We'll take your passport and twenty pounds,' they said.

'And I'll take your car,' I agreed. It seemed like a fair swap.

So, at exactly 9 a.m., I edged out into Bahrain's rush-hour

traffic in a fully airconditioned Chrysler. It was enormous. It was left-hand drive. It was an automatic. I had never driven anything like it in my life, and I was hungover. Everyone was driving on the wrong side of the road, I had a rudimentary road map from reception; this was brilliant.

Doing my best to ignore all birds and concentrate on the road and the other cars for the first half-hour at least, I gradually got the hang of Bahraini driving. I used my horn a lot more than my indicators. Having mastered basic driving, I then started paying some attention to the road signs and somehow managed to find my way onto the southbound Hawar Highway. I was off. Outside its capital Manama, Bahrain's road system is a simple one.

Within another thirty minutes, all traces of the city were lost in the dust behind me. I raced along, Arabic pop music bursting out of the stereo, the Persian Gulf to my left, the desert that takes up over ninety per cent of the country to my right. I'd never been anywhere like this before. And to think, without birdwatching, I'd be home in London preparing for a trip down to the west country right now.

A flock of somethings landed on the beach beside me, so I pulled up on the sand, got out of the car and sat on the bonnet with my binoculars. By this point I'd virtually given up on my inferior guide book, so I sketched each of the species as carefully as possible in my notebook, taking care not to drip too much sweat onto its pages. The sun was already high and incredibly fierce, not great for my blistering hangover.

Jumping back in the car for air, I kept driving south. Krazy Ken had assured me I'd find flamingos somewhere down here. I didn't. I found flaming nothing. Actually, what I did discover was a compound called Jaww Prison that loomed out of the desert, making me screech my car to a halt. This really was quite a jail. Have a look on Google Maps if you want to see just how remote it is. The highway petered out symbolically on the other side of the dispiriting buildings. This was the end of the road. I wondered if the inmates felt envy or were inspired by the sight of the birds outside their cells.

I had no option but to head north again so aimed for Askar, the only village nearby that was marked on my map. I'd only seen three or four vehicles since leaving Manama and this place was as eerily empty as the desert plains themselves. At one point I left the car by the side of the road to explore some mangroves, but after drawing shaky pictures of some seabirds I got so freaked out by the creaks and shadows of the trees that I ended up running back into my comforting Chrysler, locking the doors and peering at the birds through the window instead.

Meandering round the village I passed the odd immaculate mansion but mainly rubbly shacks, half-built concrete homes, and battered cars. The whole place looked like it was suffering from heatstroke. The odd person I passed peered at me quizzically but for the most part I glided around alone in what felt like a post-apocalyptic daydream.

At one end of the town I found an open sandy area with one rusty goalpost, a few boulders and an alarming amount of broken glass. In the distance I could just make out a small group of youths, huddled together under a makeshift shelter, half-heartedly prodding a fire. I assumed they were cooking. There really wasn't any need for any more heat.

Just in front of them I noticed a different bird to anything else I'd seen that day. A bird of prey. A kestrel, I thought. No, hang on – I checked my book – it's much more likely to be a lesser kestrel over here. No . . . wait . . . two, three, four, five lesser kestrels! All perched obligingly between me and the young chefs. Ah ha! I smiled. I've found you!

Just as I was congratulating myself, the nearest of the birds took off. I followed its flight through my binoculars and was admiring its broad, rufous back when it disappeared. One second it was there, the next it was gone. I waved my binoculars round wildly but it really was nowhere to be seen. Only when I lowered them was the grim truth revealed. The kestrel was now floundering around on the ground, just yards from where it took off. Looking closer, I saw that its legs were tangled up in some sort of twine which led all the way back to the perch. It was a prisoner on a leash. When it tried to fly off the string snapped it back like a kite.

A quick check showed that the other four were also tied up in the same manner. They all sat there glumly, apparently aware of the futility of flight. The lads nearby, I realised, were in charge. They were the captors.

I got back in my car and tried to think. What on earth should I do? The burgeoning birdwatcher inside me felt outraged. These birds should be free! How dare they tie up those magnificent birds of prey! It's disgusting! It was like my 'zoos are evil' phase all over again.

The competitive side of me was similarly incensed. I've come all this way, only to see birds that don't count on my list because some truant kids have tied them up! They're not pets! They shouldn't be captives!

But then the cowardly, perhaps reasonable, side of me stepped in. Well, there's not much you can do. There are five of them and one of you. And anyway, who are you to say what these people can or can't do? Your aunt keeps Japanese chickens, Duncton used to take you to falconry shows, is this any different?

As this debate raged on inside my still throbbing head, my attention was caught by another bird, much brighter, much closer and clearly much freer, drifting over a fence behind the car and alighting on a branch not far away. I had all the time in the world to appreciate its fine turquoise chest, brilliant yellow head and olive wings. This was the first burst of colour I'd seen in the whole of Bahrain.

I flicked through the guide and immediately found its match. This was a bee-eater, my most exotic bird so far and one which would definitely count for my list. I'd found it all by myself here, in the middle of nowhere, thousands of miles off the beaten track.[65]

Once I'd jotted down its particulars and got my fill of its feathers, I got out of the car and wandered over to where the bee-eater had emerged. It was midday now and about 400° Celsius. The land around me looked ravaged to an almost biblical degree. Broken trees, barbed wire (did they have that in the Bible?), one rotting carcass of a cow and one skeleton of a cow licked clean by flies. But amongst this desolation I found not only two more vibrant bee-eaters but a fine crested lark. Another new Middle Eastern bird, this one distinguished by its punk-like haircut. Following its jumpy flight, my eyes then fell on yet another pair of magspies! As far as I was concerned, this was the same pair of magspies that had been stalking me in the city centre! They really were quite creepy. And just as I was about to beg them to leave me alone, I heard a strange wail from somewhere in the distance.

'Helloooo! Helloooooo!'

The birds took off and I looked round. It was the lads with the fire and the kestrels, beckoning me over. Through my binoculars I could see that they were all grinning. *Phew*. But in a slightly manic way. I had three choices: stay with the evil magspy birds, get back in the Chrysler and spend another few hours by myself or go and see what the young bird jailors wanted.

---

65 Bee-eaters are very occasionally seen in Britain. In 1920 a pair nesting in Scotland was described as one of the most surprising and unlikely events in the ornithological history of the British Isles. Sadly the birds' efforts came to grief when a cat ate the male and a gardener imprisoned the female in a greenhouse until it died.

I gritted my teeth, grabbed my microphone from the car and walked over. At least if they tied me up too I'd get it on tape.

It took what seemed like hours to cross the deadly football pitch and I very nearly turned back twice. It was only when I saw that they couldn't have been more than twelve years old that I resolved to keep going. Maybe I'd even set the birds free . . .

They greeted me like I greet my brothers, with a slightly awkward wave, a big smile and a small 'Hello.'

'Hello,' I said, and glanced around. The oldest-looking boy was proudly clutching yet another kestrel. A couple of the others were tending to the fire. One stood up and offered me some food.

'No thanks,' I said, rubbing my stomach. 'I'm full.' I was actually pretty hungry by now, but I couldn't be sure he wasn't offering me barbecued kestrel.

After a stilted exchange in which it quickly became clear that neither of us could understand the other's language, I pointed to the bird and did a flapping sort of motion. This got them all quite excited. One of them scrabbled around in a sack beside them and pulled out their homemade kestrel trap: a shoe-box sized cage, with a live mouse darting round inside just below some twisted wire meshing. Gesticulating carefully now, they showed me how the kestrel would swoop down at the mouse and become entangled in the web like a fly in a spiderweb. Their mimes were tremendous. In some parallel world the six of us could be having a competitive game of charades in a draughty living room.

I knew by now there was no way I was going to liberate the birds. I wasn't brave enough, but also, perversely, it just didn't seem right. From the boys' point of view, this was a great diplomatic moment. They'd been fine ambassadors for their country. They had invited me over, offered me food and shared their ancient bird-trapping secrets. They had been utterly hospitable when they could quite easily have stabbed me and nicked the car.

They mimed brilliantly to suggest I took a photo. I showed

them my binoculars in an attempt to demonstrate that I didn't have a camera. They weren't very impressed. Eventually it seemed like the right time to leave, and I strolled back to the car, passing the kestrels on the way, unable to look them in the eye.

Back in the now familiar surroundings of my Chrysler I headed west and managed to cross the whole of the narrow country in an hour or so. I tried not to think about the kestrels. On the other coast, facing the Gulf of Bahrain, I arrived quite by accident at a beach resort called Al Jazair where instead of birds, I found thousands of sunbathers, nearly all of whom were entirely covered up by long black or white robes. Apart from the dress code it was just like being at Blackpool, kids jumping in and out of the waves, mothers worrying, grannies scoffing ice cream. I ate what was left of my withered packed lunch and admired the view.

By the time I returned the car to the hotel that evening, I'd been driving for over eight hours. Most of the time it was just me, the Chrysler and my favourite Arabic radio station, cruising around, ignoring signs for Saudi Arabia, occasionally stopping to stare at and sketch a bird. Unlike the lesser kestrels, I felt incredibly liberated. I felt like I was in a film. Not a very exciting film, admittedly, some sort of arty affair about a man birdwatching on his own in Bahrain, but a film nevertheless. I wondered if this was how David felt when touring with his band.

Going through my list with David a few weeks later he allowed me sixteen new species for the trip including broad-billed sandpiper, Kentish plover, purple heron and an Indian house crow, and I was pleased with myself. When I showed him my drawings of those most mysterious birds that had followed me round the country he instantly knew what they were too; 'Myna birds! Oh yes, you would have seen a lot of them,' he said. Apparently they were too common to include in the official bird guide. It just goes to show that no matter how ordinary the bird, it can mean something to someone.

25 April

The week that followed dragged interminably. I was pleased, of course, when Liverpool beat Chelsea 2–1 in the semi-finals of the FA Cup to reach their thirteenth final, but apart from that one jubilant afternoon I was restless. Britain seemed sterile compared to the wild side of Arabia that I'd discovered.

On the way to a gig in Stratford-upon-Avon, however, I nipped into a village called Stokenchurch and was able to sate my new hunger for a while at least.

Just off Junction 5 of the M40, where I'd seen that red kite at the very start of the year, Stokenchurch looks down on the Buckinghamshire valley where the birds of prey were reintroduced back in 1989. Since then, they've thrived, gobbling up the carrion that litters the motorway and becoming a regular sight in the skies over the nearby towns. Back in medieval times, the UK's cities were home to thousands of the birds. Chaucer mentions a red kite in *The Knight's Tale*, and in *Coriolanus* Shakespeare describes London as 'the city of kites and crows'. In fact, the birds acted as a free cleaning service for the capital, devouring any KFC-style scraps Shakespeare's contemporaries dropped. (If I was London mayor I'd think about setting up a similar system – Ken Livingstone employed Harris hawks to disperse the pigeons from Trafalgar Square in 2000.) But from being a constant traffic-warden-style fixture on every street corner, stripping carcasses and nicking bread from children, their numbers gradually shrank with increased hunting and egg-collecting, until a hundred years ago only a dozen pairs were left in Britain.

From the lookout in Stokenchurch I saw at least twenty of the birds, wheeling over the motorway, searching for the latest poor rabbit to become road kill for lunch. There are at least eighty pairs in this area alone now, the M40 providing more than enough food for the growing community. As I trudged along the tops of the chalky Chilterns at about the same height some of these birds were flying, they looked to me like ptero-dactyls. Everyone says they only eat dead animals, but if I had a cat or a baby I'd be worried.

29 April

As the length of this chapter attests, April had been a big month for me. While out in Bahrain I'd hit triple figures for the year, almost fifty of which I'd seen in the last three weeks alone. Duncton, meanwhile, had only added another eighteen. I was drawing close. I'd also gained my own personal guide in the form of David and was improving my basic birdwatching skills every day. The previous afternoon I'd been walking round Queen's Park with Rachel and was delighted to point out some ring-necked parakeets in the trees above us. No one else had seen them, but my instincts were honed. I heard their squawks, I nailed them. In the petting zoo I was genuinely disgusted to hear a man tell his grandson that a goose was a swan. I was definitely getting closer to becoming a birder.

Rachel, in turn, seemed impressed by the parakeets (if a little embarrassed by my mortification in the petting zoo). 'Oh wow,' she said, 'they're amazing.' Written down, that doesn't look like the most emotional of reactions, but to me it meant a lot. My hard work was paying off – if I could impress my wife (well, it was the pretty parrots rather than me really, but I found them), maybe one day I'd be able to impress my kids.

Getting up at 6.30 a.m. was no longer the struggle it once was. Andrew, The Welsh Harp volunteer, had told me that today was the day the Brent birders were to carry out their annual bird count (a whole day of birdwatching designed to monitor the fluctuating numbers of birds in the area) and I arrived at the carpark at 7.15 a.m. Of course, I wasn't the first to get there.

Andrew and several others had been stationed in the hide since the sun rose soon after 5 a.m. But I was there and I was going to do my bit.

Actually, I had another long drive later that day so could only stay for a few hours and didn't see a single bird that the real birders hadn't spotted before I'd even got out of bed. But it still felt good to be part of the team. There was a buzz around Heron Hide, and by the time I'd left, the names of sixty-seven species had been chalked up on the board. Sixty-seven species! In a tiny patch of land in the northwest corner of London!

I managed to see thirty-two species during my brief stint, including four new ones for my total; common swifts at last, house and sand martins and a pair of the stock doves that David was so aggrieved to have missed earlier in the month. Tellingly, though, the overall Welsh Harp total only rose to seventy-three species by the close of play. Not a single new bird was added after 5 p.m. In fact, Andrew and co only saw six new species in the final ten hours.

This made me think three things. First, those people who waited patiently for those last ten hours represented the hard-core of birdwatchers, the season-ticket holders, the fans that stand and cheer at the end of the 0–0 draws. Second, *most* bird-watching is actually like those last ten hours. You don't do a big bird count every day. You don't see exciting birds every minute. And third, the birdwatching year is a lot like this particular birdwatching day. Most of the birds are seen in the first few months. Duncton was already slowing down. Few new birds will arrive after April. So had I peaked too early? Would I be able to cope with the rest of the year? I was now just ten birds behind Duncton, but were there enough left out there for me to close that gap? Or would my year and my story simply tail off . . .

CHAPTER 5

Oddie Language

'...we had very good views of this scarce vagrant, which neither of us had seen before. There were many people present, and I suddenly heard someone answer their mobile phone with the words, "Oh, hi Lee." He turned to look directly at me and then answered a very obvious question by saying: "Yes, he is." That was the moment I realised with great discomfort that I was being watched.'

– Adrian M Riley

Alex: 112 species
Duncton: 122 species

3 May

On the first day of May I had to go to John Lewis to buy some blinds. When you work from home there are thousands of potential distractions. Tinkering about with the room you're meant to be writing in is just one of them. It's sometimes too dark, I thought, but it's sometimes too light. I need adjustable blinds! So off I went, confident that as soon as I'd got the light right I'd be able to write much better jokes.

Riding an escalator up to the home furnishings department on the second floor, I passed Liam Gallagher de-escalating back to ladies fashion below. Our eyes met. The Oasis singer seemed to be saying, 'Don't worry, I'm just going through ladies fashion to get some stationery from the ground floor on my way out – isn't it busy in here? – and yes, I often procrastinate when I'm meant to be writing too,' or something like that. I smiled what I thought was my friendliest smile. He half-smiled, half-scowled back and was gone.

Sitting on the tube on the way back to Kensal Green, a bag of blinds between my legs, I thought over the encounter, and realised there were similarities between celeb-spotting and bird-watching. Of course, you had to be at the right place at the right time, but you also needed to know what you were looking for and where they were most likely to be. Finding Liam Gallagher in John Lewis was a lucky yet fairly ordinary celebrity sighting. It wouldn't have warranted more than a sentence in *Heat* magazine's 'Spotted' column. In birding terms it was like seeing a green woodpecker – a nice story to tell your friends but not that impressive.

In fact, while focusing on my Oasis founding member, I may have missed several other celebrities because I wasn't paying attention or didn't know what they looked like. I don't think I'd recognise anyone from *Coronation Street*, for example. And if

I was really taking the task seriously, I would have gone some-where like The Ivy restaurant and put the hours in, waiting patiently all night long, listening out for the tell-tale twitter of a Keira Knightley or an Eva Longoria.

But then again, maybe Liam Gallagher wasn't such a bad spot. After all I had instantly known who he was. From the briefest glance I had registered his greyish face, stern demeanour, wiry frame and tight clothes and thought, 'That's Liam Gallagher.' Because he wasn't exhibiting the older, calmer features and shorter hair of his brother, I had known right away that it wasn't a *Noel* Gallagher. Furthermore, I knew that a Liam Gallagher could be seen in the area because I'd seen him walking down Regent Street at about the same time the year before. I knew the features and habits of a Liam Gallagher.

Bearing this in mind, I decided to combine what skills I possessed as a celeb-spotter with my more pressing birdwatching challenge and spend at least some of the next month celebrity-birdwatchingwatching. I would try to find one of the nation's famous birdwatchers and watch him watching birds, in a bid both to see how he indulged in the hobby, and maybe pick up an extra bird or two in doing so.

The phrase 'one of the nation's famous birdwatchers' needs qualification. There are clearly fewer famous birdwatchers than, say, footballers, chefs, even (and I think this is bizarre) gardeners.[66] But the nation does have some famous bird-watchers. Liam's contemporary, Jarvis Cocker, lead singer of Pulp, has often spoken of his love of the hobby. Indie bands British Sea Power and Guillemots and American singer-songwriter Sufjan Stevens (who is brilliant) have all made

---

66 In thirty seconds I was able to list eight famous gardeners. To my shame, I could only name seven Prime Ministers in the same period of time. Have a go and see the back of the book for my answers.

similar claims. In fact, Britain's most famous pop star, Sir Paul McCartney, has admitted his own fondness for birds and even constructed his own personal hide on his estate. When The Beatles got going in the late 1950s, birdwatching was also just becoming enormous, as demonstrated by a gloriously named birding programme called *Look*[67] directed by the same Peter Scott who opened the Sevenoaks sanctuary with Prince Philip, Jeffery Harrison and Duncton. In 1958 as many people tuned in to watch a *Look* episode (in black and white) on Europe's woodpeckers as did that year's FA Cup Final. Soon afterwards Macca wrote to Scott, asking, 'Can I have the drawings of them ducks if you're not doing anything with them?', signifying an interest in the subject, if not any specific knowledge or basic grammar.

Almost certainly not the Peter Scott TV programme,
but probably something similar.

---

67 For me, the word *Look* evokes both the weary instruction and excitable enthusiasm of Duncton as a youthful father: 'Look! Will you just calm down!' or 'Look! It's a chaffinch!'

Meanwhile, across the sea in Ireland, Van Morrison was busy capturing the romance of the hobby in his song 'Coney Island' with the line, 'spent all day bird-watchin', and the *craic* was good!' Birdwatching can be cool.

It can also be political. In 1910 the British Secretary of State for Foreign Affairs, the Rt Hon. Edward Grey, went on a diplomatic birdwatching trip to Hampshire with the recently retired American President, Theodore Roosevelt. On a single morning in the village of Itchen Abbas near Selborne in Hampshire they saw over forty species *and* strengthened Anglo-American relations. More recently, Kenneth Clarke has been our most notable birding politician and while it's unlikely I'll catch him stomping about the British countryside with ex-President Bush, it's an entertaining thought.

The village of Selborne lies sixteen miles northwest of Midhurst, and is often described as the birthplace of birdwatching. While Cley nurtured the hobby, it was here in Hampshire that what we now think of as birdwatching first began.

The man responsible for this *naissance* was Gilbert White, who became curate of Selborne in 1784. Much like being a comedian, the job allowed him enough free time to explore the area, and in 1789 he published *The Natural History and Antiquities of Selborne*, a compilation of letters he'd written to two prominent zoologists, Thomas Pennant and the Hon. Daines Barrington, about the birds he observed. For the first time, he'd made the distinction between species such as the chiffchaff and willow warbler by watching and recording rather than shooting and stuffing, a practice that would eventually become the norm some 200 years later.

More well-known than all of those listed above, though, are the birdwatching comedians. Perhaps the introverted nature of the comic, combined with the freedom of the occupation, make birding the perfect pastime, maybe it sounds suitably eccentric, but whatever the reason, Eric Morecombe, Vic Reeves and Rory McGrath have all expressed their love of birds. And standing at the top of this comical pile, enjoying the best view, there's the current Bird Idol, the one and only, inimitable, slightly irritable, Bill Oddie; a man with an extraordinary and often underestimated career. Having gained fame as one of The Goodies in the 1970s, he's since become even better known for his books and programmes on birdwatching. He received an OBE for his service to wildlife conservation in 2003, and chose to attend the ceremony in his birding camouflage shirt. Madonna lusted after him in her 1992 song 'Erotica',[68] and most importantly, perhaps, he voiced the part of Crow with unique ornithological insight in the 1980s cartoon *Bananaman*, which, alongside David Jason's *DangerMouse*, was one of my favourite characters on TV as a kid.

Bill Oddie is the curmudgeonly figurehead of British birdwatching. When he first presented *Britain Goes Wild*, a record 3.4 million viewers tuned in. In much the same way that Delia Smith made a nation rush out and buy goose fat, so Oddie caused sales of nest boxes and bird baths to rocket, simply by saying how good he thought they were on his TV programme. Duncton told me he'd once arrived at the bird reserve in Minsmere to find an excited huddle of birders at the entrance. 'Much around?' he asked as usual.

'Nah, not really,' came the reply. 'We did have Bill Oddie earlier though.'

'Ah!' cried Duncton. 'Whereabouts?'

I too was determined to find my Oddie. He would be my golden eagle or, even better, the golden condor in *The Mysterious Cities*

---

68 'Bill Oddie, Bill Oddie, put your hands all over my body.'

of Gold.[69] I wouldn't go so far as to stalk him, but I'd certainly do the next best thing: follow him, paparazzo-style. I swatted up on his significant characteristics: beard (naturally), glasses, portly physique, gaudy shirt beneath the more typical khaki waistcoat. I discovered his common habitat: Hampstead Heath.[70] And so, at 7.30 a.m. I was striding across the heath, keeping my eyes out not just for birds, but for Bill. Looking back now, the idea of searching for an older man on a heath made famous by a certain incident involving George Michael does seem like an obvious comedy set-up, but I was taking this very seriously. I was going to get my man.

As soon as a human loomed into view, I raised my binoculars: Male? Yes. Stocky? Yes. Beard? No! Damn . . .

After three hours, my arms were tired and my notebook full. I'd seen a total of twenty dog walkers walking forty-two dogs (including one of those professionals holding ten dogs at once like a Maypole), two businessmen hurrying in opposite directions, one photographer, three people doing t'ai chi, several panting joggers, one hilarious speed-walker and one other birdwatcher. Who wasn't Oddie. I'd also seen a great spotted woodpecker, a sparrowhawk, three types of tits (coal, blue and great),

---

69 A rival to *Bananaman* in my affections, *The Mysterious Cities of Gold* was a typically epic 1980s cartoon featuring a young Japanese-looking Spanish boy called Esteban who was searching, much like me, for his dad – and the lost Inca cities of gold. It all ended quite tragically, but on the way Esteban discovered an enormous solar-powered Golden Condor which could travel considerable distances under the sun's power alone and was referred to as an 'ornithopter'.

70 Thanks to several references by Bill in books and on TV this is common knowledge. I don't want to be held responsible for a spate of copycat Oddie Watchers. He's already something of a cult figure, with no less than twelve people at the time of writing impersonating him on MySpace. That's twelve people (one of whom may, admittedly, be Bill) spending their time pretending to be the bearded birder! That's even weirder than me spending my spare time trying to find him. Isn't it?

carrion crows, parakeets and a greenfinch. I'd had a fine morning ducking in and out of the sunlit woods, following obscure paths no one but Oddie would take, tracking him like a tribal warrior. I may not have found him, but I was learning to think like him and was convinced I was becoming a better birder in doing so. Psychologically, this was, perhaps, the oddest point of the year.

7 May

Bill Oddie's name came up several times during my second birdwatching date with David. 'Well, Oddie's a proper birdwatcher,' he said. 'He knows his stuff.' When I tested out my theory that birdwatchers were like the paparazzi, David recoiled as if I'd said they were like trainspotters. 'Oh no,' he said, 'the paparazzi are a whole lot more pointless.'

This was to be my biggest birdwatching day of the year so far. I'd slipped into bed at 1.30 a.m. the night before, following a Friday night gig in Reading, slipped out again at 5.30 a.m., whispering goodbye to the ever patient Rachel on the way ('Just don't make a habit of it,' she said, sleepily), then picked up David from his home in east London and headed out to the Kent coast. Around the country birdwatchers were celebrating International Dawn Chorus Day[71] and by 7.15 a.m. (still quite late in proper birdwatching terms) we'd had our breakfast at a service station and were watching whitethroats and blackcaps[72] buzzing about

---

71 According to the official website, 'An annual celebration of the world's oldest wake-up call – the dawn chorus – and the beauty of birdsong. Throughout the UK, people are encouraged to wake up early, just after 4 a.m., and hear the dawn chorus from their bedroom window.' As an annual event it's a bit like Easter, in that the date moves around a bit, and a bit like World Aviation and Cosmonautics Day (12 April) in that it's not necessarily the most important day in most people's years.

72 Both of which are sensible, accurate names for birds, as well as being suitable for pirates with similar attributes.

above some hedges in a place called Cliffe in Kent. On a normal weekend I'd still have hours of sleep ahead of me at this point in the day. I like sleep. But racing out of London to chase birds was fun. Would I do this voluntarily without the incentive of a challenge? Maybe . . .

. . . or maybe not. After the initial coffee rush faded I began to feel tired and just a little bit faint, and the idea of bed then *Soccer AM* under a blanket was appealing. How is it that dads like David and Duncton have so much more stamina than me? Does having a child suddenly make getting up early and 'doing stuff' all day easy by comparison?

Although at times I felt like I was sleepwalking, I had David to keep me going, and keep going I did. It was well worth it. As well as the pleasant business of strolling through the countryside, chatting about Oddie and being out of London, the birds were impressive. During the first four-hour circuit we were mobbed by countless hungry swifts gorging on a mist of midges and almost knocked out by a low-flying hen harrier skimming along the marshy fields. We walked in single file along a river wall by the Thames, stopping to see garganeys and little stints on the bank below. I finally caught sight of my first cuckoos of the year and heard my first nightingale at ludicrously close range, although I couldn't glimpse it through the thick gorse. (This was an odd stand-off. David and I stood and listened to the bush for thirty minutes, while the bird steadfastly refused to reveal itself. Instead it sat and hid and sang – strange behaviour surely?) Although David was telling me both where the birds were and what they were called, I found myself tuning into the hobby like never before. My instincts seemed to sharpen, ears and eyes working together – I felt alive. I felt like a cliché.

At lunch we refuelled with sausage rolls and acrid coffee at the Medway services on the M2 (not my favourite – probably not even in my top ten – very little atmosphere[73]) then headed down to another nature reserve called Elmley Marshes on the Isle of Sheppey in the middle of the River Swale. David was plotting our route, based on his own birding compass and regular texts from Birdline – a spoonbill had been seen in the area, so we homed in on our target. This was the last day of the Premiership season, so I was also receiving texts alerting me to goals scored. But after another disappointing domestic season for Liverpool, I was more excited when his phone buzzed than mine.

Like Anneka Rice on *Treasure Hunt*, but more subtly dressed, we followed Birdline's clues and were rewarded with the fine sight of an osprey resting before his next fishing trip, and a Temminck's stint sneaking furtively along the river. Rounding a corner to another stretch of water we came across a clutch of couples (one father and son, one husband and wife, one pair of friends) all of whom had their equipment pointing in the same direction. 'It's the spoonbill,' whispered one before stepping aside to let me have a go on his telescope. Through the blurry circle I could see a large white bird, head twisted round, apparently fast asleep. Once again, I failed to be thrilled by what I was assured was a dramatic find, but I was pleased to get yet another new bird for my total.

---

73 I thought I should probably put you out of your misery and reveal my favourite ten. So, in reverse order, we have at 10: Trowell (M1, jct 25-6 – particularly well-stocked W H Smith). 9: Fleet (M3 jct 4A-5 – excellent pedestrian footbridge). 8: Leigh Delamere (M4 jct 17-18 – the last stop before Mark's stag; we enjoyed the Postman Pat ride there). 7: Norton Canes (M6T jct 6-7 – I love everything to do with the toll road). 6: Clacket Lane (M25 jct 5-6 – Mum and Duncton bought me a fry-up there on my first journey up to university). 5: Heart of Scotland (M8 jct 4-5 – most ironic name). 4: Newport Pagnell (M1 jct 14-15 – according to The Smiths song 'Is It Really So Strange', Morrissey lost his bag here). 3: Scotch Corner (A1(M) jct 57 – the final stop before Edinburgh). 2: Woolley Edge (M1 jct 38-9 – I had a wash in the five-star, loo-of-the-year, award-winning shower there). And, you've guessed it, at No.1, it's Toddington (M1 jct 11-12 – I had my haircut at the incongruous barbershop there).

As we strolled off once more, a cry went up behind us: 'He's waking up!'

We arrived back just in time to see the spoonbill stretch his wings, look lazily round and stagger off into the air. It was quite a sight. Its bill did look exactly like a spoon. I'm not sure if that was what the other birdwatchers were excited about, but I loved it. Imagine a massive bird with a massive spoon for a nose. That's worth getting up at half-five for.

By the time my watch had struck 5.30 p.m. (it's an idiosyncratic timepiece), we had to think about getting back to London. I had a gig in Greenwich that evening and had to start switching focus back to my 'job'. So, after watching some brilliant yellow wagtails cavorting in the fields – my twenty-second new species of the day – we headed home in satisfied silence. I did check Radio 5 once to confirm Liverpool's final position[74] but I knew David wasn't interested, and I was enjoying our mutually contented exhaustion after a whole day outside. Summer had just begun, and I sensed I'd caught the sun. I went on stage that night with tired legs and such a ruddy complexion that I felt I had to explain myself. For the first time, I told the audience I'd been birdwatching. I think some of them thought I was joking, although there was no punch line to the story. Either way, it felt good to tell them the truth.

12 May

Immediately after that high came the inevitable low. Birdwatching without David suddenly felt unsatisfying, frustrating, pointless. I was impatient. I couldn't see the same sights on my

---

74 They ended the season with a 3–1 win away at Portsmouth, but Man Utd were busy thrashing Charlton 4–0, so took second place behind Chelsea by a single point. Liverpool had made it into the Champions League once more, but had still finished below the top two. Not good enough.

own. Before a particularly testing gig in Bournemouth, in which the entire audience was made up of men in Hawaiian shirts (not one of whom was Oddie), I'd stopped and stomped around Stanpit Marsh near Christchurch for two hours. My *Birdwatcher's Yearbook* said I should be able to find a bearded tit.[75] I found a tree sparrow. And although this was a new bird, and although I was in a beautiful place, passing parents with children in boats and horses with foals galloping along the beach, beneath another warming sun, I wasn't happy. I couldn't find the birds I wanted.

Following a tip-off from the London Birders forum, I bought tickets for England's Test Match against Sri Lanka at Lords, where a common crane had been spotted flying over the previous day. I had vaguely planned to go to the game at some point, so this wasn't as extravagant a gesture as it might sound, but it was fun to go to a cricket match with an ulterior motive. Lots of people had binoculars, but few were aiming them high above the action.

In fact, few were aiming them anywhere at all, for there was very little action. Rain fell consistently throughout the morning and everyone looked damp and bored. Was watching cricket any weirder than watching birds? To be honest, I didn't have a great time doing either, seeing only four tight overs of cricket, a cormorant high above the sodden wicket and a balloon in the shape of a dolphin which I was sure wouldn't count for my list. It wasn't a captive, it wasn't a pet, it wasn't dead; but then it also wasn't a bird. Like the child who had let the inflatable mammal slip, I was upset. Something was missing.

---

75 Clearly a funny name. The bird itself, however, sports more of a moustache than a beard – a long, drooping Chinaman-style tash. I particularly like it because on the same page there's a bird called a sombre tit, which doesn't look amused at all by the facial hair.

That evening I had a text from Mat out in Africa:

We had a birding competition today and saw or heard 74 species! Who scored England's runs in the test and who won the UEFA cup?[76]

I texted him back wearily, glad he wouldn't be able to sense the lack of enthusiasm in my reply.

13 May

Another text combining sport and birds from another member of my family epitomised another day of birding frustration.

At the beginning of the month, Duncton had casually slipped into the conversation – just as I am now – that he and Mum were off to Romania this week for a trip up the Danube. What I hadn't comprehended was that this was a specifically birdwatching mission. The holiday was organised by a birdwatching company and featured trips to several nature reserves and famous birding hotspots, rather than anything cultural or traditionally touristy. As I have said, and indeed believed, Duncton rarely goes bird-watching outside Sussex. He occasionally strays into Kent and Norfolk, but I was under the impression he'd be stuck on the Sussex coast while I sashayed round the world for much of the year. This birdwatching trip to Romania represented a departure for Duncton. A birdwatching trip abroad, something he confessed he'd always wanted to do, was extraordinary behaviour. And once again I felt that I had kick-started his passion and in so doing severely limited my chances of winning the competition.

The lengthy text, from Mum, read:

---

76 Trescothick and Pieterson both got centuries in a rain-ruined match that was eventually drawn, while Sevilla beat Middlesborough 4–0.

On v. noisy stretch of river tonight. 2 types of frog + fire-bellied toads all croaking. 134 different birds seen (not by me tho), 50+ new ones so far for dad! My brain needs a rest! Someone here got texts as goals happened so kept up to date in the cup – but she was West Ham ... Well done Liverpool! hope all OK with you both, AML Mum x x x.

Note the superior texting technique to Duncton's: use of symbols, not in capitals, abbreviations and not a single mistake. Good use of exclamation marks too, the first ('50+ new ones so far for dad!') definitely being an exclamation mark of danger rather than humour. I had been so close to catching up. I thought this was the month I'd slip past him, winking as I went. Now, in one Romanian fowl swoop, he'd charged off into the distance without even a word cast back to his struggling son.

I was consoled by the fact that Liverpool had indeed beaten West Ham in the FA Cup final – thanks to some Steven Gerrard heroics that evoked memories of Istanbul the year before – but even that was a bit of a worry for me. So exciting was the game, so thrilling the finale and so good the result that I was already looking forward to the World Cup next month. Good things come in threes, I thought, and if Gerrard could lead Liverpool to European and domestic cup glory, surely the World Cup would be next? But how was I supposed to go out birding if England were going to win the World Cup for the first time in my life? All logic, I admit, had gone out of the window, but my loyalty to the Big Year was threatened. I'm not going to win now anyway, I thought, what's the point?

My progress was infuriatingly stilted: two steps forward – but only when assisted by my carer, David – then no steps anywhere at all. Duncton's meanwhile, was fifty-plus steps forward, so far that he could no longer even see his son faltering behind him. As I used to on family walks, when Duncton strode purposefully ahead and my legs just weren't long enough to keep up, I sulked.

16 May

I'd been neglecting my garden birds for some time now so, with just a hint of petulance, I decided that while Duncton was flouncing up and down the Danube, I'd get down to some grassroots birdwatching in Kensal Green. At a particularly sticky stage of the Cup final, when Liverpool were 2-1 down and I was planning how to laugh off their loss to my friends, I'd seen my first goldfinch on the Defender II, but was so caught up in the game that I hadn't really given it credit. With another football season finally at its futile end, and three weeks to go before the World Cup, I would now devote myself to my loyal local birds.

In my second edition of *Birdwatching* magazine, I'd read an article on mealworms. The article suggested you should treat your birds by giving them a regular supply of these creepy crawlies, ideally creating a mealworm farm in your back garden so they could have a regular supply. I'm not particularly squeamish, but I am quite badly organised, and so I didn't dare grow my own mealworms. I'd forget all about them and then come home to find they'd eaten my wife. So I followed an RSPB advert on the same page and ordered myself a batch.

I'd been working the night before, so had got up late, thrown on a dressing gown and was eating my breakfast. It was about 11 a.m. Rachel had indulged in a more conventional takeaway the previous evening with some friends, so I was eating their leftover curry. If you've never tried it don't judge me yet – cold curry in the morning is a treat everyone should enjoy at least once a month.

Because I'm out most evenings, I tend to watch my requisite hour of telly in the morning. This morning, however, there was nothing on. I couldn't cope with Jeremy Kyle or tolerate Trisha, so I flicked through the sports channels and settled on a game of netball. Now netball may be a women's sport, but it's not beach volleyball. It's a proper sport, like basketball, played by proper sportswomen in proper sports clothing, so I wasn't being pervy. I just wanted some entertainment as I ate my curry, and about halfway through my garlic naan I was really getting into the game.[77] I think men can get obsessed with any sort of competition – Badminton, *Big Brother*, Birdwatching – if they spend enough time sitting in front of it.[78]

Even so, when a delivery man knocked on the door and was greeted by the sight of me in my dressing gown, clutching a bowl of curry, with women's netball blaring out in the background, I was just a touch ashamed. His nonchalant expression suggested that this wasn't such an unusual sight, but I was still uncomfortable. 'I work nights,' I tried to explain, vaguely suggesting I do something worthy like medicine or road building.

'Sign here,' he said, handing me his futuristic electronic notepad. I scrawled my name and scurried back inside my den, clutching the package and feeling quite sordid.

---

77 Team Bath eventually beat Loughborough Lightning. They also eventually beat pretty much everyone else and won The Super League both that season and the next. I got quite into Team Bath in much the same way as I had once got into Liverpool.

78 Actually, thinking about it, my ability to watch any sport on TV is a talent (yes, a talent) learned independently of Duncton. He can't. A couple of months before I got married he suffered a detached retina. It was as painful as it sounds, but it did mean he got to lie on a sofa for a week while a big snooker tournament was on BBC2. I would have watched every ball struck. He said he couldn't watch more than two minutes before getting bored. Birdwatching, however, is a whole different ball game.

It was then that I noticed the package was making noises – a rustling sound, a crawling hum and, I noticed, an unnatural movement just beneath the surface. The mealworms were alive.

I checked the advert again. Yes, there it was, 'live mealworms' – just slightly more expensive than 'dried mealworms'. Why was I such a snob when it came to buying stuff for the garden? Midway through my already stomach-churning breakfast, I was holding a bag stuffed full of stretching, tetchy worms.

I sprang into action. I could deal with this. I made sure I was recording the netball (I now had to know who had won before I could carry on with my life), stuffed the remains of the curry back in the fridge and peered at the bag. So, I thought, I've got a lot of live worms. I need to store them somewhere. I don't want Rachel to be cross. What should I do?

I was stumped.

I phoned up the RSPB for help.

'Oh,' they said, 'just put them in a container with holes for air and a lid so they can't get out.'

'Great,' I said, 'thanks.'

A container with holes and a lid. Easy. I glanced around the kitchen. There must be something here. Aha! The teapot!

For twenty seconds I contemplated pouring the larvae into our one and only teapot, a cherished wedding present and much used kitchen item. It was only really the nagging thought that they might be able to crawl out of the spout that stopped me.

What else? I know, perfect . . . the piggy bank!

This was, to me, a much more sensible option. The piggy bank had holes, obviously, so you could put the money in. This could be ideal. Unfortunately, this was a piggy bank with a history. I'd bought it for Rachel as a surprise gift one afternoon. She was as surprised and pleased as you can be about a gaudy china pig.

One evening between then and now I was hosting a comedy quiz show with Key and Mark (the stag). Not having a budget that stretched to buzzers, I grabbed the only thing I could see that would make a noise on the way out of the house, and later that evening handed one of our contestants Rachel's piggy bank to shake if they wanted to answer a question. Rachel was in the audience. I hadn't asked to borrow her pig. Halfway through round two the contestant got particularly excited and gave the pig a thorough rattling. The pig exploded. Everyone laughed. Except for Rachel and I. I'd done a bad thing.

The pig was now superglued back together and wrapped in a bandage to remind me of my mistake. I was duly warned. Filling Rachel's romantic pig present with mealworms would not be a good idea.

I was stumped again.

I texted Mum for help. Despite being on a river in Romania, she texted back in a matter of seconds:

Try a Tupperware container or an ice cream tub. Pierce it with a fork. Good luck! x

That's what mums are for – sound advice and perfect texting ('Tupperware' isn't even in predictive text). But we didn't have any Tupperware containers and the only ice cream tub we had was full of ice cream. I think people only keep empty ice cream tubs when they have children. We didn't have children. We had worms. I scooped the remaining ice cream into a bowl, stuck it in the fridge next to my curry (mentally marking it 'lunch') and washed out the tub. I was nearly there.

*

'Most bird people would probably tell you that there are roughly eight sub-clans in the tribe – scientist,[79] ornithologist, bird-watcher, birdwatcher, birder, twitcher, dude and robin stroker,' writes

---

79 Despite being at the top of the knowledge tree, scientists can, of course, make mistakes, as demonstrated by a certain Scottish (or, more likely, Icelandic) swan.

Mark Cocker in *Birders: Tales of a Tribe*. That's a complicated tribe. The first two 'overlap pretty much completely'; bird-watcher, Cocker explains, is only included 'in a bid to banish (it) for ever . . . If you need to stick a hyphen between the two words you've obviously never been involved in the enterprise in your life.'

Twitcher, of course, we've covered. But dude was news to me. 'His central feature,' writes Cocker, 'is ignorance . . . "dude" also carries a vague moral implication, suggesting a person who purports to know things they patently don't. A dude is the most unwelcome character in any rigid hierarchy . . .' This got me a little worried. Was I a dude?

When I was younger, I wanted to be a dude. Brad on *Neighbours* was a dude and he got to marry Beth. But I'd never actually thought of myself as one before. Now, though, dude apparently meant something different, something less cool, less relaxed, something more morally flawed. Thankfully I was fairly confident I hadn't purported to know things I patently didn't. I had claimed a dodgy woodpecker, yes, but that was different. That wasn't feigning knowledge; that was hoping for the best. But I did have to be careful. I could easily see myself becoming a dude. At the Wetland Centre with Tim I was very nearly a dude. I no longer wanted to be a dude.

Cocker lists 'robin stroker' last. 'They are the most lukewarm in their enthusiasm,' he says. 'Like my parents, they heap food on the bird table. They watch from the living-room window. They join the Royal Society for the Protection of Birds.' I couldn't really deny any of this. I did heap food onto my bird tables, I did watch from the living-room window, I had joined the RSPB. And, most damning of all, I was about to try to stroke a robin.

I was Mark Cocker's parents, he was my dad. I didn't think this was good news.

I knew I had a long way to go before being a birdwatcher or a birder, but after nearly six months it was frustrating to be stuck at the bottom, with the perilous dude level still to negotiate. Still, I'd started, so I'd have to finish.[80] At least I was in one of the clans. I was on the ladder. And besides, as Cocker concludes: 'Robin strokers are the vast bulk of decent folk without whom bird conservation would have no real teeth. We should all learn to love and stroke them fondly.' Absolutely. We should all do a bit of robinstrokingstroking when possible.

18 May

Mealworms aren't really worms. They're larvae that will in time metamorphose into mealworm beetles. They're the caterpillars' ugly sisters. But the birds love them. Illustrating the article I read in praise of the humble mealworm, the sort of article few magazines ever dare publish, was a photo of someone feeding the worms to a robin. But instead of placing the worms on a bird table or scattering them across her lawn, this lady had both the worms and the bird in the palm of her hand. She had the bird eating out of her hand. I wanted to do that. I wanted to hold a robin in my hand. I wanted to feel the feathers, the weight, the tiny life (I imagined it would have the texture of a tennis ball, the mass of a squash ball, and the little heartbeat of a mouse).

So on the day the worms arrived I poured a few of them into the Defender and only had to wait a matter of minutes before a blue tit and the robin (yes, the same portly chap as before) were gleefully tucking in. I watched with a bowl of curry then a bowl of ice cream from the kitchen.

---

80 I've used it there but the statement: 'I've started, so I'll finish' has always struck me as quite illogical. Just because you've started something, that doesn't mean you *must* finish it. If you've started eating a meal and realise you'll be sick if you eat it all, you don't have to finish it and then be sick. There is always the option to pull out. It's just that being stubborn men, the eating it all and being sick option is often the only one we see.

The next day, I placed a few more of the mealworms on a plate on a table in the garden, closer both to the house and human activity, so the robin would learn to trust me. Again, before long, three birds (the robin again and two starlings), were standing on the plate, mercilessly attacking the poor larvae, plucking them from the china, snapping them in half and gobbling them down. I'd never seen them so happy (the birds, not the poor worms).

Now, on the third day, it was time for me to be that plate. At about 11 a.m. – well before their lunch but ideal for a mid-morning snack – I took my position on one of the chairs, shut my eyes, wrinkled my nose and reached into the ice cream tub for a highly unusual scoop. They didn't actually feel that bad. Reasonably firm, like boiled rice, the creatures wriggled as if in slow motion on my hand, occasionally twisting one end (presumably a head but both ends looked identical) up as if to look me in the eye. I, meanwhile, did feel quite bad. All of a sudden I was uncomfortable with the idea of condemning these worms to certain death. To leave them out in the garden to do their best was one thing, but to actually hold them out for their beaky murderers felt cruel. Still, this was what the RSPB had recommended, so this was what I would do.

An hour later, I'd had no customers. Three worms had actually writhed their way to freedom, dropping off my thumb on to the patio below, and were making a bid for the flowerbed, so I felt a little better. My arm, however, was aching, so I was now resting it along the table. I was also trying to read a book to pass the time, but was finding concentration and page turning tricky.[81] One blue tit had alighted briefly on the seed shack but was so put off by my presence that he hadn't even stayed for a bite to eat there.

---

81 This was particularly frustrating as the book in question was that rare thing, an ornithological thriller: *Pelican Blood* by Chris Freddi. It's a murder mystery about birdwatchers. Like I say, everyone's got a story about birds; this one's the bloodiest I've encountered so far.

I had experience of robin stroking. This is my first mention
of birds in print, written at the end of 1983.

By midday, three things had happened. First, the robin landed on a branch about a yard from me and watched me beadily for several minutes. I watched him right back. Occasionally our eyes darted down to the worms, who may well have been watching us too. All three corners of this food triangle were nervous. We couldn't all win. The worms might escape and the robin and I would lose out. The worms might be eaten and the robin and I would be happy. Or the worms might be a Bahrain-style trap and I might crush the robin in my hand. Not wanting to take that risk, the robin flew next door for some time out and much safer sesame seed. Stalemate.

Second, a vast throng of starlings swooped onto the fig tree above me. There must have been about thirty of the noisy, agitated things. With summer coming the figs were swelling, something I hadn't noticed, but which the starlings clearly had. They crash landed on the branches with such a clatter that I jumped, startled, and a couple more worms fell from my hand.

While I held out my wriggly offering they then tore into the fruit with savage energy and I prayed they wouldn't do the same to my hand.

Third, one of the occupants of the flat above ours appeared at the window and watched me warily, much like the robin. As I've mentioned, the house next door belonged to an Anglo-Italian family, who were always friendly, kind and welcoming – even if their bird feeder was annoyingly superior. The flat above us was being rented by an Italian family. Again, they were lovely, quiet and trouble-free (except when there was a big Italian football match), but having only recently arrived from Italy, they were unfamiliar with the whole concept of birdwatching. Having been puzzled by my CD tree decoration the year before, this painstaking attempt at feeding must have looked quite bizarre.

Birdwatching isn't massive in Italy. There are hundreds of fantastic species to find, but it's not a national pastime as it is here. Being something of an Italophile – he takes Italian lessons and holidays on Lake Garda – Duncton subscribes to *Ali*, the Italian birdwatching magazine. (The Italian for birdwatching, by the way, is '*il birdwatching*'. They don't have their own word for the activity, so foreign is it to their culture.)

Interestingly, British and Irish robins are far more trusting of humans than their European counterparts. The traditional British Christmas image of a red-breasted robin perched on the fork handle of a nearby farmer is one of the more realistic festive pictures you'll find. But anywhere other than these islands, robins are far too wary to go near a human hand. That American robin in Peckham may have been seen by countless birders, but none would have dared get too near, for fear of scaring him back across the Atlantic. Italian robins don't sit on Italian gardeners' shoulders.

When I caught the eye of the Italian father of the house, watching me, watching a robin, watching me, watching the worms, watching the robin, watching me, watching the Italian father of the house, it was a peculiar moment. I nodded seriously as if this was a normal but important everyday activity. He nodded back, admirably masking shock or dismay.

I continued with my experiment for another hour without success. Even if he'd stayed watching, my neighbour wouldn't have seen me with a bird in the hand. He must have thought I just fancied sitting outside for the morning with a handful of worms. He may have thought I was airing them, or even showing them off. I couldn't face trying to explain myself.

19 May

By now I'd set the London Birders Forum as the home page on my laptop. It had been the official Liverpool FC site. Now each time I logged on to the internet I'd find out which birds were playing where, rather than footballers. I was determined to shake off my dip in form, whatever it took.

I'd read reports on the site the week before, not of a special bird but a special birding occasion – the inaugural 'London Birders Drinks'. Harnessing the power of the internet and acknowledging the social side of birding, a few of the more prominent posters had suggested a night in a pub, catching up with old friends, putting names to faces that they saw every week out in the field, and finding out who was using what pseudonym on the forum itself.

Now that I was officially friends with David and had met Andrew at The Welsh Harp, I thought I should go along. But on the tube down from Kensal Green to Baker Street where the drinks were scheduled to be consumed, I was nervous. Despite my job, I hate walking into a room and having to say things to a group of people. I'm bad at introducing myself, embarrassed by everything, socially awkward and naturally shy. Will David be there? I thought. If not, who will I speak to? What will I speak about? Will I fit in? Will they suss me out as a fake or a dude? These doubts continued to build as I neared the pub, but I knew my only hope of staying close to Duncton's total was with the help of other, more experienced birders. So with two hours to fill before a gig in Soho, I poked my head into The Globe Pub on the dot of 6 p.m., far more anxious than I ever am before going on stage.

All I could see inside was rugby, on about eight separate screens. Below this the sort of men you'd expect to be watching rugby in a pub stood about in various masculine poses. Large men in large groups. There were a couple of stag parties there too, warming up for their own scrummage later on. Surely these weren't the London Birders? I circled the room, but saw no binoculars, no khaki, no fleeces and no walking boots. I was secretly relieved that no one but me had shown up. I'd been let off.

Then, behind a particularly sturdy supporter, I noticed some stairs. That must be where they were. I tried to psych myself up again: I can do this, I've done this before, you're fine, everything's OK. I climbed the stairs, practising my opening line on the way; 'Hi, I'm Alex and I'm very nearly a birdwatcher . . .'

But there was nobody on the second floor. No rugby groups, no stags, no birders, nobody. Again I felt a surge of relief. I'd been stood up, but I'd done my best. Now I just had to go and make a roomful of strangers laugh. I fled.

To my surprise and delight, David came to my gig. He'd thought about going to the birders' drinks but, like everyone else apparently, decided he liked the remoteness of the hobby and wasn't quite ready to turn it into something else. 'To me,' he'd said during our first outing together, 'a lot of birdwatching is about solitude. I do go with other people occasionally, but mostly I'm on my own. It's often the only chance I get to be alone . . .' I felt honoured and touched that he hadn't minded meeting me.

20 May

Turning on my computer the next morning, I was confused to see photos of what looked like a highly successful first London Birders' outing. I scrolled through the banter to see what had happened. Surely these weren't the rugby fans in the pub? Or had they just hidden when they saw me coming up the stairs?

It was my mistake. The day before the event someone had changed the venue to the Metropolitan Bar on Marylebone, having heard about the televised rugby match in The Globe. It seemed that proper birders check the forum even more regularly than me, and the ensuing night was indeed a triumph. London's birdwatching community had amassed after work and stayed in the pub till closing time. The pictures showed a joyful band of normal, sociable people. I imagined them, sharing stories, comparing equipment, singing birdsongs, generally having a very nice time, and I kicked myself.

A phone call to Duncton, who had arrived back from Romania that morning, did little to improve my mood. He'd seen a total of eighty new species for his year list, fifty-five of which were lifers. He was full of stories about the red-footed falcons, hobbies and little bitterns he'd seen from the deck of the boat. 'There was no engine!' he told me with inexplicable excitement. 'We were pulled along by a tug so we could all just sit there with our binoculars. It was amazing.'

They'd walked up into the Carpathian Mountains and tried and failed to see bears, but that didn't matter to Duncton. He was Charlie, just back from the chocolate factory, full of stories and high as a kite. More interesting to me, however, was Mum's perspective. This was also her first birdwatching holiday. And while Duncton knew he'd have an amazing experience, Mum had been worried both that she might not have quite as much fun – and that this might become a regular occurrence.

'I did enjoy it,' she told me, with that intonation that leaves you in no doubt that a 'but' is lurking just round the corner. 'But it was a bit too much. It was OK. But I got extremely bored by some of it. Sometimes we'd only walk ten yards before the tripods went up because they'd seen something or heard something, and was it this kind of warbler or that kind of warbler? And I didn't really care to be honest. Some of the basic stuff was great, I was really pleased to finally see a cuckoo – we saw a cuckoo every day which I loved. But the finer details and the notching up of numbers just wasn't my scene really. And there wasn't an awful lot else. I do enjoy birdwatching to an extent, but not to that extent.'

It seemed an ornithological holiday was where the birdline was drawn between my parents. He had loved it, she had not. She was more than happy for him to go on another trip like it in the future, as long as she didn't have to go too.

I understood how she felt. Despite my determination to win the competition, I had already lost patience with the warblers and thrushes that, to me, looked identical. To be trapped on a boat that stopped every twenty yards in front of yet another small brown trilling thing wouldn't be much fun if you weren't really into that small brown trilling thing. Maybe I was more like Mum than Duncton in this respect. My interest in birds might always be superficial. I liked them, sure. Some of them were brilliant. But I didn't love them. I loved other things – football like my brothers, jokes by myself and words like my mum. I might just be able to become a birdwatcher, but I doubted I could ever be a true birder. Perhaps it was a good thing Duncton hadn't taken me to Fair Isle.

26 May

After ten days of trying to sweet-talk a robin on to my hand, I gave up. I had a lot of time to think while sitting uncomfortably, arm outstretched, still as a statue, and had decided that ten days was enough of a trial period. It had dawned on me gradually that this may not be a good way to experience birdwatching. I do, after all, have a perfectly adequate set of binoculars that would allow me to see a robin close up without being stuck in one spot. Spending more time walking round rather than sitting in my garden might also mean I saw other species of birds.

The final straw came when I talked to someone who'd actually had the experience of feeding a bird by hand. It was Tom, the merlin man from the stag and he was more than happy to share his bird-handling experience. Birds, by the way, were now dominating nearly every conversation I had. If, like me, you find social situations tricky, it's great to have something you can talk about with nearly everyone. After all, everyone has a bird story. And recently, somewhere out in the country, Tom had fed a robin from his hand.

'Do you want to know what it feels like?' he asked me.

'More than anything,' I said.

'OK, well hold your hand out like this . . .'

If you're reading one-handed feel free to join in at this point. I stretched my hand out, hand upturned, just as I had been doing every day for the last ten days.

'OK,' continued Tom, 'that's what it feels like to hold a robin.'

'What?' I asked, puzzled.

'That's what it feels like. They're so light, you can't actually feel them at all.'

Hmph, I thought, tremendous. In theory, a robin might have landed on my hand while I was dozing or looking up at my Italian neighbour. Well, at least now I would avoid the anticlimactic moment by calling a halt to the experiment on my own terms.

29 May

I turned my back on those pesky weightless red-breasted tease-balls, and the end of the month heralded a brand new favourite bird. Not some shallow, insubstantial airhead either, but a good, honest bird: a pigeon. A woodpigeon, to be precise. To be even more precise, it was the woodpigeon that lived on my street corner. For the first time this year, my favourite bird was an individual rather than a particular species.

Every day on my way to the shop or the tube I'd pass this particular chubby pigeon, distinguished by a bizarre white vertical stripe down his forehead, strutting about on someone's hedge or pecking away at the fag ends at the entrance to Kensal Green station with all the confidence of a drug dealer who knew he was king of his turf. I'd always found the pigeons in my gardens amusing, particularly when they started attempting to mate in the spring. Despite feeling that I shouldn't really be watching, I couldn't take my eyes off the bizarre ritual. First, the female would walk meaningfully back and forth along the wall, completing about five or six lengths under the steady gaze of her partner, before stopping on what I imagine she consid-ered the most romantic spot. Facing away from the male she would then hop twice and crouch down. At this cue, the male would clamber enthusiastically on top of her then sit perfectly still for ten seconds. Without warning, he would then twitch. Without fail, he would then fall off. This happened pretty much every day in March at 10 a.m.

On this particular May morning, the drug-pushing Harry Potter lookalike wasn't in any of his usual spots. I felt disap-pointed. But as I came down onto the station platform I saw him sitting by one of the benches, calmly preening, as if waiting for the train. I sat down beside him. We waited for the train. After mis-measuring the window the first time, I was returning to John Lewis for a new set of blinds.

To my great satisfaction, when the train pulled up Harry followed me on. In fact, it was almost as though he politely let me go on first: 'No, after you – humans first.'

Of course, the atmosphere in the carriage was instantly charged. Normally a dreary London trek into town, for once the commuters smiled at one another, spoke even! For the pigeon is a mood-enhancing bird. A humble pigeon can make everyone feel better. Think of Wimbledon. Even if the crowd has had to sit patiently through rain-break after rain-break, the sight of a pigeon landing on the net will cheer up every single person on centre court. 'Look! It's a pigeon!' someone will cry. The players will laugh. One of the quirkier ones might do an impression of a chicken. 'This is wonderful!' the commentator will say, and everyone will agree. 'It's a pigeon on a tennis court,' people will sigh as if trying to convince themselves it might possibly be true. 'We paid to watch tennis. But now we're watching a bit of tennis *and* a pigeon! Wonderful!'

All these thoughts and more buzzed about the carriage. We all knew this was a story we could dine out on for days. But then, at Queen's Park, the very first stop, the pigeon calmly hopped out again. The mood in the tube reverted to its normal gloom. People looked back at their free papers and tutted at celebrities. Everyone was miserable again, except for Mr Potter-Pigeon, whom I could see through the window cheerfully looking about, pleased that he'd made such good progress without any effort, let alone having to pay. When I returned home that evening, Harry was back under his normal lamppost, touting for business.

I wondered if I could share this pigeon story with members

of the London Birders' Forum. It seemed relevant, but I knew they were more into rare bird sightings than anthropomorphic adventures. Still, I was further cheered by two items of particular interest in that month's RSPB newsletter. The first, a typically quaint letter from a lady who wrote to say that while gardening, 'A robin landed in my garden hat!' I presumed someone had pointed this out, since there was no way she'd be able to sense the slight bird's presence, but either way I liked the image, even if I had no idea what a 'garden hat' was like.

The second was news about Oddie. 'For two weeks from 30 May,' the article read, 'Bill Oddie will be presenting this year's BBC *Springwatch* programme.' Perfect, I thought, a chance to take my mind off the World Cup and maybe pin down Oddie. 'And for all you Goodies fans,' it continued, 'they will be performing at this year's Edinburgh Festival, so book your tickets now!'

Ah ha! More good news. I would have at least two bites at this cherry, surely more than enough bites, considering the size of an average cherry.

CHAPTER 6

Football Crazy

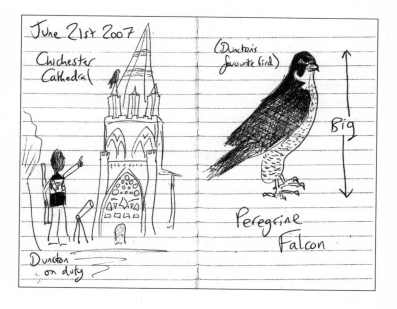

June 21st 2007
Chichester
Cathedral

Duncton
on duty

(Duncton's
favourite bird)

Big

Peregrine
Falcon

'My total was on 308, and it was now becoming obsessively the most important thing in my life.'

– Adrian M Riley

Alex: 137 species
Duncton: 203 species

6 June

For most of the year, I tried to go on birdwatching trips either in my local area or near where I was working. Like most people with ears, eyes and a brain, I'm all too aware of my carbon footprint, and didn't want this vaguely green project to turn into one enormous gas-guzzling road trip. Duncton's patch-birding is clearly the most sound, both in environmental and birdwatching terms. He spends most of his time in his own county, caring for and about the birds around him; he's never tempted to charge up the M1 to join in the latest mega-twitch. He's more like the supporter of a local Sunday league side than one of the best teams in the Premiership.

I, however, have always supported Liverpool[82] and do occasionally travel a long way to see a big match and probably have a lower ethical threshold with regards to the odd unnecessarily long journey. So when Mum emailed me to say she'd read in the *Radio Times*[83] that Bill Oddie was going to be filming *Springwatch* on a farm in Hatherleigh, Devon, just a hundred-mile round trip from a gig I was doing in Taunton, I didn't think twice about making the detour.

By now I'd made several trips to Hampstead Heath and had covered pretty much all of its 800 acres without once bumping into Bill. Statistically this wasn't surprising. There will always be only one Bill Oddie (despite evidence to the contrary on MySpace) and there was only one of me. In contrast, there are hundreds

---

82 When I say 'always', what I really mean is, 'ever since people started saying Chip (my then blond little brother) looked like the blond former Liverpool player and current Liverpool assistant manager Sammy Lee (I don't remember watching him helping Liverpool win their fourth European Cup in 1984 but I do remember him performing the role of "super sub" in the following season) and definitely before they did the double in 1985–6'. Like one's first kiss, the moment one picks one's football team is unpredictable but precious.

83 A magazine the Hornes have always subscribed to. First issue: 1923.

of great spotted woodpeckers on the heath alone, none of whom have other commitments like making nature programmes or occasionally appearing on comedy shows. So, by dropping in to a place I knew he would definitely be, I figured I'd save myself an awful lot of time in the long run. I was twitching Bill Oddie.

Mum's instructions were vague ('Well, it just said the farm was in or near the town . . .') and after pulling up at quite a few farms that seemed to concentrate more on making food than TV, I started to worry. I couldn't dip Oddie again. Then, rounding a corner, I saw the tell-tale telly signs of a man with a yellow high-visibility jacket and earpiece next to an enormous sign saying BBC OB (standing for 'outside broadcast', not 'Oddie Bill' I later found out).

I suddenly felt quite shifty – as if I actually was a member of the paparazzi – and so instead of stopping and asking after the programme's presenter, I drove straight past the entrance, pulling up in a layby a few hundred yards down the road. 'Come on Alex,' I said to myself in the rear-view mirror. 'Everything's OK. You're a good person, you're not a stalker.'

These stern words did the trick, and I managed to pull myself together sufficiently to drive back, doing my best to look as normal and non-threatening as possible. I pulled up to the entrance of the farm. The security guard sidled over.

'Hello,' I said cheerily.

'Hello,' he replied, cleverly throwing the ball right back in my court.

'Is this where they're filming *Springwatch*?' I asked, with wonderfully feigned ignorance.

'Yes it is,' said the man.

'Is Bill here?' I probed, sounding just a bit too familiar.

'Yes he is.'

'OK. Can I come in and just, you know, have a look at him?'

'No you can't,' he said, firm and surly all of a sudden. 'That's not possible. Health and safety. Goodbye.'

'Goodbye,' I said, trying to sound jovial through clenched teeth. I drove off, seething.

Health and safety? I wasn't going to infect Bill with anything! Nor was I going to put him in any sort of danger! All I wanted to do was watch him watching birds. Did Bill attract so many stalkers that he had to have a full-time security team? Or, more likely, was this just standard practice?

Either way, I was put out. But I wouldn't give up yet. I drove further on down the road and pulled over again. I'd seen a few episodes of *Springwatch* and knew the set up. Yes, they were camped on a farm, but most of the filming was done outside (that is the best place to watch spring after all). Surely I'd be able to find another way on to the set? Surely there wasn't a man with a high-vis jacket and a huge sense of his own importance at every entrance?

I got out of the car and tiptoed off through the nearest field. I was off-roading. Now I actually was going to do something wrong.

But no. I was denied again. Despite my best trespassing efforts I made absolutely no incursions into the farm. Staggering about aimlessly for an hour, I spotted four Jurassic-like buzzards circling above me, but absolutely no way into the *Springwatch* camp. Every direction I chose I came up against a high barbed-wire fence or water. I just wasn't prepared to get scratched or wet. I was also keen not to lose my car and so didn't want to wander too far off-piste. Eventually I gave up, shouted, 'Damn you Oddie!' and returned to the car where I sat for the next two hours, watching the gate to the *Springwatch* site through my binoculars. Now I really was a paparazzo.

Once again I was thwarted. He must have snuck out of a secret exit, hidden in the boot of one of the suspicious-looking cars I'd seen, or set up camp inside the farm. I contemplated buying a tent and pitching it outside the gate – he'd have to pass me at some point! I'll just wait him out!

But then I remembered my life and drove off to Taunton to vent my frustration on a very lovely Devon audience.

9 June

Apparently I wasn't the only person who felt that the England team definitely was going to win the World Cup. With the four-year wait nearly over, the English press were now talking of little else, hyping up our chances at every possible opportunity. World Cup fever had infected the nation, and unlike bird flu, nearly everyone was affected. I freely admit that by the time Germany kicked off against Costa Rica at 5 p.m. on Friday, 9 June, all thoughts of birds or birdwatching were at the very back of my mind. Maybe even in a different part of my body altogether.

Blinded by this football flu, the day after my latest failed Oddie quest I did something of which I am still quite ashamed: I went into my local Kensal Green newsagent and bought 200 packets of Panini stickers (football players, not toasted sandwiches). I hadn't really planned to collect football stickers during the World Cup, but I do occasionally buy a copy of the *News of the World*, just for the sports section obviously, and one of their special football issues in May came with a free 2006 FIFA World Cup Germany Official Sticker Album. A free sticker album! How can anyone say it's not a clever newspaper?

By the opening day of the tournament I was only five stickers short of completing it. I still hadn't got Ronaldhino, Jermain Defoe (yes, I know, he wasn't even in the squad but you still want him in the album, don't you?) and three (yes, three!) Japanese stickers – the shiny team badge, Takayuki Suzuki (a 5ft 10" midfielder from Ibaraki) and Keiji Tamada (a nine-and-a-half-stone striker who plays for Nagoya Grampus Eight).

I was twenty-seven years old.

The thing is, you can't chuck a Panini Sticker Album in the bin. Especially when the paper throws in a free packet of stickers that includes Wayne Rooney and Thierry Henry. It was a sly and crafty ploy by the publishers, and I was well and truly ensnared.

In the halcyon days of Mexico '86 – when the Hungarian keeper Peter Disztl amused kids with his beard and the tournament's mascot Pique (an anthropomorphic chilli pepper) proved especially elusive – the football sticker system was simple. You spent your pocket money on as many packets of stickers as possible, gradually built up your collection, then swapped duplicates with like-minded collectors in the playground (using the only two words in the swap lexicon: 'need' and 'got').

Now things had moved on. Yes, the playground option was still available, but as I said, I was twenty-seven years old. Hanging round schools had to be a last resort. Unfortunately like-minded, similarly aged collectors were much harder to find. I did have a few friends who had also, independently, decided they would collect pictures of all the faces of all the footballers at the tournament and adhere them to a book, but not enough to guarantee the completion of my album.

Luckily, in the twenty-first century a grown-up sticker-obsessive could trawl the internet, using sites like eBay to buy, sell or, ideally, swap stickers with people from all over the world. In the weeks leading up to the World Cup, I sent off twenty-eight envelopes containing between one and nineteen stickers to everywhere from Rotherham to Bishop Auckland, and in return heard the pulse-quickening thud of twenty-seven (Ian Duffy from Stansted failed to keep his side of the bargain) similar packages on my own doormat.

Most of my fellow collectors claimed that they were looking for stickers on behalf of their children, and for a while I felt that if I wanted to have any myself (children, not stickers) I'd have to put this sort of thing behind me. But then I decided that these people were probably lying about their 'children' to save face – much more devious a crime than being upfront about one's childishness – so I carried on. Internet swapping was, I felt, a rewarding and efficient method, although when sending a solitary sticker first class I did wonder if I was getting value for money.

Unfortunately I couldn't find anybody with a spare Fernando Torres, and my patience had been so severely tested by the wasted trip to Devon that I snapped. Being twenty years older than I was the last time I'd collected the stickers, I now had a credit card in my wallet instead of the traditional demi (current school yard slang for 50p, apparently). So when I realised I could ask for the entire box of stickers instead of the usual two packets I went on a mental safari and did it. In fact, I bought two boxes. I felt like Veruca Salt. And, at the time, that felt good.

It took me thirty minutes to go through every single sticker in the packets, and I found only three I needed. Just three! Out of a thousand! It then took me another hour to arrange the remaining stickers into numerical order so I could alert my swapping contacts to these fresh spares. By the time I'd finished, the initial euphoria of my outlandish purchase had worn off. I still had two stickers to find and now I just felt dirty. I'd behaved badly.

It shouldn't be about filling up your album as quickly as possible. It's about the chase, the rareties, the Zeljko Kalacs. It's about meeting up with an old friend for the first time in five years, just to trade the Tunisian keeper for Stuttgart's Gottlieb-Daimler-Stadion (53,200 capacity); sharing a knowing smile with a stranger at Nuno Valente's impossibly fat face; people on eBay saying they're collecting for their sons when we all know that's only half the story. It's about a small but happy community sharing this intimate, beloved, pointless knowledge. It's like birdwatching.

10 June

In what was a predictably anticlimactic start to England's World Cup campaign, the team just about managed to scrape past Paraguay 1–0 thanks to a lucky own goal. Instantly the media tide changed and the unjustified belief of the nation lurched into unwarranted pessimism. 'We're never going to win this tournament again!' shouted pundits, 'Dire!' and 'Dismal!' screamed the headlines, while I remained quietly confident that we would emerge victorious. In order to back up my gut feeling with some research, I watched pretty much every match shown on TV. I didn't see any new birds.

My only bird-relief was that Duncton was also following the World Cup with some interest. He was still out at a nature reserve at least once a week, but he seemed just a tiny bit preoccupied by the tournament. I'd never thought of him as a particularly fanatical football supporter but maybe that's because he's a Tottenham Hotspur fan. They haven't had an awful lot to shout about in recent years. But in the glory days of the early 1960s and the early 1980s, he'd often been there in the stands, cheering them on. When I was looking through my old scrapbooks for evidence of early birding, I stumbled across a couple of Duncton's:

This one was from 1961, when Duncton was twelve years old. Every page is filled with cuttings lovingly taken from the sports pages, featuring headlines like: 'Blanchflower & Mackay Keep Spurs on Top', 'Greaves can put Spurs Back on that Pedestal' and 'Spurs Beat Wednesday to Win Championship'.

Nowadays Duncton makes at least one pilgrimage up to White Hart Lane each year and has even persuaded Mum (the staunch Motherwell and Queen of the South fan) to become a member. Each year they get birthday cards from the skipper and gaffer,[84] as well as much-treasured club scarves, credit card wallets, clocks and tie pin badges.

Somehow, therefore, Duncton combines his interest in sport with his birdwatching. Like David with his music, Duncton is no one-dimensional obsessive; birds are a part of his life but he's able to do other things. Since retiring he's taken up the sport of real tennis[85] and somehow finds time to play a game or two every month.

Meanwhile, I spent nearly every day of the month watching, thinking and talking about football. I couldn't do anything else.

15 June

England beat Trinidad and Tobago 2–0 and still the critics weren't happy. 'Not good enough', apparently. I'm generally an optimistic person – I always think Liverpool are going to win and everything is going to be OK and, I guess, that has generally been the case – so I couldn't understand the stick the players were getting. More important to me was the fact that I had finished my Panini album. It had taken me about a month but when I stuck in the final face[86] I was genuinely happy. I'd done it.

---

84 The first year of Mum's membership she read out a birthday card from a 'Mr Hodie'. 'Who is this Mr Hodie?' she cried. It was Glen Hoddle. The four male members of the family found this very funny.

85 By 'real tennis' I don't mean that some people play fake tennis. 'Real tennis' is the original version of all racquet sports and was first played in twelfth-century France. The best thing about it is that every player gets a world ranking. Duncton is the 7,342nd best real tennis player in the world.

86 Sticker 570: the Tunisian goalkeeper Ali Boumnijel. Aged forty, he was the oldest player at the tournament.

I admit that I was a tiny bit worried about my life. Was it normal to be collecting stickers at my age? More to the point, was it normal to be collecting stickers with such ruthless efficiency at my age?

I realised that I might be a touch obsessive compulsive. If I start something like a sticker album (or a birdwatching year or a meal), I have to finish it, as illogical as it might be to do so. What's more, I like starting things like sticker albums. But then several of my friends also *had* to finish their Panini sticker albums. My brother Mat *has* to find out who got the runs in the test match. A lot of men, it seemed, have this urge to collect – whether it be stickers, stamps or statistics, there's something about the process that appeals to the male of the species. I can't really speak for women, because I don't know many and don't completely understand the ones that I do, but as far as I can tell, they don't have quite the same urge. Rachel has got a lot of pairs of shoes and handbags, but not a ridiculous amount (I ended up with about 750 spare stickers).

Laying these concerns about my behaviour to one side, my only remaining worry was that having lovingly placed the completed album in a cupboard (not on a table where people might, God forbid, touch it) I now had quite a large gap in my life. How would I cope without my daily packet purchase ritual? I could go out birdwatching, but then I might miss a good match. I clearly needed to focus on the football. Otherwise England might not win.

Instead of stickers, then, I went back to W H Smith the next day and bought *Shoot*, *Match* and *FourFourTwo*. I still wasn't really enjoying the birdwatching magazines – they'd been gradually stacking up in the sitting room, making me feel guilty and Rachel annoyed – but I did like the idea of subscribing to something. I suppose I was a little jealous of people who went to the special interests section each month, who hadn't abandoned their youthful passion, who still cared about ridiculous things. Even my interest in football, I realised, wasn't strong enough to be classed as a hobby. I liked it, yes, but I didn't subscribe to a magazine. Well, not till now.

20 June

After watching the first two matches on my own or with Rachel I met up with a big group of friends to see England take on Sweden. It's at times like these that I appreciate how different my view of football is to that of other people. My friend Owen (who had joined me in the kitchen for some hungover stag bird-watching in January), knows the height, weight and birthplace of every player, Key has strong opinions about the formation Sven chooses and what impact each substitute might make, while Phill the Stratford romantic has even stronger opinions about absolutely everything. By half time it was clear that they all thought England were rubbish.

I tend not to worry so much about details like whether we're actually any good or not. The final score was England 2 Sweden 2, enough to see us through to the next round. That, to me, was all that mattered. We were still on track to win the thing. To my disappointment I'd struggled with my new football magazines – the only bits I really enjoyed were interviews with Liverpool players. I'm afraid that sums up my whole relationship with England football. I enjoy the matches, but I'm really just hoping that the Liverpool players will do well. When England beat Germany 5–1 in their own backyard back in 2001 (probably their best result of my lifetime) I felt particularly proud not because I'm English but because all the goals were scored by Liverpool players (Owen 3, Gerrard and Heskey). There's no real logic to these feelings. I'm not from Liverpool, I don't know these people. But I have spent most of my life caring about the club, so much so that it has become a part of me. I am a Liverpool fan. In the same way that Duncton is a birder.

But why am I not also a birder? Duncton spent as much time showing us birds as football during our formative years, so why did I turn my back on one in favour of the other? For now, too late, it seemed to me that I might have chosen the wrong hobby. My passion for football was flawed, it was shallow, and it didn't seem nearly as fulfilling as birding was for Duncton. I love the whole business of the World Cup: the achingly long build-up, the conjecture, the politics. I love the fact that because it only comes up every four years, each tournament represents a distinct time in your life. I remember bemoaning Maradona's Hand of God with my family in the living room in '86; I watched USA '94 while on a school trip in Italy, witnessing the Brazilians beating the Italians on penalties while drunkenly failing to chat up some Italian girls; Ronaldinho's flukey free kick that knocked us out of the tournament in 2002 marked the end of my and Rachel's extended studenthood.

But a three-week burst of emotion every four years isn't a great return for a hobby, especially when really I'm only watching the two or so Liverpool players on the field. Duncton is thrilled by birds every day. Of course the Premiership does provide that constant appeal, the rolling of the seasons reflecting the annual cycles of our birds. But while the daily dramas of birdlife – the great struggles with predators, the death-defying migrations, the nest-building, the song-singing, the gliding, soaring, hovering, swooping – are weighty, important, natural things, the Premiership seasons seem slightly ludicrous, silly, even ugly in comparison.

While we worship our heroes for kicking a ball about forty odd times a year, the modest swift travels 14,000 miles, eating, sleeping and copulating on the wing. That's gruelling and skilful. A swift can stay airborne for three straight years. The tiny hummingbird, weighing no more than a penny, can cross the 600-mile Gulf of Mexico in a single flight, determinedly beating its little wings 200 times every single second. And it's not just flying that sets birds apart. The flightless erect-crested penguin has been known to travel 4,000 miles from their home in New Zealand, hopping over icebergs and swimming through waves 120 feet high in the Drake Passage, to finally land at the Falkland Islands a few months later. That's incredible.

Sure, the FA Cup occasionally throws up romantic surprises like an American robin in Peckham, but the preposterous prices, the petulant tiffs and the pathetic play-acting that dominate the Premiership just didn't seem so important to me all of a sudden.

21 June

With the tournament grinding on and even my interest, for perhaps the first time, waning, I broke up the month with a trip down to Chichester. Every year about sixty pairs of pere-grine falcons, in Duncton's opinion the most majestic of Britain's birds of prey, take up residence in some of Britain's most imposing buildings, taking the place of cliffs as the birds have moved inland. From the heights of the enormous funnels of Tate Modern in London, Peterborough's power station, or the cathedrals in Derby and Lincoln, these raptors have been thrilling city residents in increasing numbers over the last thirty years.

Just twelve miles south of Midhurst, Chichester Cathedral has been home to a pair of the birds since 2002. Over the last four years they'd produced at least twenty-three young, and as part of his volunteership, Duncton has manned an RSPB tent pointing telescopes at the birds on their turrets each breeding season.

This was the first time I had seen Duncton in full RSPB mode. In fact, when I emerged from the cathedral's quaint coffee shop to see him clad, SWAT-team-like, in a fine RSPB flak jacket, siastically chatting to innocent members of the public, it was the first time I'd ever seen him in any sort of uniform. It was an impressive sight. The birds wheeling around the spires above may have incited gasps from the gathering crowd below, but I was mostly proud of my dad.

There were five RSPB volunteers on duty that afternoon, mostly bearded, obviously, and all energetic, knowledgeable and funny. Initially I was standoffish, slightly embarrassed even, but their bonhomie was infectious and I gradually relaxed.

Their role was to make visitors to the cathedral aware that there were peregrine falcons about, in effect playing the part of big arrows labelled 'Look! Big Birds!' pointing up to the nest in the southeast turret and their larder[87] in the southwest turret. But they were also there to provide the equipment with which people could see just how impressive the birds were. As well as top notch binoculars and telescopes, this equipment included a yard-long wooden stick, the same length as the falcons' wingspan, which the volunteers wielded with panache while fielding questions. This answering service was where Duncton really excelled. Like an expert compère, he put people at ease with his assured banter.

'So, how long do they live then?' asked one curious visitor.

'Oh about eleven to twelve years on average,' replied Duncton, firing out statistics from his big stick like an ornithological machine-gun.

'A bit like a dog then.'

'Yes,' said Duncton, quick as a flash, 'it's a dog's life.'

Duncton may well have laughed loudest, but everyone was definitely amused by the joke.

The highlight was when a middle-aged couple proudly announced that they were called Mr and Mrs Twitcher. All Duncton really had

---

87 Always thinking ahead, peregrine falcons often harvest more snipe and woodcocks than they can eat in one go and store them in their homemade fridges for a later feast.

to do was pass on this information to anyone else who arrived, but in doing so he managed to make everyone chuckle. It was the way he told them.

Late in the day, one of the birds was spotted bringing some food back to the nest. 'It's a she,' said Duncton. Two of the people standing next to him thought he'd said, 'It's a sheep.' They laughed, because by now Duncton was well established as the joker. Recovering well, Duncton suggested that it was actually a baby, a darker joke, but still popular.

I stayed over in Midhurst that evening. Mum had dug out my last Panini Sticker Album from 1986, and as I leafed longingly through the pages, twenty-year-old memories flooded back. It was alarming to realise how little my life had changed over the last two decades – if anything, my stickers this year were stuck in with even more childlike care.

Duncton and I had planned to go out looking for some bizarre nocturnal birds called nightjars that evening, but they would have to wait. We drank too much wine toasting the falcons at dinner and Duncton couldn't drive. Besides, Holland were playing Argentina, so we bonded over the TV instead.

25 June

I watched England's first game in the knockout round on my own. It wasn't a great spectacle. Beckham eventually sent England through with a trademark free kick, but by the end of the game I was quiet rather than jubilant, thoughtful, not triumphant. The thing that was perplexing me, apart from England's mysterious lack of passion, was why Mat had stayed with birdwatching, while I hadn't. Was he more like Duncton than me? Was it something to do with their relationship, or more to do with Mat himself? Mat, of course, was in Africa and unable to answer such questions, so instead I turned to Duncton.

During the course of another epic phone call, after we'd briefly dismissed the England performance, he told me how he'd started to get into birds. Most of the stories that first trickled and then poured down the line were brand new to me. I said very little, but scribbled notes frantically. I was surprised he'd never told me this before. But then I suppose I'd never asked.

'Well, my first memory of birdwatching,' he began, 'and I remember this quite clearly, was sitting in an apple tree in the garden and looking at a blackbird. I must have been about seven years old . . .'

That's about as sweet an image of my now grey, grizzled, bearded dad as I've ever had: a young boy, in the mid 1950s so presumably in black and white and shorts, sitting in a tree and becoming fascinated by a blackbird. I'd had a similar moment myself, perched on my sofa, watching my blackbird devour a worm in January this year, but that didn't perhaps evoke such innocence.

Duncton was still reminiscing.

'And I remember the first bird I came in close contact with. We had a museum at our school and someone had brought in an injured lapwing. I remember being struck by its fabulous colours . . .'

Again, this was a charming if slightly bizarre picture. A museum in a school, to which people brought wounded waterbirds? I didn't remember any such establishment at my school. But then again, we did have a 'museum' at home. It was just a set of shelves in the playroom, crammed full of the things we'd found on walks or holidays – shells, fossils, the odd animal skull – but to us, it was the 'museum', inspired, perhaps, by Duncton's schooldays.

'. . . then when I was eleven or twelve I discovered the British Junior Naturalist Association and went up to Yorkshire for this week-long summer natural history course and I remember they said if you like birds you must come back for the winter course. That would be pure birds. Well, that was that. In January I went straight back to some sort of youth education centre in a village called Hutton Buscel. We were taken to all the great birdwatching sites. It was really tough, we were whisked off first thing in the morning and had to walk around all day. I remember it being dark at seven in the morning but we saw everything. And there were kids from all over the country . . .'

I began to see how his enthusiasm for birds had stayed constant for more than half a century.

'I also went to a conference by the Junior Bird Recorders Club at their lodge in Sandy, absolutely fantastic. There were individual bedrooms, meals in a lovely dining room, the most fantastic bird feeders I'd ever seen. They were the predecessors of the YOC. You were in the YOC weren't you?'

Yes, I was still part of the conversation, and yes, I was a member of the Young Ornithologists Club.[88] We all were. It

The Junior Bird Recorders Club Conference in Sandy in the 1960s.
A young Duncton is the last lad on the left.

---

88 It's now called the 'Wildlife Explorers Club', a change of name that I don't support. I liked being a young 'ornithologist'. For a while, at least, I was at the top of the birdwatching tree. Sure, exploring is fun, but being an ornithologist sounded much more important.

didn't mean much more to me than a shiny badge, but I could see now how significant our membership must have been for Duncton. He told me he'd organised all these early birdwatching exploits on his own, and was justifiably proud of himself.

'Soon after that I started going to Sevenoaks and met Jeffery Harrison. Going up to Fair Isle was the natural progression. I think I'd met Mum when I went up the first time – that was in the early seventies. And that's a great memory. I remember arriving there the first time by boat – the ferry was still the *Good Shepherd* then of course . . .'

Of course, Duncton.

'. . . and all those seabirds were wheeling around. That's the best way to approach. I'll never forget that. I took Mum there, then kept going back, eventually with Mat of course. It's funny, I remember one of the wardens saying to Mat that he should come back without his dad for a young person's course – just like all those years before. And Mat did – he went back with his friend William the next year. And I think he volunteered as a warden at Loch Garten like I did too. We both must have done that when we were about nineteen, keeping egg collectors away from the osprey nests. They're one of the biggest success stories, ospreys. Of course they'd become extinct in Britain but came back in the sixties . . .'

I had to interrupt him. I could see how both his and Mat's passion for birdwatching had snowballed. But mine had never even started to roll. What about Duncton's own brother, Johnny? And his chicken-keeping sister Polly?

'No, Johnny and Polly didn't go on any of these trips. They both went on sailing courses with Grandpa. Although of course now Johnny's getting into birdwatching – a bit like you. You can get into it late. Unlike sailing. You know we all went on a sailing trip recently? I couldn't do it at all! They assumed I'd been with them on those trips when we were kids, but I'd always been off birdwatching so I displayed a complete and utter lack of any nautical understanding!'

I knew the feeling.

Grandpa, Duncton's dad, was called Trader. Well, his first name was really John but I guess he set the precedent for shopping around for a more interesting name.

'... needless to say, Trader was interested in all aspects of natural history. He enjoyed looking at birds from boats. That's another early bird memory, sailing on the Suffolk coast at the age of about ten. I remember watching the avocets breeding on Havergate Island. They're a big success story too. The symbol of the RSPB of course. And the Isle of Sheppey, that's where he kept his boat ...'

And that's where I'd seen my osprey with David the month before. I was following in his footsteps, even if, like Johnny, I was doing so a few years later than Mat.

'... my parents gave me my first binoculars in 1962, when I got a scholarship to Westminster, a great pair of 7 x 50s. I've still got them somewhere. They did encourage me. But Trader was always into his sailing and, of course, his rocks. I remember he had this little collection of precious stones at home. They were fascinating. Not as fascinating as birds but interesting. He had this one long stone that you could bend for some reason. I don't know what it was but if you tensed it carefully it would curve in the middle. One day I bent it so much it snapped. But he didn't say a word. I think I might have glued it back together!'

Trader, Grandpa, was a mineralogist. When I started writing this I was procrastinating on the internet and found a book on Amazon that he'd written, called *Towards the Twenty-first Century. A Discussion Organized Jointly for the Royal Society and the Mineralogical Society by J E T Horne and Sir Kingsley Dunham*. At reasonably great expense I bought it, couldn't understand a word of it, but did draw some inspiration from the solid fact of its publication.

He would have been ninety in November 2008, a few weeks after Duncton's sixtieth and my thirtieth, but he died in 1999. His funeral was on my twenty-first birthday. His obituary in *The Times* mentioned that he'd been one of the first men to examine moon dust brought back from the first landing in 1969. I'd never known that either. But then I suppose I'd never asked.

CHAPTER 7

Penalties

'Slowly, day-by-day, I was finding the game less and less amusing. In fact, I was beginning to understand that it was not a game at all.'
– Adrian M Riley

Alex: 139 species
Duncton: 206 species

1 July

I kicked off the second half of my year trailing Duncton by sixty-eight species. This deficit seemed to me so massive, so insur-mountable, that I forgot about the respectable total of 139 species I had managed to find and took to shaking my head wearily when anyone enquired how my birdwatching challenge was going. 'Don't ask,' I'd reply grimly.

Unfortunately, lots of people did ask on 1 July, the day of England's quarter-final reckoning. With Germany and Italy safely through, it was our turn to try to book a place in the semis, against either Brazil or France. Now that the final and World Cup glory were just two games away, the pendulum of the nation's affections had swung back towards the centre and a few more people were thinking that England might just sneak it after all, even if we were playing awful football. So I joined about fifty of my friends in a pub not far from Kensal Green to watch their tussle with Portugal.

'Tussle' was about the right word for it. 'Scrap', 'scuffle' and 'ugly clash' would also be fine. There wasn't a lot of the balletic football that the compilers of highlights must hope for. There were no goals and very little 'goal mouth action'. Seeking some other form of entertainment, quite a few people asked me why I was spending so much time birdwatching rather than watching the game. A few told me about a bird of prey they'd seen or an unusual bird they'd had in their garden ('Probably a jay,' I said). Two people said to me, 'I've got a question: are birds animals?'[89]

Over in Germany, Wayne Rooney got sent off. Cristiano Ronaldo acknowledged his part in the dismissal with a cheeky wink. Man Utd's best two players were responsible for what then looked like England's downfall. 'How could they?' I shouted.

---

89 Easily number one in my Frequently Asked Questions chart for the year. The answer, by the way, is yes. Of course birds are animals. What on earth were you thinking?

But England didn't roll over. Oh no. Instead, they managed to grind out a dull 0–0 in normal time, before gritting their collective teeth and shutting up shop throughout extra time too, dragging the game into a penalty shoot-out.

'Well, we've had it now,' sighed the pub as one, remembering games against Germany in 1990[90] and 1996, Argentina in 1998 and indeed Portugal in 2004.

'No, we'll win this one, I can feel it!' I countered, remembering games against AC Milan in 2005 and West Ham in 2006.

I was wrong. We lost 3–1 in a pathetic shoot-out. Gerrard and Carragher both missed their kicks. Liverpool's best two players were responsible for what actually was England's downfall. 'How could they?' I whispered.

5 July

Of course I couldn't stop watching the football just yet. Even without England it was an all-European final four. How could I take my eyes off Italy's stunning last-minute extra time win over hosts Germany, or France's narrow defeat of Portugal and a justly booed Ronaldo?

Without England the tournament burst back into life. The football seemed better, more important and much more entertaining. In the first semi-final, Italy's two late goals were greeted with so much jubilation from the flat above that it seeped through into our sitting room below. Zinedine Zidane was man of the match in the second, setting up Henry's winner and somehow booking his and France's place in the final. I watched both games with close footballing friends instead of everyone who happened to be in the pub, and remembered why I loved football.

---

90 Well, West Germany, but it was still Germany.

9 July

For once, the final wasn't an anticlimax. Again I watched it with the friends I talk, play and watch football with throughout the rest of the year. It's all very well for the England team to unite the country during a big tournament, but standing up for two hours, with a rubbish view of the fuzzy screen, too scared to disagree with the general mood of a football-obsessed crowd isn't nearly as much fun as poring over a big game with your best mates.

It was, of course, Zinedine Zidane's final. He opened the scoring after just seven minutes with a penalty that rattled in off the cross bar. That's how you take them. Materazzi equalized from a corner twelve minutes later. The game fizzed, France looked dominant, but the game went into extra time.

Then something extraordinary happened. I'm struggling to think of a birdwatching equivalent. Materazzi said something naughty to Zidane. Zidane head-butted him in the chest. Zidane was sent off. Materazzi went on to take one of the penalties that gave Italy their first World Cup triumph in twenty-four years. For us, this made the 2006 World Cup a cracker. Sure, it was a violent moment, a shameful conclusion to Zidane's career and an unpleasant end to the tournament, but we knew right away that we would all remember it. This would go in our collective World Cup memory bank, alongside Maradona's hand ball and young Michael Owen's wonder goal. This was breathtaking.

Reactions around the world were brilliantly mixed. In our little flat we didn't bother trying to make sense of the flawed genius's actions (we called it 'the head-butt challenge') and instead got drunk and celebrated football. Over in France, President Jacques Chirac proclaimed Zidane a national hero, 'a man of heart and conviction'. *Time* magazine described the incident as a symbol of Europe 'grappling with multi-culturalism'. FIFA fined him £3,260 and slapped down a three-match ban which, because he'd already retired, Zidane voluntarily substituted for three days of community service.

So is there a birdwatching equivalent? The master of the game, choosing the closing minutes of their final outing to go mad and bash someone to the ground with their famously bald head? Probably not. Oddie would have to do something pretty remarkable to Kate Humble on the final edition of *Springwatch* to come close. The only story that seems remotely relevant is that of Eric Hosking, whose career as a bird photographer was marked by an attack from a tawny owl that resulted in the loss of his left eye. This was an isolated moment of violence that has gone down in birdwatching history. But it also marked the beginning rather than the end of Hosking's career. His photos were soon published in the wake of the strike, as was his autobiography, brilliantly entitled *An Eye for a Bird*. Also, only a couple of people saw that owl assault Eric, while over a billion witnessed Zinedine's eccentric head punch.

So, the World Cup fantasy was over for another four years. Well nearly, anyway. The next morning I walked out of our flat and was congratulated by no less than three people on Italy's victory. Glancing back I saw that our upstairs neighbours had decorated the entire façade of the house with green, white and red sheets, blue scarves emblazoned with the word *Italia*, and a football shirt with Materazzi's name on the back. I smiled and thanked the well-wishers. I was glad the dream had come true for someone near me, but even more chuffed that people thought I was Italian. If my face was swarthy enough to be Mediterranean, I was doing something right.

12 July

I had kept an eye on the garden during some of the more tedious matches, but with London now throttled by the grip of summer, the birds were much harder to see. Next door's fig tree had flopped entirely over our patio, providing welcome shade, but also stealing all of our sunlight and hiding all of our birds. My female blackbird was my only constant feathery companion during most of June and July, but when she gobbled up all my carefully nurtured strawberries in one terrifying binge, I stopped paying her much attention.

During the entire footballing period I saw just one new bird, a herring gull on a beach not too far from a gig in Exeter. But I now had at least five weeks with virtually no distractions and, to kick things off, a couple of shows up in Scotland. Keen to get back out in the field, I dug up my *Birdwatcher's Yearbook* once more and planned a couple of trips around Edinburgh and Glasgow. I was way behind Duncton, but I had a car and I knew how to use it (even if I didn't have the slightest clue how it actually worked).

14 July

The last time I had a couple of gigs in Scotland, I spent almost the entire trip in my hotel room watching snooker. I did go out to Piemaker[91] a couple of times, but that was pretty much the extent of my cultural excursions. I'm not proud of myself. I got sucked into a gripping Embassy World Championship final between Shaun Murphy and Matthew Stevens and just couldn't escape. Something happens to me when I'm away from home with whole days to fill. Suddenly the chance to explore a new place becomes oppressive, any outings seem exhausting, and televised sport wields an unnatural pull.

But this time in Edinburgh, on the advice of both of my bird guides (the yearbook and David), I phoned a lady named Mrs

---

91 Perhaps my favourite Edinburgh shop, it does what it says: makes pies. Tremendous pies. All day and till quite late at night. Why haven't these taken over London yet? Or the world?

Marr as soon as I woke up. 'Yes,' she told me in her sprightly Scottish accent, 'there are sailings to Bass Rock today. In fact it's a perfect day out there so we'll be going to Fidra too.' So straight after breakfast I left my room without even turning the telly on and bravely stepped out into the world.

Bass Rock isn't a type of music;[92] it's an island in the Firth of Forth, about a mile off the coast of North Berwick, a town thirty miles east of Edinburgh. David had told me this was a must for my birdwatching year. He'd taken his girlfriend there a few years ago and even she, a non-birder, had been blown away. Thinking back to Mum and Duncton's trip to Romania, I knew how much that meant.

I'm usually up in Edinburgh during August for the Edinburgh Festival Fringe, so it was a refreshing change to wander down to Waverley Station and not have flyers thrust in my face by eager drama students and weary comics. For me, though, the city will always be associated with the festival, whatever the time of year, and as the train and I zoomed along the coastline, I couldn't help but think of my trip to Bass Rock in terms of an Edinburgh show. How would this day out compare to normal Fringe fare?

North Berwick, to my naive surprise, was brilliant, well worth a visit if you want to escape the mayhem of the city during the festival. A bit like Ibiza, but without the noise, drugs and idiots, the seaside town used to be a fashionable holiday resort in the nineteenth century and still boasts stunning white beaches and glorious views out to the North Sea. As Mrs Marr[93] had said, it

---

92 If it was, I imagine it'd be a fusion of rock and bossanova, the rhythm made famous by the Casio keyboard we and many other families had in the 1980s.

93 I should explain that I got Mrs Marr's name and phone number from my *Birdwatcher's Yearbook*. When I told Duncton about her he wasn't surprised by this personal service, it seems there are a fair few characters who help the birdwatching community in this way. 'When I went up to Shetland,' he told
(cont. on p 214)

was a perfect day, and the place looked like a postcard: gleaming sand, perfect rock pools, families having fun. Of course, it was Scotland, so everyone was wearing quite a lot of clothing, so it looked pretty much the same as that beach in Bahrain.

From the shore I could see Bass Rock itself, a big, almost symmetrical, bright white lump of, yes, rock. Worth coming to see? Well, it was a very big rock . . .

Happy to play the role of a tourist, I popped into one of those modern touchy-feely visitor centres called the Scottish Seabirds Experience. In a bid to reinvigorate the town's tourist industry, it was opened in May 2000 by Prince Charles (Duncton once saw him in a *Footlights* show at university. He was in a dustbin. Have I mentioned that?), and boasts contemporary gadgets like inter-active displays, *Big-Brother*-style webcams, and 'spectacular light and sound shows'. Worryingly, I ignored all these attractions, drawn instead to a row of high-powered telescopes trained on Bass Rock and its neighbours. Ah ha, I thought, now for some serious birding! Then I caught myself thinking that and went a bit red.

After waiting patiently for a couple of minutes, I sidled up to the first available telescope and looked out to sea. All I could see was the sky. When I stepped back, it seemed to be pointing in the general direction of the rock and the water, but every time I bent down to peer into the eyepiece, I seemed to lose all sense of direction. I was tempted to ask for help, but knew that wasn't what men do. Eventually I managed to aim it at what I thought was the big white rock. It was out of focus. I wiggled a couple of knobs. Nothing. Finally, I decided to read the instruc-tions that were printed helpfully (condescendingly, I'd thought at first) on the wall by the scopes, and zoomed in to see that I

---

93 (cont.) me, 'I was told to give Bobby a ring. Bobby was a famous birder up there, and I was nervous about calling him, but he said, "Oh, you're coming up to Shetland? Well I'll meet you off the ferry then. We'll make an expedition of it! Bring a friend!"'

wasn't looking at a big white rock at all, I was looking at hundreds and hundreds of big white birds. So many big white birds that I couldn't make out the colour of the big rock.

The birds were gannets – 100,000 of them. (That's what it said on one of the 'information walls', although it was a rather suspiciously round number.) This was the world's second largest gannet colony. I was impressed, but mostly I wanted to get a closer look at them. According to Mrs Marr, the boat would leave in twenty minutes, so I rushed out of the centre and raced down to the pier to take my place in the queue for the sailing. Actually, I was the only person there, so I was the queue.

I was soon joined by several families, none of whom recognised that I was a queue and who stood in haphazard groups on either side of me. I held my tongue. That seemed like the right thing to do. When the small roofless boat arrived, I even waited till a couple of parents with very small children had got on before grabbing a good seat. I could do this parenting thing.

'When will you be back?' asked one lady who'd put her husband Charlie on the boat, like a mother might a child.

'In an hour or so,' said the gruff Birds-Eye-style captain, 'but that'll be round the corner. The tide's coming in so this here will be under water when we're back.'

'Ooh,' squealed the lady in reply, clearly impressed by his nautical knowledge and appearance.

'I'm married to a woman who can walk on water!' quipped a fellow passenger. Everyone laughed, including me. This was proper banter! We were off.

As we chugged gently towards the rock, the skipper (who was, by the way, a proper man – gnarled, bearded, dour, with a fine line in gallows humour) gave a dry running commentary about the area:

'Further east, down at Sea Cliff Beach, there's a long sloping red rock close to the shore. On the other side of that lies what's reputedly the smallest manmade harbour in Britain. But it's a bit pointless me telling you about it because you can't see it from here . . .'

That sort of thing.

After about twenty informative minutes, we were closer to the rock than the shore and could appreciate just how many birds 100,000 gannets were. The noise was terrific, constant shrill screeching and screaming; it was like being the only adult on a plane full of babies, but without any of the responsibilities that situation would entail.

We could smell them too. Cries of, 'Oh, that stinks!' went up as forty noses were immersed in the all-pervasive gannet perfume. The sky was thick with gannetness – their sounds, their scent, them: enormous beaky white wings, some diving around us, others gliding on the sea breeze. Everywhere you looked there were gannets. Long white necks, glowing yellow heads, swarming around like massive freakish bees. I'd really never seen anything like it. And then I remembered that Duncton had: 'And all those seabirds were wheeling around. That's the best way to approach. I'll never forget that.' This was my Fair Isle moment.

We circled the island, admiring the remarkable clouds of gannets, gannets and more gannets, from every angle. During an hour-long Edinburgh show, the audience's attention will begin to flag after about forty minutes. Everyone on this boat was transfixed for a full hour and a half. It was the perfect Edinburgh performance. Unless you don't like gannets. There was one man who'd made it clear he was going to be an awkward customer by spending about five minutes getting on board, grumbling that the boat was moving too much ('Can't you stop all these waves for a bit?'). 'This is rubbish,' he muttered over the noise of the engine and loud enough for everyone to hear. 'Gannets are rubbish. Not as good as swans.'

But it wasn't all gannets either. In amongst the stinking quilt of white feathers, the captain pointed out guillemots standing to attention on the rock, like penguins but a bit more serious. I also notched up the tough-sounding razorbills and my first shag of the year. Then, at that tricky forty-minute mark, the first puffin flew past.

'Puffin!' shouted the skipper. Everyone missed it.

'There's another!' he cried.

This time I saw a flash of something whiz past the stern[94] and shouted, 'Yes, puffin! Definitely!' Soon we'd all seen plenty of the little tinkers, perched on the rock, their famous clown-like faces looking out at us with just a hint of melancholy. I never knew they could fly with such bullet-like speed. Short and stocky, they punch through the air like gaily painted torpedoes.

Back at the harbour, the captain announced that since the weather was so good, he'd be taking a trip out to the island of Fidra too.

'What's on Fidra?' asked one man.

'More gannets!' said the captain.

The gannet-hater scuttled off the boat far quicker than he'd got on. 'And more razorbills, guillemots, herring gulls. We should be able to see kittiwakes too,' our skipper continued. Kittiwakes! Another new species! I stayed on board, as did about half of what was now a pretty tight crew.

But this trip wasn't so successful. Perhaps it had come too soon after the highs of Bass Rock; like watching a newish, experimental comedian after a Billy Connolly video, it just wasn't quite right. Yes, we saw lots more puffins resting on ledges and yes, they were now my new favourite bird, but it was the island itself that made me feel uneasy. Unlike Bass Rock, we were

---

94 I have no idea if that's the right word. Like Duncton, and unlike Trader, Johnny and Polly, I am no sailor. If you think something like port, starboard, keel, helm, ballast, boom, foremast, tiller or ketch is more suitable, please do cross mine out and put yours in.

allowed to get off the boat and wander round Fidra, and while it was uninhabited by humans, it was home to countless gulls who'd just had countless chicks. So, as our merry band of mums, dads, children and I marched around, we soon realised that we were endangering the lives of tiny baby birds who lay virtually hidden under the tufts of grass and whom we would only just see, cowering in the shadows of our boots, as we went to take our next step. Quite justifiably, their parents were spitting and shrieking at us from the air. Our captain had given us sticks to hold above our heads to protect us from aerial attacks.

It was all quite odd and a little uncomfortable. When he instructed us to use these sticks to defend ourselves against angry birds I could see the faces of some of the kids light up, while others crumpled with fear.

I didn't think we should be there. This was the birds' island and the young ones in particular were so unused to humans they didn't know they could or should run away. We shouldn't have been there, but proper birdwatchers should. I could see why Fair Isle was run almost exclusively by genuine ornithologists rather than tourists like us who just wanted to get a few close up pics of furry chicks. Then again, I did see kittiwakes, and a schmaltzy pair of fulmars, so I got what I came for.

After three hours on the water, I noticed with some pleasure that my face was a little sunburnt. I'd got sunburnt in North Berwick! It might have been a touch painful but I felt a whole lot healthier than I had after my snooker marathon on my previous visit.

16 July

Instead of driving straight from Edinburgh to Glasgow, I stopped at a place called New Lanark where, according to my yearbook, I could get 'unrivalled views of breeding peregrine'. Since

Duncton had shown me tremendous views of exactly these birds the month before, I wondered how much better the experience could be. Do they mean you can actually see the peregrines breeding? Do I want to see such behaviour? I want to experience birdwatching fully but I didn't know it involved that ... The book also promised dippers, pied flycatchers, skylarks and barn owls, none of which I'd seen before, so all things considered, I was excited. I had another whole day ahead of me and was determined to bag them all.

I never really got to grips with New Lanark. It's near Lanark, which is a normal Scottish town,[95] but New Lanark was some sort of bizarre homemade tourist village. The signs indicated that it was an old mill town, but I couldn't tell if anyone lived (or milled) there any more. The houses seemed empty, but there were signs of life everywhere. The lights were on but no one was home, and after three days on my own I found it just a little bit eerie. I'm sure I could have discovered more about its history if I'd wanted to, but I was here to see birds, not learn about culture, and the site with these 'unrivalled views' was a mile outside the ghost town at the Falls of Clyde, a fine-sounding water feature, high up in the hills.

So I marched off, up a well-kept footpath that climbed the bank alongside the river below. Thanks to my regular walks around The Welsh Harp, Kensal Green Cemetery and countless other nature reserves, I was now reasonably fit (although I still didn't think I could run very far without wanting to cry) and I strode with giant, dad-like steps, overtaking the other dawdling visitors, until I reached the peak from which water tumbled down into the pool below and presumably once powered these rumoured mills.

---

95 The hundredth largest settlement in Scotland, apparently. That's a satisfying claim to fame.

Once again, I was the only birdwatcher there. Well, the only person with binoculars anyway. Some of the dads leading their families along the path looked like they could easily out-bird me, but I seemed to be the only person on a strictly birdwatching mission. At the time I felt quite proud of this fact. Looking back, I can see that someone like Duncton would have got much more out of the day by combining his birding with a look around the village. But I was determined to be single-minded.

This meant that for the first hour I saw nothing except families, dogs and water, all things I like, but none of which would help me beat Duncton. There were no birds of prey at all, let alone any saucy sights to rival those at Chichester Cathedral, and there was no sign of the other species my book had promised. I felt ripped off.

But then, just as I was about to turn back to the mysterious city of old, I caught sight of a tiny bouncing bird, about a hundred yards below me, bobbing up and down at the edge of the plunge pool. It really was very little. I don't know how I managed to see it. But somehow it had appeared on my radar and, training my binoculars upon it, I confirmed what I'd initially thought – it was a dipper!

There was no doubt about it. It was small but chunky with a white bib[96] and, best of all, it was dipping. Every few seconds it would bravely poke its minute head into the bubbling brook of freezing Scottish water then bound back onto its step. Completely charmed, I watched it for ages. It might have been drinking, fishing or washing its hair – I didn't care which: it was dipping! And I was watching. Families arrived and peered down to see what I was staring at. It was like that childish game in which you pretend to be looking up at something in order to try to

---

96 A bad colour for bibs, I think. Babies' bibs seem to be white too. This makes no sense to me. If that's the bit that's going to get messy, make it brown, green even. Anything would be better than white.

make other people look too, so you can then think, 'Ha! I fooled you and now you're looking up at nothing!' (That's pretty much how birdwatching seemed to me for twenty years.) Except that now I could see something. I could see a dipper! And without binoculars no one else could see my diminutive friend, so I felt smug.

I skipped back down to my hire car. But even then my bird-watching senses were firing. Passing through some dense trees I connected with a pied flycatcher! At first I wasn't sure it was a pied flycatcher, it was small and compact and seemed to be catching flies,[97] but it was flitting round too much. Then, for a few seconds, it alighted on a pine tree just yards from where I was standing and I could see that it was indeed pied – neatly dressed in black and white. I forgot all about the other birds, the breeding peregrines, the owls and the skylarks. I'd found two brand new birds, all on my own. I felt good. I punched the air. Then I felt embarrassed, but still good.

19 July

I'd seen ten new species on my own up in Scotland and was well and truly back in the birdwatching groove.

Back home, a second heatwave hit London. Well, I say heat-wave: it had been quite hot for two whole days and I heard a lady in the post office say, 'It's this heat! It's unbearable!'

At 7 a.m. I was confident that I would be able to bear it. For the tenth time in as many weeks, I drove over to Hampstead Heath soon after dawn to search for Oddie. For the tenth time in as many weeks I searched in vain. Perhaps he'd decided he couldn't bear the heat. Nonetheless my spirits were lifted by the

---

97 To be honest, it was a little way off and if I couldn't tell what bird it was I definitely couldn't tell what insect it was eating. But I guess they were flies. Most small flying things are, aren't they?

sight of three young kestrels learning to hunt on Parliament Hill. From the comfort of a bench I watched them rise and fall, fluttering more precariously than their parents, then plopping down impatiently on imaginary mice below. I felt like applauding their efforts, then recalled their captive cousins in Bahrain and saluted instead. This time I checked there was no one else watching first.

On my way over to the lido, I saw a particularly tame jay and was again pleased both to spot and identify the bird without recourse to binoculars or books. I hung around its tree for a few minutes in the hope that someone might come along and ask me what that exotic-looking bird was, so I could impart my wisdom, Duncton-style, in a knowing yet offhand way. But no one else seemed interested. What was wrong with these people?

Over at the pools, I'd been casually leaning against another tree for another couple of minutes when a flash of blue caught me by surprise and I lost my balance. This was my first solo view of a kingfisher and it literally knocked me off my feet. I only just managed to regain my composure in time to stop myself stumbling head first into the water.

So, an enjoyable morning, but no new birds and still no Bill. Dissatisfied, I dropped into what was actually the closest patch of open land to our flat, Wormwood Scrubs. I hadn't appreci-ated what a large green space it was until it was featured on Oddie's *Springwatch* as an example of a birdable urban environ-ment. Obviously it's hard to squeeze a big field into London, so in functional fashion Her Majesty's Prison of the same name is situated at one end, while Linford Christie's athletics stadium, a whole load of football pitches and a pony centre have each got their own spot on the common itself.

It was midday and the field simmered in the heat. The scrubs were aptly named. All I could see were huge swathes of, well, scrub. With the prison behind me and the dry tufts of dead grass in front, it felt like a cross between Jaww Prison in Bahrain and the Serengeti, where I imagined Mat was busy getting his fill of new birds. Unfortunately, here in Brent there was nothing much about,[98] save for a few shifty looking magpies and a couple of crows. I quickly got hot and bothered and felt like going into a post office to let off steam.

20 July

Worn down by yet another day of sun (three in a row!) I looked despairingly at my figures. Despite my successful foray over the border, I was still miles behind Duncton. The groove I'd felt I was in just twenty-four hours earlier seemed more like a rut, so similar to a groove but not nearly as much fun. Sure, I could spot the most common British birds with some confidence now, but I needed more. I had a gig in Winchester that evening, so I decided to get my fix with a sneaky trip to a place I knew wasn't strictly legal, but where I could definitely get what I needed: Birdworld.

If you haven't been to Birdworld, you might imagine it's a birding utopia, an ornithologist's paradise, a whole heavenly world of birds. If you have been to Birdworld, you'll know it's not nearly as good as that. It's more a friendly compound for birds, taken there against their will, but which on looking round probably think they haven't got too bad a deal. 'Birdworld!' They must think when they see the colourful signs, 'Fair enough. No more pesky humans, just birds!' Unfortunately there were pesky humans, loads of them, mainly kids, most of whom didn't particularly want to be there on the sweltering day that I visited.[99]

---

98 Another birdwatching phrase I was now unconsciously using.

99 I later found out that I too had visited Birdworld as a kid – in 1984, the year my very first 'writing book' was published (well, written). Once more, however, I seem to have wiped this birding memory from my mind.

After buying a ticket and trying not to spend any more money in the gift shop on the way in (yes, they're on the way in nowadays), the first enclosure that greets visitors to Birdworld is a spacious cage full of brightly coloured hummingbirds. 'They're all right,' said a kid in a Man Utd shirt, against whom, for some reason, I took an instant dislike. After watching these rare and remarkable birds for two more seconds he turned away and demanded, 'Right, now where are the monkeys?'

'No,' said his teacher patiently. 'I've told you already, this isn't a zoo, there aren't any monkeys. Only birds.'

Only birds. Music to my ears, but apparently the droning of hell to this young hooligan's: 'Oh no Miss, you can't be serious! That's games! That's lame! That is well rubbish!'

If he wasn't impressed by the hummingbirds, how would he cope with the rest of the world? Luckily, the Birdworld leaders had thought of that. For this wasn't just a bird zoo, this was more like a bird circus! In one tent a toothy wide boy carelessly flung fish at penguins before a packed and gasping crowd who'd rushed to see this captive bird highlight. In another, a birdman (not really a birdwatcher, not really an ornithologist, but clearly someone who knew his birds) mucked around with a whole load of owls that he'd trained to swoop and twit twoo on cue. In an adjacent block a very young man showed off some parrots he'd instructed to ride bikes and talk. I couldn't understand how someone so young had found himself in this profession, but it struck me that these were two things I'd some day have to teach my own offspring to do, and so paid close attention. Unfortunately the only word his parrot could say was 'parrot'.

'What are you?' the young trainer asked each time the parrot did a wheelie.

'Parrot,' said the parrot.

To my shame, this struck me as quite funny. It was, I suppose, incongruous. And, if every animal in a zoo were trained to say what they were, it would save a lot of the money currently spent on signs. No need for a laminated page reading 'Elephant' if the elephant barks the word when requested. Another scheme for *Dragons' Den*, perhaps.

After about the fifth 'Parrot!' I'd got the message. If his young coach had only asked a few more imaginative questions ('Name a world snooker champion from Liverpool.' 'Parrot.' 'Correct! How about a famous Monty Python sketch beginning with "Dead"...' 'Parrot.' 'Correct!'), he might have kept my attention for more than four minutes. Still, I guess that'll come to him with experience.

I had mixed feelings about Birdworld. It was great for kids to be able to see such amazing birds close up, but the kids seemed far more interested in the gift shop. The birds were remarkable, with far more varieties than there are at London Zoo. From the gate of one enormous field I watched two emus, birds I'd previously thought were fictional. In another, two ostriches sprinted about, 'Reaching,' according to their sign, 'speeds of up to fifty-nine miles per hour.' Surely one of them must have broken sixty by now, I thought,[100] and why don't we harness these birds? Literally. Surely these are the ultimate twenty-first-century transport? They don't break the law and they don't leave a carbon footprint. If I was in charge, everyone would have an ostrich ...

Next door, four vultures sat around in their own pen looking disdainfully at the very British bushes. Not quite as manic as the ostriches, they looked decidedly glum, even when a pair of herons swooped down and landed nearby. I was reminded of the bird that had visited the penguins at Regent's Park and was wondering if herons are a particularly curious species of bird, when a compact family of three generations of humans drew

---

100 Although, on further consideration, I remembered the pointless fact that the terminal velocity of a falling cat is sixty miles per hour (after which their fur acts as a parachute). Could this be relevant?

up next to me.[101] The grandmother and her daughter debated for some time why the six birds didn't all look alike. 'Those ones over there, they must be vultures,' said the grandmother.

'Well, what about them then?' said the young mum, pointing at the herons. 'This is the vulture bit so they must be vultures. How else would they get in here?'

'I don't know, do I? But anyway, I think they're all ugly looking birds.'

I was trying not to be judgemental about either their birding ignorance, or their respective early motherhoods, but this, I felt, was quite an ironic comment. You can't just go round slagging off vultures! To their faces!

I trooped back towards my car and my gig, but not before hypocritically succumbing to the temptations of the gift shop. No cuddly bird toys for me, though. No, I bought a shiny blue bird bath for my classy birds back home which I've since carefully refilled each week but which the birds have ignored. 'Poncy,' I suppose they think. 'That's just a posh puddle.' Perhaps I am a bit of a snob.

21 July

I hit 150 birds with a trip down to Midhurst and a bird called a woodcock that wasn't quite as glamorous sounding as I'd have liked. In fact, Duncton and I got our first woodcocks of the year together when we finally got round to going on the 'nightjar expedition' we'd aborted during the World Cup. Nightjars are one of the few species found more often in southern England than anywhere else.

I was touched when I realised he'd planned a whole evening round the trip. In true manly fashion we drank beer, barbecued

---

101 Three generations of women, in fact, the eldest of whom looked no older than thirty. The youngest was in a pram.

meat then set off in search of birds. No one else was at nearby Ambersham Common at 9.30 p.m., just the two woodcocks we scribbled down in our respective notebooks. Then Duncton set down his rucksack. 'It's time,' he said.

Nightjars join ostriches, penguins, parrots and puffins in the group entitled 'Fun Birds'. They're quirky for a number of reasons. First, they're nocturnal. Second, they have tiny feet on which they can barely walk. Third they're one of only two species of birds that hibernate during the winter. Tremendous. Fourth, their name sounds like a swift drink in a pub. And fifth, their nickname is even better: goatsuckers. People have been calling them this for centuries after mistakenly believing that they feed by sucking milk from goats. How can you make that sort of mistake? An adventurous nightjar must have had a tiny swig from a teat way back in the past, and then whoever witnessed it must have told everyone what they'd seen.

Apart from this, my favourite thing about nightjars is that you attract them by holding up two white handkerchiefs and waving them in the air like a morris-dancing air traffic controller. According to birdwatching lore, the goatsuckers think you're a moth, their actual favourite food, and fly towards you. Only when they work out either that you're not a moth or, if you are, then you're an enormous bloody moth, do they fly off again.

Amazingly, after Duncton had flapped his handkerchiefs for just a couple of minutes, a weird alien-like chirruping rose up around us. I had drunk quite a bit more beer than Duncton, but was mightily impressed – moved even. The spooky noises edged closer in the deepening murk of the night until eventually five large, flappy birds loomed out around us. Nightjars!

Best of all was Duncton's wonder. Even though he'd performed this ritual and seen these birds a hundred times before, he still grinned throughout the whole show. And I felt sure that letting me into this strange club was adding to his enjoyment.

22 July

I didn't sleep very well that night. My normally facile dreams were interrupted by strobing images of Duncton beating an enormous pair of moth wings in a bid to attract a goat. When I awoke my head hurt. I couldn't really remember what had happened the night before. This wasn't what I had got into birdwatching for.

My morning only got worse.

The last big bird flu headline had come in May, when two fatal cases of the H5N1 virus were reported in Indonesia. Since then, the panic had largely died down. The spectre of the whooper swan in Scotland still raised the odd scare, but other stories had taken over the front pages. And most of those other stories came from the Middle East. And involved Lebanon. And Israel.

On 12 July, a conflict broke out between the two countries that became known in Lebanon as the July War and in Israel as the Second Lebanon War. Whatever you want to call it, ten days after the violence erupted, both sides had suffered hundreds of casualties as the world watched in horror.

I'd been following the international news with more interest than usual. The wedding we'd been invited to in Israel, my one chance to catch Duncton up, was now just a month away. As the violence escalated it became obvious that Israel wasn't a safe place to go. Hundreds of thousands of Israelis were displaced from their homes. The wedding, sensibly, was called off.

Well, not called off exactly. It was moved. To Barnet.

As well as being grim global news, this was a huge blow to my birdwatching year. Despite Lee G R Evans's pessimism about the heat, I was looking forward to the 'returning warblers in the wadis and larks at K40 and flamingos at K20 Reservoir' that he'd promised. Now, thanks to this conflict, I wouldn't get to see them.

I don't want to make light of a bloody and tragic war, but there was something grimly amusing about this complicated political and religious struggle having the power to reach as far as England and influence a birdwatching contest between a father and son. War. What is it good for? Well, I haven't got the political nous to say for sure, but certainly not for my Big Year.[102]

29 July

I spent the following week trying to work out what to do next. Rachel and I now had a two-week gap in our diary that was meant to be filled with this trip to war-torn Israel. I looked into holidays around the Barnet area, but couldn't find anything to suit Rachel's desire for relaxation and stimulation and my need for exotic birds.

With all wedding plans relocated to the UK, Rachel was off to the hen weekend down in Wales. I needed to get out of the house and stop worrying, and so I phoned David. He was spending the weekend with his family, but recommended I take a trip east for some birding. That's what he did when he needed to clear his head.

So I called Tim, my other main birdwatching companion, who said he was free and up for anything. He hesitated when I said I'd be round to pick him up at 7 a.m. the next morning, but

---

102 However, as Peter Marren explains in his book, *The New Naturalists*: 'In a way war encouraged birdwatching. It is often said that war consists of five per cent wild excitement and fear, and ninety-five per cent boredom. Stationary soldiers and, still more, prisoners of war need a hobby.' As do stand-up comedians and the recently retired.

kept his word, and by 9 a.m. we'd arrived at a place called Lakenheath Fen nature reserve in Suffolk, aiming to regroup with another amateur birdwatching adventure.

It was still very hot. I know I shouldn't go on about the fact that it was actually hot in summer in Britain but it really was very warm. So warm that Tim had decided to wear an entirely white outfit: white shoes, white shorts and a white T-shirt with a picture of a stick bird printed on the front. When I picked him up – I was now wearing good birdwatching gear: I'd replaced my yellow shoes with brown walking boots, was wearing dark trousers and an unlikely khaki shirt. I probably looked like a prat – he realised he'd picked the wrong clothes for the occasion. 'It doesn't matter,' I told him. 'It's very hot.'

According to David, Lakenheath Fen was one of the few places in Britain where golden orioles breed each year. These were still Duncton's birds of the year, so I was determined to see them for myself. I'd come to terms with the fact that I probably wasn't going to find my own childhood favourite, the golden eagle, but if I could spot a golden *oriole* (it sounds the same if you say it quickly) that would be almost as good. So for a good couple of hours we ambled round the woods and fields surrounding the sweetly named Little Ouse river, an odd but chirpy couple strolling in the sun and looking out for orioles (Tim insisted we refer to them as Golden Grahams. He had a point. They do sound more like a breakfast cereal than a bird[103]).

Once again I revelled in Tim's inquisitiveness. I'd brought a fair amount of bird literature, which I hoped would help us find these elusive birds, and every sentence we read aloud prompted more incredulity. 'OK, apparently the golden oriole is "a summer visitor …"', he read from the bird guide, '"… shy, restless,

---

103 Other examples of birds that sound like you could eat them in the morning include corncrakes and capercaillies, whimbrels, kittiwakes and a nice bowl of honey buzzards.

mobile, keeps concealed high up in foliage ... blends into the sun-dappled leaves and escapes detection ... Nests suspended in branch fork Walt Disney-style, high in canopy," says our playful author. "Often emits" – and this is what I'm looking for – "a screaming hoarse *VEEAAHK!*"' (He really went for that sound.) 'So if we hear that we'll know we're getting warm.'

I'd also printed out a few pages from the internet about other birders' successful oriole-finding missions. In one blog someone mentioned that Lakenheath Fen was the place to go because as well as golden orioles, this was where he'd seen his 'favourite ever woodcock'. Tim couldn't get over this tremendous statement. 'Who's got a favourite ever woodcock?' he asked, flabbergasted. Disturbingly, I could relate to the sentiment. I've got my favourite kingfisher, I thought to myself.

By lunchtime we'd incorrectly identified a marsh harrier (we were told by a 'proper' birder that it was a buzzard), discovered what we were sure was a brand new goose (it looked a bit like an Egyptian goose so we thought it was probably Moroccan or Tunisian) and had triumphantly spotted another great crested grebe, still Tim's favourite bird from the Wetland Centre trip back in February. We also found two frogs (that we thought might be toads because they were warty), ten cows (definitely cows) and a donkey-sized, long-haired Alsatian whose owner tried to reassure us with the words: 'Don't worry, he likes faces!' No idea what this meant, and no sign of any orioles. According to my notes there were only six of the birds in the entire reserve. This was the needle-hunting aspect of the hobby I found frustrating but which, I guess, makes successes like Duncton's so sweet.

Lunch was the highlight of the day. We found a lovely café in a town neither of us had ever heard of and scoffed down a lot of cakes.

Refreshed, we drove three miles to Weeting Heath, where David had insisted we would see a bird called a stone curlew. I'd been disappointed by this sort of promise before, so was healthily sceptical, but the warden told us one had been seen that morning. Taking a long look at our attire and our single pair of cheap binoculars he offered to show us the bird himself and led us down to the relevant hide, where he set up his own telescope and pointed it at the field. Neither of us could make out anything through the lens. The warden said things like, 'Can you see that yellow flower? Look just below that . . .' This didn't work. It was like trying to spot the image in a Magic Eye poster with someone whispering, 'Well, squint, look *through* it, gaze at the fifth dot from the middle . . .' in your ear.

Also, our attention kept being grabbed by a couple of stoats cavorting in the foreground. Apparently they're the bane of the stone curlew's rare lives (and are therefore closely 'controlled' by the wardens) but to us, they were the most interesting things we'd seen all day. Stoats! Like in *The Wind In The Willows!* Eventually, we did manage to spot the vaguely bird-shaped lump our warden was employed to protect, but it was fast asleep. We were not impressed.

Neither of us had heard of a stone curlew before. I'd assumed it would either look like a stone or be quite curly. Unfortunately, all we could see was its sleepy head and neck, so Tim read me the description from the *Collins*:

'Stone curlew. Here it is. It's in the "Thick Knees" section. In fact it's the only bird in the "Thick Knees" section. It must have very thick knees.'

I had a look through the warden's scope. 'I can't see its knees,' I said, 'it's sitting down. It's still asleep.'

'In Dutch it's called a *griel*,' Tim announced with great pleasure. 'In Swedish it's a *tjockfot*. That's very useful information. And it's forty centimetres long. Is that one forty centimetres long?'

'Yes, it's exactly forty centimetres long.'

The warden didn't look amused.

'Long, heavy, pale yellow legs,' Tim continued. 'Are its legs heavy, Alex?'

'Well, I still can't see the legs but I guess if those knees are as thick as you suggest they'd have to be pretty weighty.'

'Flight usually low, with deliberate wing beats. So ignore all birds that seem to be accidentally flying . . .'

'Will do . . .'

'OK, well I should probably take this back to the centre,' the warden interrupted us, snatching up his scope.

'Thanks for your help!' we both chimed.

Alone in the hide I asked Tim what he thought of the stone curlew.

'Lazy bastard,' he pronounced.

It may have been one of only 300 pairs in the UK but to us, the bird was disappointing. We'd paid £2.50 each to see an utterly unmajestic bird having a nap in the distance.

Still, we'd had a nice day out and lots of cakes for lunch. What's more, the stone curlew was another new (and rare) bird, and for the third time that year I'd got a bit sunburnt. I'd been pleasantly distracted if not overly stimulated. In fact, it was only when I called Duncton for our monthly round up later that evening, and he told me he'd seen loads of stone curlews out in Romania, that I thought again about my massive bird shortfall. I'd gone all that way for one bird that he'd already seen.

To confound matters, when I read out my entire list of species for the year (our conversations in 2006 must have been really quite dull) he pointed out several birds that I'd included but couldn't actually count. Without meaning to cheat (honest) I'd snuck Polly's Japanese chickens, the Aylesbury duck and Egyptian goose from Manchester and a snow goose from the London Wetland Centre into my total. 'The first few are all domestic,' he explained, 'and strictly speaking, snow geese aren't count-able. There are a few proper ones over here, but they're only rare vagrants to the most northerly isles. I'm afraid what you saw was almost certainly a "plastic" one – another captive.'

At the beginning of the year, he would have tried to sound sympathetic when breaking my third bout of bad news that month to me. But I could tell from his tone that Duncton was happy with his lead. He'd only added one extra bird himself, but had spent nearly every day of July enjoying the sun in his garden. I'd travelled to every corner of the British Isles, added just six new birds and was knackered. With just five months to go, I'd seen 145 species, compared to Duncton's 208. And he'd seen a golden cheerio and I hadn't.

I turned to Adrian Riley for some inspiration, but he too was struggling. At the same point in his year he was on 328 species and wrote:

'I was so low on emotional fuel that I found I did not even care about the bird. I phoned Nessie and told her in a broken voice that I had had enough. I simply felt unable to carry on driving myself into the ground. I could not even face the long journey home. I was beaten. I sat with my arms crossed over the steering wheel of *The Enterprise* and wept with sheer unadulter-ated exhaustion.'

OK, I suppose I didn't feel quite that bad. A good night's sleep would probably sort me out.

CHAPTER 8

Beyond the Fringe

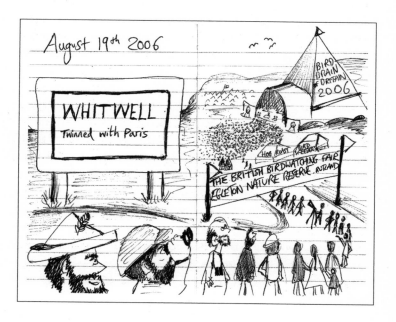

'If one is going to put oneself in this sort of situation, one had better expect the proverbial to hit the fan at some stage. The best policy is to face it head on – not try to avoid it, as this is impossible.'

– Adrian M Riley

Alex: 145 species
Duncton: 207 species

7 August

You'll be relieved to know that Riley soon picked himself up, dusted himself down and took himself off to the Scilly Isles for some serious birdwatching. That's how he faced his 'proverbial' head on. I had different priorities. So a week into the month I packed a bag, said goodbye to Rachel and drove north to somewhere I hadn't thought I'd visit during the year, the Edinburgh Festival. The Goodies were performing for the first time in twenty-five years and I'd bought myself a ticket. I was going to face my Oddie. He was my 'proverbial'.

I'd gone up to Scotland the month before by train. This time I was driving, so with my *Birdwatcher's Yearbook*, I planned a route that seemed sure to yield at least a couple more birds. And so, despite leaving at 9.20 a.m., I arrived in Edinburgh at 7.20 p.m. I spent ten hours travelling 400 miles on A-roads, eating four Ginsters sausage rolls and listening to entire shows by Ken Bruce, Jeremy Vine and Steve Wright on Radio 2. All this because of birdwatching.

Spending that much time on your own, you could do some pretty profound thinking. You could ponder your career, your family, politics. You could consider the state of the world, the wars, poverty. Or you could contemplate memories past and dreams for the future. But for ten hours, I thought almost exclusively about Bill Oddie. What will I say when I see him? How will I greet him? Should I tell him I've been following him for the best part of six months?

By the time I arrived, I'd answered all these questions and more. I was focused.

My three bird stops were the only breaks to this concentration, and I was really treating them as fodder for my conversation with Bill. The first stop was The Lodge at Sandy, where

Duncton had stayed as a child[104] and where, I later discovered, we had stopped as a family in 1987 on our way to a holiday in Yorkshire.

> Are Holiday in Yorkshire :.
> Daddy was on duty so we didn't set off to Eleven in the morning. We drove for a few miles to Sandy, where we had lunch at the R.S.P.B H.Q. Then we had a little walk round.
> Then we drove on to Yorkshire. On the way we had supper ax at a happy eater. Then we got to our house at 7:30. The house had a big garden and a stream and also a tennis-court.

I'm not sure what's better for you, a Ginsters sausage roll or a meal in a Happy Eater restaurant. It's probably a close run thing.

Until I found this scrapbook I had no memory of this stop, and on my unwitting second visit I didn't recognise anything about the stately RSPB building or its pristine woods. I remember the holiday itself, in a lovely house with, as I described, 'a big garden and a stream', but I have no recollection of the RSPB HQ.[105] I guess that means that by 1987 I had entirely lost interest in birdwatching.

In 2006, however, I explored the nature reserve with unbridled enthusiasm, still full of adrenaline at the thought of finally meeting Oddie and not tired by the mere fifty miles I'd covered so far. I was even a little impatient, and probably didn't make the most of the grounds, but I did sit for a good half-hour in one of the immaculate hides, watching no less than six great spotted woodpeckers dine, dinner-party style, on a breathtaking

---

104 And where Lee G R Evans had also spent many of his formative birdwatching years.

105 The longest abbreviation in the book.

bird feeder. 'That is state-of-the-art stuff,' I murmured to myself. I was perhaps more impressed by the bird table than the birds, but then I noticed something to my right, creeping up a tree.

It was a treecreeper, my first for the year and instantly one of my favourite species, mostly because their name is both accurate and appropriate. This was a shuffly sort of a bird, well camouflaged against the bark of the oak, nervously going about its business and doing its best not to get involved with the more flamboyant wood-peckers. It reminded me a lot of me.[106]

Nipping into the visitors' centre, I found out that they were using a couple of Duncraft Super Cling-a-Wing Bird Feeders hung on Single and Double Shepherd Staffs, a Meripac Bird Banqueting Hall, three Squirrel Baffles and several Rabbit Shack Flatpack Rosedale Bird Tables with Hexagonal Ceramic Effect Rooves. Pleased to have a new species under my belt, I got back in the car, ate a sausage roll and drove another ninety miles up to the Lound Gravel Pits in Nottinghamshire, where my guide said I might find the dramatic-sounding Manx shear-water, killdeer or great skua. Not many people would break up a journey with a refreshing trip to a gravel pit, so again I felt pleased with myself.

This was, however, no Welcome Break.[107] This was a frustrating break. As soon as I'd paid my £4 entrance fee (which immedi-ately aroused my suspicions) I realised most of the birds I had heard from outside the gates wouldn't count. These were more captive birds. When signing up for this Big Year, I had no idea that there were so many birds imprisoned in this country. I saw

---

106 Usually a cringe-worthy statement but hopefully I can get away with it because I'm comparing myself to a tiny bird.

107 The second most widespread service station operator, with twenty-seven stations, beating Roadchef (twenty) into third place, but not really coming close to Moto, who run no less than thirty-eight, including Woolley Edge, Trowell and Pease Pottage.

birds like a fulvous tree duck, a cinnamon teal and an Indian spotbill, but couldn't include them in my total. It wasn't quite a zoo and it certainly wasn't Birdworld. It was a nature-reserve-enclosure hybrid, and I was in the wrong half, with my binoculars. So while kids were being picked up by their dads and shown a stork on one side of the fence, I was peering out through the wire with my birdwatching equipment. Yet again, I felt foolish.

Only later, when I looked up the pits on the internet, did I discover that if I'd been a little more patient I may have seen some legitimate birds. Rareties do drop in there – earlier that year something called a gull-billed tern had got everyone excited – but you needed to put in the hours. I hadn't. I'd just finished my second sausage roll, packed up my binocs and left.

Piqued, but focusing once more on Oddie, I ploughed on for 200 miles, stopping at a narrow strip of marsh called Bemersyde Moss in the Scottish Borders. This time, to my relief, there was no one else there. There was just a single hide, untouched by axe and unsullied by the words SEX HUT. I brought out sausage roll number three and munched happily away, gradually blending into the landscape. Dusk was settling and the cows, sheep, fields and skies were appropriately moody. I hoped I'd see one of the site's breeding black-necked grebes, a relative of Tim's great crested, thanks to which the Moss has gained limited fame.

Unfortunately, I'd used up my bit of luck back in Sandy. The notes neatly written in the hide's log book informed me that the last black-necked grebe had packed its bags and emigrated the week before. But I didn't really care. I'd found peace here in the Moss. The setting alone was better than a mocha from Caffè Ritazza, more exciting than GameZone and more relaxing than one of those massage chairs, where you put in a couple of quid, sit down, and get poked about for ten minutes. I made the final approach to Edinburgh and Oddie with a smile on my face (and the fourth sausage roll in my stomach).

Hi Bill, my name's Alex and I'm a birdwatcher.

8 August

That smile stayed on my face throughout the next day. The sun was shining, the festival was in full swing. Eager drama students and weary comics thrust flyers in my face every step I took down the Royal Mile, but I didn't mind. I didn't have to perform a show every night for a month. But Oddie did. And I'd be there to claim my prize.

Or so I thought. I arrived at The Goodies' venue a full hour before their show started but already a queue bigger than any I'd seen at a nature reserve meandered down George Street. As the minutes ticked by, staff at the venue skipped down the line dishing out bright yellow stickers that read 'Do the Funky Gibbon', 'Goody Goody Yum Yum' and 'Anything, Anytime, Anywhere', the last of which I slapped on my chest with pride. Anything, anytime, anywhere, I thought, that's right. But more specifically, Oddie, now, here!

The audience was made up almost entirely of people older than Duncton, so when we were finally allowed to enter the auditorium I managed to overtake a couple of my rivals and grab a seat in the very front row. I'm not proud of myself, but after my six-month search I was determined to get a good view.

The lights dimmed. I was more nervous than I ever am before one of my shows, more excited than at anyone else's. Then out they came. The Goodies! Tim Brooke-Taylor, Graeme Garden and ... and ... and that was it. Where was Bill? While the rest of the audience laughed, I sat up straight, mouth agape with confusion and distress.

'As I'm sure you all know,' said Graeme, 'Bill's not actually on the tour with us . . .'

What? You're sure we all know? I didn't know! I've driven 400 miles on A-roads to see Bill!

'But don't worry, we have got video inserts of Bill throughout the show and I've got my Bill ventriloquist's dummy!'

Don't worry? I hadn't pinned down the rules of my Oddiewatch, but I knew that a virtual reality Bill, on screen or a puppet on the end of Graeme's fist, wouldn't count.

The show went down brilliantly. I was gutted. I spent the rest of the evening getting drunk in a way I would never have dared to do if I had to perform myself the next day.

I later found out that Bill hadn't committed to the tour due to his birding obligations.

9 August

I was staying with some friends who were doing shows at the festival, but who happened to have their one day off the next day, and we didn't get in till 5 a.m. that morning. Four hours later, Tom (the merlin man) banged on my door. Apparently we'd agreed to spend the day birdwatching. Key was also invited but once again declined. At that moment, with that hangover, I saw his point.

Nevertheless, with a splash of water on our faces and a bacon and cheese slice from Piemaker slithering down our throats, we were driving out of Scotland again, along the east coast this time, waving to Bass Rock as we passed it. We did our best to ignore the fragile state of our bodies, aiming for the Holy Island of Lindisfarne where we hoped, by some miracle, to be cured.

Tom had been taken here as a kid by Janet and Jamie. It was his turn to retrace steps and rekindle old memories. As soon as the tides let us cross the momentous causeway and the island's castle rose up ahead, I could tell that this was another Bass Rock, another Fair Isle. This was somewhere that would stay with us for ever.

We acted like children. We gorged on cockles, prawns and salmon from a fresh fish stall, followed by a fry-up in a café for lunch. We got lost and competitive in an enormous maize maze (you see what they did there?) ingeniously carved out by a farmer. We wandered round the island for hours, scrabbled up hills and over walls, exploring kilns, throwing pebbles and, occasionally, looking at birds.

At the northeast corner of the island we stood with our hands on our hips and gazed out to sea. All we could see was sea. Denmark sat about 500 miles away, but my binoculars weren't that good. Then we noticed a few gullish birds floating on the water between us and the Danes (quite a bit nearer to us) and before I knew it, I'd got two new birds for my list. The first was a Sandwich tern, named not for its eating habits but after the town in Kent where the species was first identified, whose Earl would go on to name the bread-filling-bread recipe and after whom Captain Cook would name the Sandwich Islands, now Hawaii, and so confuse people into thinking Sandwich terns are from the Pacific Ocean. Is that clear?

The second was the eider duck, who gave its name, of course, to the eiderdown, one of the most comforting words in the English language.[108] The female eiders line their nests with their own soft feathers, but nowadays pillows and quilts are mostly filled with feathers from domestic geese, although 'eiderdown harvesting' (a lovely, gentle-sounding job) is still done today to eider ducklings, but in a way that doesn't harm the birds. So that's a relief.

---

108 According to Tolkien (and the film *Donnie Darko*) the most pleasing combination of words in the English language is actually 'cellar door'. To me, however, this has quite creepy connotations. So I vote for 'cheese pillow'. That sounds nice. Especially if it's a 'cheese pillow' filled with 'eiderdown'.

Out on Lindisfarne, however, eider ducks aren't called eider ducks. They're cuddies, or cuddy ducks, in honour of the Northumbrian Saint Cuthbert, one of the world's earliest wildlife conservationists, who lived on the Farne Islands in the seventh century AD.

He had quite a varied life, Saint Cuthbert. For many years he travelled round Britain, gaining a reputation for performing miracles on sick poor people. He founded an oratory at a brilliantly named town called Dull, in Perth and Kinross, a site that later became St Andrews University (I'm afraid I don't know how that saint muscled his name onto the place). Soon after that, he retired and lived as a hermit in a cave.

Presumably realising, like Duncton, that now he had all this spare time, he could do more than sit in a cave (he couldn't even watch snooker), he came out of retirement, moved to Lindisfarne, became a bishop and instituted what were probably the world's first bird protection laws in a bid to safeguard the eider ducks and any other seabirds nesting with him on the islands.

11 August

Still thrilled to be off the festival leash, Tom and I spent that evening drinking the health of my two new birds in a fine Edinburgh establishment. Generally giddy, he told me how much he'd loved his day on Lindisfarne. Our faces were ruddy with sun, the birds and the drink.

Comedians spend very little time together. We share an occasional journey to a gig or a dressing room before a show, but mostly we work alone. Edinburgh is different. For one month of the year we socialise, gossip about our peers and agents, tell horror stories about gigs in Nottingham and sneakily test out jokes. Everyone comes to the festival: brave acts taking a risk on their beloved shows and people like me, who just can't stay away – even though they're meant to be taking the year off. So as Tom and I relived our day with St Cuthbert, other comics dropped into the pub and sat down for a quick drink and a chat. As well as the usual festival banter, Tom and I described our trip to the island. Every single person we spoke to responded with their own bird story.

'Oh yeah, I saw a golden eagle once,' said one act, famed for his tall stories both on and off stage, 'it was on my shed. Massive great thing.'

'My dad used to race pigeons,' said a more introspective comic. 'Every weekend he'd be out there with his birds. I think he spent more time with them than us!'

'So tell me this. Is a bird an animal?' asked another. He was quite drunk though.

By the end of the evening, my mind was made up. With the help of Tom, my friends and quite a few Tennants, I'd determined both my short- and long-term future. I'd be back at the festival next year. For, while I was enjoying the year's freedom, what everyone really loves is the pressure, the problems and the publicity of their own show. If you're not doing a show, you're not really part of the festival. So I'd come back and do a show about Duncton. I'd tell our bird story.

And I wouldn't waste the two weeks we'd planned to spend in Israel. I decided (with the help of a call to a sober Rachel) that we should visit Mat. We should spend time with my brother on his big year. We should go to South Africa. The rest of my family were heading out to see him the following year, we should grab this opportunity and pay him a visit right now. And we just might be able to see a couple of extra birds while we were there . . .

But in the meantime, I had my Oddie to find. And through an older member of the comedy guard who'd joined us for a drink, I'd managed to discover one of the birding obligations that had kept him away from the festival.

The next day I raced back from Edinburgh along the A74, M6

and M1, stopping only once at the Charnock Richard Services (a Welcome Break, of course) for a Coffee Primo and a panini (toasted sandwich not football sticker).

19 August

'Are you going to the birdfair?'

Those were the words in the Edinburgh boozer that changed the course of my birding year.

Not 'doing' the festival for the first time in four years was like my retirement. Rachel and I could do whatever we wanted for a month. But when a fellow comedian told me about Rutland's British Birdwatching Fair, 'The World's First and Largest Birdwatching Event', I knew our time would no longer be quite so free. The middle weekend of the month would be spent in the smallest county in Britain.

Obviously, I didn't want to make Rachel trudge round a bird-fest while I got excited by things like bird feeders and binoculars, so I phoned Duncton and invited him and Mum along. This would be a wonderful family outing. After spending the night in a nearby B&B we drove in stately convoy through the village of Whitwell to Oakham, where the event had been held for the last seventeen years. We passed an official council sign welcoming us to 'Whitwell, twinned with Paris'.[109] I couldn't believe it. They got Paris! Whitwell, a tiny village (population: 550) in a tiny county (population: 38,300) had got the administrative, historical and cultural capital of France (population: 2,167,994). This was the

---

109 Coventry became the world's first 'twin city' when it was twinned with Stalingrad during World War II. Lucky old Stalingrad. They've since gone a little bit mad and twinned themselves with twenty-four other cities including Dresden in Germany, Kingston in Jamaica and Sarajevo in Bosnia Herzegovina. London is far more conservative in its choice of siblings, twinned with Beijing, Berlin, Moscow, New York, Tokyo and, interestingly, Paris.

geographical equivalent of the film *Twins*, with Whitwell played by Danny De Vito and Paris Arnold Schwarzenegger.

As soon as we got back home from the birdfair I tried to find out how this situation had come about. The answer was delightful. Apparently my request to the Secretary of State for Northern Ireland was not without precedent.

During the 1970s the regulars of the Noel Arms pub in Whitwell decided they ought to put their village on the map. As I demonstrated in Edinburgh, that's the sort of decision people make in pubs. And like me, these drinkers were determined to follow through with their plan.

The very next day they wrote a letter to the then Mayor of Paris and future ex-French President and Zidane-fan, Monsieur Jacques Chirac, proposing the link between their town and his. The letter was almost identical to the one I'd sent to Paul Murphy. 'We appreciate that you're a busy man,' they wrote, 'and not always able to deal with every item of correspondence coming your way. So if we do not get an answer within fifteen days of posting this letter, we will take that to mean assent.'

Accordingly, when no reply came from Chirac's office within the allotted time-frame (which was, coincidentally, exactly the same as Murphy's), the village declared itself twinned with Paris and erected road signs to that effect. A few years later, Rutland County Council backed the initiative in a rare display of council humour and replaced these wooden signs with the official metal ones I had driven past. As far as I know, there are no such corresponding signs in Paris. Yet.

If you want to imagine the British Birdwatching Fair, think of the Glastonbury Festival, then age the revellers by about thirty years, keep the wellies, add a downpour of proper beards (no intricately whittled facial hair, please) and substitute drugs and alcopops for plastic glasses of real ale. Keep the festival spirit. In fact, double it. The 19,000 people that gathered for the birdfair were united in their love of birds. Artists displayed works featuring birds, writers sold books about birds and distributors sold CDs and DVDs starring birds. Countless stalls sold bird food, with one in particular stocking some truly magnificent feeders, more impressive than anything I'd seen before. I asked the holder which one was his best.

'Well, this one's bulletproof,' he proclaimed proudly, gesturing like an auctioneer at his yard-long prize item: 'The Metal Conqueror' (yours for just £44.95). I'm fairly sure he was implying that squirrels wouldn't even get a sniff of your nuts if you bought this model, but I couldn't help thinking that if there was a drive-by shooting in your garden, the bulletproof perspex might in fact be dangerous for the birds, what with the ammo pinging off in every direction. I bought a brand new *Collins Bird Guide*[110] from the stall next door instead.

Rachel and Mum were bearing up well. In fact, I began to suspect they might actually be enjoying the peculiar experience. My suspicions were confirmed when Rachel rushed off to a shoe stall and returned with a pair of really quite feminine walking boots. 'Perfect for South Africa,' she beamed. I led her over to a couple of South African stalls where we chatted to some eco-tourism guides about the sort of birds we might see and bought books that told us how. I was getting excited about our holiday. Rachel, I imagine, may have been starting to worry about hers.

I took another step closer to becoming a birder by buying my first pair of 'proper' binoculars. My salesman was quite clearly a fanatical birder himself, who told me he'd seen 5,000 species through his binoculars. This hooked me in completely. I had to buy something from this man. So after much experimentation and under the expert guidance of him and Duncton, I chose a

---

110 'Illustrated by Killian Mullarney and Dan Zetterström, with text by Lars Svensson and Peter J. Grant, this is the strongest team ever to produce a field guide,' was the bit of the blurb that sold it to me.

beautifully sleek pair of lightweight Delta SL 8 x 42s. It was like buying my first cricket bat. I turned each potential purchase over in my hands, feeling the weight, admiring their newness. Then, when I picked up the Deltas, I knew immediately that I wanted them, and logic and reason went out the window. They felt right. Thankfully Duncton approved and I handed over my credit card.

As I left the stand, a photographer from the *Rutland and Stamford Mercury* approached. 'Do you mind if I take a picture of you with your new binocs for the local paper?' he asked. I didn't. In fact I was only too pleased to pose with my new favourite thing.

There were elements of the Edinburgh festival here too, with talks, events and performances staged in packed tents. In one tent a birdwatcher was doing a show about comedy. I'll be fine in Edinburgh next year, I thought.

At 3 p.m. on 19 August we lined up to watch 'The Bird Brain of Britain 2006'. This was what the comedian in Edinburgh had told me about. And this was how it was described in the fair's glossy brochure:

The most popular event at Birdfair by a curlew's bill so make sure you arrive early to get your seats. Representatives from our associate sponsors will be answering questions on chosen and general bird subjects with Bill Oddie at the helm. An unmissable hour – who will walk away with the much coveted great crested grebe trophy this year?

Unmissable indeed. Never mind who won the trophy, it was the quizmaster who represented my moment of birdwatching glory. I raised my new binoculars twitchily at the edge of the marquee, aiming towards where I thought the helm of a tent might be. There, resplendent in the Hawaiian shirt I'd been picturing all year, but a tiny bit shorter than I'd expected, was the mighty, the elusive, the Oddie.

We weren't as punctual as I had been for The Goodies, and so we had to stand at the back. It seemed that all 19,000 festival-goers had come for Oddie too. In fact, he was so mobbed by fans afterwards that I wasn't even able to give him my opening line. But I didn't care. I watched, mesmerised, as he handled the crowd with consummate ease, being funny while discussing birds. That was enough for me.

The questions were tricky:

Bill: 'Who first unsuccessfully introduced the little owl into Britain?'

Sponsor's representative: 'I think it was a nun.'

Bill: 'A nun, why? What? No! (Much laughter in the marquee) I think we'll call that a pass . . .'

Oddie managed to make it accessible and entertaining for everyone (including novices like me and Rachel and Mum) by adopting the stance of a cuddly Jeremy Paxman – but a Paxman whom you believed actually knew the answer:

Bill: 'The man who in 1843 unsuccessfully introduced the little owl into Britain was Charles Waterton. And the mistake he made was . . . he only introduced one! (Even more laughter – gales even – in the marquee.) Fortunately (Oddie was now surfing the laughter) it was a long-lived and very virile bird. It lived for forty-six years (now Oddie was laughing too) until Lord Lilford brought in another one! Whom the first one bred with, or humped, and I think he probably died in the attempt, but nevertheless, that's how little owls came to Britain!' (Applause)

It seemed to be his perfect gig. He could entertain and talk about birds. And, unlike on *Springwatch*, he could even curse a little, which he did with relish and charm. I added 'occasionally coarse' to my description notes for 'Bill Oddie' (along with 'shorter than you might think'[111]), and ticked him off. Got him at last!

Oh, there were birds at the birdfair too by the way. Behind the swathes of bearded birders and camps of canvas tents, the Rutland nature reserve stretched far off into the hazy distance. But, like most people, I barely turned my head in that direction. Like most people, I was far more interested in the people. That was where the fun lay for me. And while I stand by my statement that everyone was united by their love of birds, they were all still susceptible to the very human traits of jealousy and rivalry. As people passed on the paths, eyes would lower, first to the other's binoculars, then to their waterproof jacket (necessary on the day we went) and then down to the walking boots. I'd never heard the term 'binoc envy' before Duncton muttered it to me as we queued for the reassuringly sweet-smelling loos. Apparently a jealous birder had been eyeing up my Deltas.

24 August

Infused with the festival spirit, Rachel and I spent most of the next week getting ready for our trip to South Africa, booking a place on a safari, plotting a route down the Garden Route and

---

111 'He's actually 5' 3".' Almost a foot shorter than Natasha Kaplinsky.

making sure we could meet up with Mat and Morri in Cape Town. After a short diplomatic conference, she also agreed I could book a professional birdwatcher for one day only so I messaged Mat and hired a guide.

Two bird events marked these intermediary days. First, the sighting of a wren in my garden. Along with the dunnock, the modest wren is perhaps one of the least flamboyant of the British birds, but I was pleased to see the tiny brown ball cock its tail in my garden and be able to tick another bird on my garden list. I might not reach Duncton's total of fifty-nine, but I was well on my way to double figures.

Second, after two days of postings on Birdguides about a yellow-legged gull in Kensington Gardens, I hurried to the right spot in Hyde Park and found the bird on the exact post in the exact lake opposite the exact statue of Peter Pan indicated on the website: a normal sort of seagull, but with bright yellow legs.[112] It was almost too easy. But I guess that's what I'd paid my Birdguides joining fee for. And I liked to think the symbol of eternal youth had some sort of significance for my adventure, although I wasn't quite sure what.

Finally, we attended the relocated wedding itself, not on the coast of Israel but in Barnet. If I'm honest, it was in a glorious location called Wrotham Park, three miles north of Barnet, a Neo-Palladian English country house that features in *Peter's Friends*, *Jeeves and Wooster* and *Gosford Park* and which was the perfect setting for a brilliant day – but calling it 'Barnet' sounds funnier.

The service took place on the house's immaculate lawns,

---

112 Gulls can be notoriously difficult to tell apart. Luckily, some of their names give at least a bit of a hint: slender-billed gull, black-headed gull, ring-billed gull, lesser black-backed gull, great black-backed gull, glaucous gull, ivory gull, sooty gull, white-eyed gull, little gull, laughing gull and the tanned Mediterranean gull.

affording us stunning views out across its 300 acres of parkland. As the couple exchanged rings and vows I noticed two large eagle-like birds circling above us. Unfortunately I'd been banned from bringing my binoculars (not good form at a wedding apparently) so I couldn't find out what they were.

29 August

It takes quite a while to fly to South Africa, but we did get to watch *Mission Impossible III* and eat peanuts, so the experience was generally fine. After landing in Cape Town, we flew another six hundred miles north on one of those small flimsy frightening planes to Port Elizabeth, then picked up a more sturdy car and drove for another ninety minutes before triumphantly arriving at Lalibela Game Reserve on the Addo Elephant Park, where we'd planned to spend a few days before heading back down to Mat and Morri in the capital.

As in Bahrain, I had trouble concentrating on the road with foreign birds flashing all around me, but with Rachel at my side, emphasising just how keen she was to survive long enough to see a giraffe, we made it to the camp.

This was a reserve unlike any I'd visited before. Hides were unnecessary. Every building – the kitchens, the dining room, the lounge area and our bedroom – was perched high in the trees, looking out over a seemingly endless jungle forest. But it was the sounds that were most impressive. I had no idea what I was listening to, but it was definitely more exotic than a wren or even a yellow-legged gull. I wasn't even sure if the noises were being made by birds or some poor mammals being trodden on by elephants, but I wasn't bothered. This was terrific. This was like a film. This was how I wanted to go birdwatching.

After dumping our bags on the floor of our room I stood on the balcony, looked out at the tree tops and immediately saw seven or eight new species. Brilliant. Unfortunately I didn't have a clue what any of them were. I'd done my research at London Zoo in March and had the African guide books I'd bought at the fair, but they weren't enough. I didn't even have my primal training Duncton had instilled in me as a child. These birds really were all new to me and with no guidance, I couldn't confidently identify them. Luckily, I would soon meet a man who could.

We went out for our first safari drive that evening. There were six of us altogether – Rachel and I, a middle-aged American couple who both wore Harley Davidson bracelets and a quiet retired couple from Dublin – and we all sat royally in a jeep driven by our smiling guide, an Arsenal fan called Ben.

'Before we leave, are there any special interests?' he asked us. This was my chance. I could come out as a birder . . .

'I like lions,' purred the American lady, 'and zeeebras.'

'Hippos and elephants,' growled her husband.

'Scrub hare,' offered the Irish chap. I think this was a joke.

'Giraffes!' shouted Rachel, getting into the spirit of things.

'. . . er, birds?' I tried, without much conviction and probably too late. But at least I'd had the courage, eventually, to admit my fetish.

'OK,' said Ben. 'I will try my level best but I am afraid to make some promises because all our animals are afraid of me!' Much like Duncton at Chichester, Ben's smile was pretty much permanent, and I was confident that definitely was a joke.

'Right, sit back, relax and enjoy yourselves,' he grinned. This was much better than trudging round a graveyard.

To the delight of Jim (the American – he'd introduced himself loudly to the group just as Ben had told us all to shush by a bush: 'I'm Jim and this is Judy! We met on the internet four years ago, which was great . . . Oh sorry, yes, shhh! Sorry Ben! Wow! What is that thing?'), the very first animal we came across was a hippo. An enormous hippo. As big as a boat. Big enough to fill our entire garden. We were all very impressed.

But then, for the next half-hour, it was all birds. Perhaps because they are easier to spot than lions and scrub hares, perhaps because Ben himself was a birder (his knowledge was awe-inspiring), or maybe because he had appreciated my plaintive bird request, Ben only pointed out things with wings, using phrases like: 'That should be a jackal buzzard above us', 'That should be a yellow-bellied stork over there', and 'That should be a hadada ibis up ahead.'[113] Everyone else made admiring noises, but I was positively whooping. These were spectacular birds with spectacular names and I could count them all!

We saw proper Egyptian geese that Duncton couldn't quibble over, African hoopoes, blue korhaans and an orange-throated longclaw, all looking as exotic as they sounded. Ben would point them out and shout out their names for me to scribble down. I felt a tiny bit like I was cheating, but he'd also give me a titbit of information about the bird that made me feel I was learning something.

'Those fork-tailed drongos over there,' he told us, 'are often found near rhinos. They like to swoop in and out of their slip stream, eating the insects the rhinos stir up.'

'Brilliant,' I said. These were the birds I wanted to see: fearless birds that tailed rhinoceroses, the little ones that sit in the mouths of crocodiles, ostriches breaking the speed limit.

'Do you know which bird has the most feathers and which has the least?' he asked the group.

No one wanted to look stupid, so no one said anything.

---

113 Ben always began his identifications, 'That should be . . .' At first I worried he'd go on to say, 'But, it's actually a wren.' I soon learned that Ben was always right. His 'That should be . . .' represented supreme confidence. If something wasn't what it should have been, I imagine he'd have had serious words with the offending species.

'Well, the swan has the most with 25,800 and the humming-bird has the fewest,' he said, breaking the tension. 'Can you guess how many the hummingbird has?'

Now we got involved. We could guess numbers. 'How about 10,000?' said Jim confidently. 'Or 5,000?' offered Rachel. 'No,' I said, thinking I was being pretty clever. I was, after all, the bird expert. 'It must be about the same: 25,500?'

'Oh no,' Ben laughed. 'The hummingbird has 950 feathers. It is the smallest bird in the world but it does proportionally have the largest brain.'

The words 'bird' and 'brain' struck a chord. Must not be a dude, must not be a dude . . .

We did, of course, see mammals too; wildebeest, buffalo, kudu, impala, springbok, warthogs and wild dogs. Jim got tremendously excited at anything that looked like something he'd seen in America and asked a lot of questions about Ben's gun. 'So have you killed one of those?' he would enquire menacingly, staring at each new animal.

Rounding one dusty corner into a more open plain we came across a herd of giraffes just yards away from our vehicle.

'Giraffes,' gasped Rachel. This was what she had come for.

'So, could I break and ride that?' drawled Jim. A brilliant question. If I was Veruca Salt and Duncton was Charlie, Jim could only be Mike Teavee. Eyeing Ben's gun, he fondled his enormously long camera as if it too were a weapon: 'This is only a 1.4; if you get a 2x you start losing some of your clarity.' *Click, click.* 'Come into the sunlight little son.' *Clickety-click.* 'Got you.' *Click.*

Soon we were back to the birds. If I'd had to choose a favourite (I didn't) I'd probably have picked the glossy starlings that shone out from a perfect African tree like my old CD bird-baiting trap. They were shinier and far bigger than a British kingfisher, and managed to impress everyone on the jeep, which was no mean feat. I offered to lend John, the burly Irishman, my binoculars for a closer look. 'No! I can see it ... I don't need your binoculars,' he said in a peculiarly defensive way. I think he thought I was insulting his eyesight.

But then I also really liked the anteater-chat, even if that was mainly because of its casual-sounding name. An 'anteater-chat' immediately made me think of my New Year birdwatching friends up in Yorkshire, nattering away, taking the mick out of each other, but nibbling on insects rather than orange segments.

As our first African night fell and we headed back to the almost embarrassingly luxurious camp, we saw lions for the first time and my birdwatching priorities were suddenly under threat. We heard them first, a spine-tingling guttural roar that vibrated through our bodies. 'Lions,' whispered Ben, still smiling but serious for the first time. We sat in breathless silence, the only light Ben's torch searching for the source of the rumble.

A scrub hare jumped right over the bonnet. 'Yes!' shouted the Irishman rather too loudly. He hadn't been joking.

Then Ben's beam caught a much larger pair of eyes – cat's eyes, but a dangerous design. He switched on his floodlight and there, about ten yards from the jeep, we saw a majestic male lion, yes, a lion king, resting on his haunches and apparently ready to pounce. Behind him two noiseless lionesses smiled dangerously. Ben's earlier joke didn't seem quite so funny now. [114]

The gasps of everyone on board were testament to the power of the animals. Words like 'beautiful', 'graceful' and 'sinister' were whispered. Jim's clicks came thick and fast as he did his futile best

---

114 See if you can spot two of my favourite anagrams in that paragraph. They're sitting next to each other.

to capture the scene. It was a bit like the Alpine swift on Hampstead Heath, but far less specialised. No one could fail to be moved by a lion. If you ever get the chance to go lionwatching, take it at once.

But then Jim's Daytona Beach[115] baseball cap blew off and the whole thing descended into farce. Ben said he should leave it. Jim said he couldn't. Ben had to rev the engine to scare off the lion then sneak out of the car and grab the hat. Then we all went home to bed a little bit cross with Jim.

31 August

The next two days followed a satisfying pattern. At 5.30 a.m. Rachel and I would get up (quite happily, we were on holiday!) and indulge in a full breakfast feast. It would be freezing cold. It was winter in Africa and while it was warmish during the middle of the day, at either end it was more like New Year's Day in Northern Ireland. In fact, it was so cold and often so wet (too wet, sadly, for the jeep to be able to cross to the part of the park where the elephants hung out) that it was just us, Ben and the American couple on the first morning and just us and Ben on the last. The Irish couple told us they preferred the evening trips, and liked to lie in and read in the morning. Fair enough.[116]

The birds we saw on these private trips were, frankly, ridiculous. Just reading the names scrawled into my notebook brings back vivid memories of Ben, the jeep, the broad skies and the Wormwood Scrubs-like landscape. We saw brown-hooded kingfishers, a sort of streetwise version of the English one,[117] yellow

---

115 Where Jim and Judy lived. I didn't think it was a real place but it is. It's in Florida.

116 Well, not really fair enough. Don't go on holiday to a safari in Africa then!

117 Actually, not as beautiful a kingfisher as the British kingfisher, something that made me feel jingoistically proud of 'our birds' back home.

canaries, like the ones people in Britain have in cages, but not in cages, black-eyed bulbuls, red-winged starlings, rufous-naped larks, spur-winged geese, tawny-flanked prinias, a bar-throated apalis and several crowned plovers, all warranting distinctive compound adjectives, because they were all so incredible looking.

I may have missed my golden oriole at Lakenheath Fen, but here I was spoilt with perfect views of the black-headed variety; just as bright, just as golden, except, of course, for its jet-black head. I found my first officially gloomy bird in the sombre boubou. And I saw blacksmith plovers and speckled mousebirds, the first with a call sounding almost exactly like someone hammering metal, the second sociable birds, bathing, preening and roosting in huddles.

We even saw our very own ostriches, not travelling at great speeds but strolling languidly over the plain. Definitely would still be a good way to travel, I decided. Ostriches are the largest, heaviest and tallest of all birds, they also have the largest eyes of any land animal (fifty millimetres in diameter). But I'm sorry to report that they don't bury their heads in the sand. That's a myth. They do, however, sit with their necks outstretched along the ground to protect their eggs or chicks (presumably by acting as a sort of tripwire), so they're undoubtedly some of the most Fun Birds in the world.

*

One bird was genuinely ridiculous. Replacing the glossy starling as my favourite bird of the holiday, the secretary bird made even Ben's smile grow. We saw it near the end of our final, private trip out on the reserve and, remembering my chosen specialist subject, Ben gave me time to sketch a picture. A cartoonish cross between a bird of prey and a waterbird, it had the body of an eagle, the legs of a crane and a wingspan of over two metres. It had a crest of plumes on the back of its head that resembled, according to legend, the quills of a secretary, and long black shorts that look to me like something a secretary might wear on a night on the town. Brightly coloured Fun Birds. Why Birdworld hasn't yet managed to nab some, I do not know.

I loved the exoticism of these birds. It was great to see zebras and giraffes in the wild, but we've all seen them in zoos and so they weren't all that surprising. OK, the lion really did knock my socks (and Jim's hat) off, but there was so much more diversity and colour among the birds, so many more quirks and calls. And besides the exotica, there were birds here that I had grown up with, and that I recognised with genuine excitement: a house sparrow nibbling on a worm, grey plovers and curlews digging about at the edge of some hippo-infested pool as though it was the most normal thing in the world. Most thrilling of all were the swallows, the exact same swallows (I liked to think) that I'd seen in Sevenoaks earlier in the year. There were just a few here in Addo, but they were on good form, wheeling round, chasing the jeep, skimming the grass. We watched them duck and dive around four rhinoceroses, tank-like animals that tried to blink away the birds like flies.

On the final morning we arrived back at camp, soaking wet but glowing with excitement, bubbling over with the names of everything we'd seen. The Irish couple were sitting in the kitchen in their khaki pyjamas, Maria, the wife, looking slightly upset.

'Do you want to see my photos?' she asked right away.

'Yes, thank you,' said Rachel, polite as always.

'The trouble is that they look like photos of photos in a book,' Maria complained.

We had to agree.

'I took them from this book here,' – she brandished one of the lodge's glossy coffee table books – 'but I wanted them to look genuine. No, it's no good. They just look like photos of photos from a book.'

That's because they are photos of photos from books, we thought. You've been bookphotographphotographing, and that's not normal.

I don't think she was planning to pass these photos off as her own sightings – I wouldn't have to contact the Rare Men – but it was strange. Rachel and I packed our bags hurriedly and bade farewell to Ben, wishing him good luck for the forthcoming football season, my fingers tightly crossed behind my back.[118] On my final stint on the balcony, I'd texted Duncton to say I'd already seen forty new species. Just before pulling out onto the N2 and the Garden Route south, Duncton texted back with a short and apparently grumpy message:

**I JUST GOT ONE AGAIN THIS MONTH. HAVE A GREAT TRIP.
LOVE, D.**

I was going to have a great trip. I could almost see his total, just ahead of me down the road.

---

118 Arsenal had already had a shaky start to the season, drawing one and losing one, while Liverpool had drawn away at Sheffield Utd then beaten West Ham at home so I could afford to be reasonably generous to my smiling rival.

CHAPTER 9

Hornes of Africa

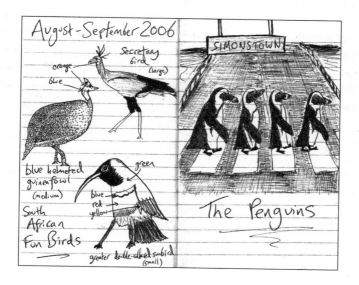

'I shall never forget the backslapping and self-congratulation on arriving home from that trip. I had never met Mike before yet, from then on, consider him a friend. Journeys such as these have little to do with birding; they are more about achieving something as a team.'

– Adrian M Riley

Alex: 189 species
Duncton: 208 species

1 September

My birdwatching in South Africa differed from Duncton's bird-watching in Romania in several ways. First, birdwatching wasn't the sole point of our trip. It wasn't even the main point of our trip. We were there to have a holiday. Birdwatching was some-thing I did on that holiday, like reading a book. I noticed the birds. Second, we weren't stuck on a boat with twenty committed birdwatchers for company. Third, the birds that we did see weren't little brown jobs. They were resplendent, spectacular, unbelievable birds. In fact, they were eye-catching birds. They caught my eye. They did all the hard work. I'm sure there were little brown jobs darting around just out of sight, happy to get on with their lives in the shadow of these stars, but I didn't notice them, couldn't identify them, or just didn't care about them.

In South Africa, I came to the conclusion that I'm a glory birdwatcher, in the same way that I'm a glory football supporter. I like the flashy stuff, the glitz and the glamour. Unlike Duncton, I'm not patient enough to spend hours watching little brown jobs or non-league teams (or Tottenham). I wanted ostriches and FA Cups, secretary birds and the Champions League. I admire people who do spend their time doing 'proper' birdwatching or supporting 'proper' football teams. I appreciate that they are the true fans, the bedrock of both activities. But I was comfort-able with this realisation. I was happy to be a glory supporter. Glory supporters, like robin strokers, have their place too.

And even without Ben, I could indulge myself in South Africa. As we sped down the Garden Route I couldn't help but notice more Premiership birds.

As it was winter in South Africa, the roads were virtually empty. Even better for us, the hotels were offering cheap rates in the low season, so we treated ourselves to some luxurious rooms overlooking the coast on our way to my brother's. The first, in a sleepy village called Nature's Valley, was a wooden beach house with a verdant garden round the back, where water splashed from fountains and bells tinkled on trees. It was designed, George the owner told us, for maximum relaxation. Rachel's face lit up.

While she was being pampered by a masseur I explored. On the balcony round the corner from our room I found four bird feeders. By now I thought of myself as something of an expert in the bird feeder market – I knew my bird feeders, I was a connoisseur of cylindrical seed dispensers – but these were different. For a start, they were spherical. Perfect globes, each with a five-inch diameter, each filled with something liquid, golden, gloopy and, I imagined, sticky. It looked delicious. This was the first time I was actually tempted to try bird food. It looked far more appetising than mealworms.

As I admired the winter light bravely straining to shine through the nectar on to the white wall behind, a small bright bird landed on the perch, stuck its beak through an opening and drank deep. It clearly *was* delicious.

The bird wasn't too shoddy either, as small as a goldcrest, smaller perhaps, but even more slender, graceful, and brightly coloured. It looked like the hummingbirds I'd fallen for in Costa Rica.

On my way out of the house and down to the beach I chatted to George again. He wasn't a birdwatcher, he explained, but then he didn't have to be. 'The birds are here anyway,' he told me, 'they're a part of the whole soothing package.' Yes, he put up the bird feeders to draw them closer to the rooms, but that wasn't birdwatching, that was common sense. 'I just like the birdsong,' he said, 'that's where I find my peace.'

It sounded to me as though George was a robin stroker. He was a birdwatcher, but a lowly one. What's more, over the course of our brief stay he helped me identify every bird that came to dine.

'They're our sunbirds,'[119] he said proudly as one arrived for a quick drink. 'And what you've got there is a greater double-collared sunbird. Ah ha! And *that* one . . .' – another shiny red and green bird had arrived – '. . . is a southern double-collared sunbird. Great.'

'Great,' I agreed.[120] Perhaps he wasn't a robin stroker. A birder in denial? Not a dude surely . . .

A third bird dropped into the bar, a darker, more mysterious customer. 'My favourite,' said George quietly, 'an amethyst sunbird. Beautiful.' He was definitely a birdwatcher. I thanked him and headed off to the beach. But only after finding out that the spheres were simple Opus Garden Ballet Hummingbird Feeders, filled with a liquid wittily entitled 'Perky Pet Instant Hummingbird Bird Feeder Nectar-red'.

I'd visited the sea far more than I usually would this year thanks to birdwatching: Al Jazair Beach, North Berwick Harbour, the Exe Estuary, Pagham Harbour and now Nature's Valley Beach, perhaps the most impressive of all. It was perfect: golden sand, blue sky, shimmering sea, every cliché you could want and no other people. I paddled in the bracing water, gasped and looked out at the Southern Ocean, a watery no-man's-land between the Atlantic and Indian Oceans. Next stop: Antarctica.

Further out on the still water I could made out a handful of birds: a couple of large African seagulls called Cape gulls, and a few large African cormorants called Cape cormorants (I didn't know their convenient names until George helped me out later).

---

119 A much fairer name than 'hummingbird' I thought. 'Humming' sounds so facile, so mundane, so pointless. 'Sun' is far more powerful and symbolic. These birds may not have been as mighty as the Golden Condor, but they wouldn't have looked out of place on one of Esteban's adventures.

120 This was the longest bird name of my year so far. I like statistics.

Returning to the shore, I almost bumped into three large black waders with red eyes, red legs and long pointy beaks, waddling along the beach, the only other walkers beside me. They marched in single file straight past me without even so much as a hello.

This time I knew what they were called. I'd passed a sign on my way down through the dunes to the sand, welcoming me to this corner of the Tsitsikamma National Park with the words: 'No dogs, no guns, no fires, no tents, no picking the flowers.' I wondered if there were dog-loving, flower-collecting, fire-starting, hunter-campers about, at whom this was aimed. Below these rules was a picture of some black and red birds and a paragraph of description. They were African black oystercatchers, a rare, distinctive and raucous wader. Just a few years ago theirs was an endangered species, threatened by human behaviour. The chicks were disturbed by bathers, nests crushed under the wheels of off-road vehicles. But here at the national park, where most things were banned, they were thriving once more. While the numbers of noisy humans were down, the numbers of noisy oystercatchers were up. Like the red kites back home, this was a success story. I felt hopeful. But I probably didn't feel as relaxed as Rachel.

2 September

Between Nature's Valley and Cape Town we made a couple more stops, at Plettenberg Bay and Knysna. Waking up in Plettenberg, we lazily watched dolphins cavorting in the waves below our bedroom window before heading out on a boat to watch whales hurl themselves in and out of the water just yards from our fragile vessel, spraying and splashing us till we were drenched. I'd never seen whales or dolphins in the wild before. They really were mind-boggling – more so, even, than the results of the RSPB's Big Garden Birdwatch. I'm not sure if whalewatching is a hobby (or if it is, whether I'd want to do it every day), but it was an experience Rachel and I will never forget.[121]

Further along the coast at Knysna, I'd been tipped off about a particular bird I had to see, the Knysna lowrie. Found only in the forests of South Africa (and the forest around the town of Knysna in particular), it belongs to an outlandish family of birds called turacos, one of which I'd seen in the zoo back in February. This variety has a particularly long tail, an orangey-red bill and bright green plumage. Its bright green crest is tipped with white: it is ridiculous looking and rare, the perfect birdwatching combination. Rachel and I wandered through the woods for hours, eyes trained on the tree tops. This was similar terrain to the rain forests of Costa Rica, the bird a similar quarry to the quetzal. But on this occasion, we had no guide. I was the guide. And I didn't find the bird. It wasn't nearly as much fun as watching the dolphins in bed or the whales from the boat and for perhaps the first time in the year I felt like I'd overstepped the birdwatching mark with Rachel. I was forcing my bird obsession on our holiday, and although she said nothing, I can't imagine it was all that much fun for her.

But then, as we neared Cape Town, we did see a bird that both of us fell in love with: the blue-helmeted guineafowl, an unlikely hero both in name and appearance. We saw these overblown chickens with increasing frequency by the side of the road as the city slowly built up around us. They were quizzical, silly, unnecessarily elaborate birds, distinguished by a bony casque perched on their heads like a top hat, and we found ourselves becoming terribly excited whenever we saw one. They formed large groups and chased one another, bursting into a

---

121 I was blown away by the gannets around Bass Rock and I was knocked out by the whales on the Garden Route. But which is better – 100,000 gannets or five whales? According to my comedy hero, Harry Hill, there's only one way to find out: *Fight!* That's a skirmish I'd pay to see.

clumsy follow-my-leader-style flight when disturbed. They made our journey fun. They kept us going. If there'd been kids in the back of the car, they wouldn't have got bored. At times Rachel and I even stopped the car to have a good look at their funny heads and wobbly legs. They weren't mind-boggling, but we loved them.

And while the whales and lions would inevitably muscle their way into our stories and memories, it was birds like these that really made the trip for me. I did have the ulterior motive of defeating Duncton, but the more birds I saw, the more I appreciated them, thanks largely to their sheer variety. The birds here were all so different.[122] In just this first week of the trip, I'd seen vultures, ostriches, sunbirds and these ridiculous guineafowl; big birds, small birds, majestic birds, birds that looked like jesters, birds that looked like models, noisy birds, graceful birds, soaring birds, sprinting birds, shuffly birds and stunning birds. The whales were very big, the dolphins very playful, but they looked like whales and dolphins. The birds were surprising.

We arrived at Cape Town late in the afternoon, in good time to meet Mat and Morri for an evening of food, drink and catching up at a bar in the heart of the Victoria and Albert Waterfront. We dumped our bags, and headed eagerly down to the harbour. I hadn't seen Mat for five months and was excited. I had the same tingly feeling as when I climb the steps at Anfield and emerge to see the fans on all sides and the pitch stretched out below. Walking into the bar, I scanned the faces for Mat and Morri with animated impatience.

---

122 I've been fascinated for a while by the dog spectrum. I find it amazing that a tiny Chihuahua can look at a Great Dane and think, 'Yes, we're the same animal, everything's fine,' and then run round, trying to sniff parts of the bigger dog's body that it can't really reach. But these are different breeds of one species. There are 'only' hundreds of breeds. There are thousands of species of birds.

People always look slightly different when they're in a strange place and you haven't seen them for a while. I think that's sometimes why the first hour or so after a long-awaited reunion can be a little awkward. They might look tanned, more relaxed, or just be in clothes you don't normally associate them with. Mat also had a beard. Mat's got a beard, I thought, just like Duncton! We raced over to their table and hugged without thinking, hesitating or flinching. It was a great moment. Unfortunately I had also been abstaining from shaving for the past week, so I had half a beard. Our faces became stuck together like Velcro, and we had to tear ourselves apart with a loud ripping noise.

We all gabbled about how good it was to see each other. Mat was clearly as excited as us. He and Morri had travelled all over Africa in the last few months and they'd been looking forward to seeing familiar faces and sharing their stories. Mat had bought a bottle of fine South African wine and had four large glasses at the ready. With great ceremony, he proudly glugged out four generous measures and raised his own glass. 'Here's to you both. Welcome to Africa!' he pronounced with a broad grin beneath his beard. At that exact moment a Cape gull (and thanks to George I was able to say for sure that it was a Cape gull) shat in Mat's glass. Cape gulls are big birds. The shit made quite a loud splash. The wine turned decidedly murky. The four of us were briefly stunned then laughed a lot. Mat ordered another bottle of fine South African wine. Any awkwardness dissolved. We were off.

5 September

That fine South African wine became something of a feature of our time with Mat and Morri. On our second day we took a minibus out to the vineyards around Cape Town and 'tested' far too many varieties in the Stellenbosch region. So when it came to the one 'Designated Birdwatching Day' that Rachel had granted me the following morning, the early start was not necessarily welcomed by all.

Birding Africa, the group I'd met at the Rutland birdfair, had sent me a laminated itinerary explaining what was in store for us, complete with a checklist of the birds we might see. It was an awe-inspiring document. It was like a Panini Sticker Album. This was going to be a big day. Mat and I, at least, were as excited as we'd ever been as kids on Christmas Eve when the four of us arrived at the Kirstenbosch National Botanical Gardens at 9 a.m.[123] Our guide was called David, which I liked. Perhaps I could have a birdwatching guide on each continent called David. Already, thanks to this David and my London David, the name David had overtaken Chris and was only one place behind John in my 'most popular names in Alex's mobile phone contacts' chart.

What I hadn't known was that this David would be quite so professional, quite so young, or quite so heroic. We got out of our car looking dishevelled and hungover. David was waiting for us by his in pristine khaki shirt and shorts with a stout pair of walking boots and a fine pair of hard-worn binoculars round his neck. He must have been six foot three inches tall, tanned and weathered, but not weather-beaten: this man looked like he'd been in a battle with the weather and won. He was hardy. A telescope was slung casually over his shoulder, like a toy. I'm probably not a good judge of these things, but he must have brightened up the day for Morri and Rachel. I thought he looked tremendous.

'Hi guys,' he said in a tremendous voice, 'are you all ready to go birding?'

---

123 Not even that early, I know. But unlike the safari, this was voluntary, this was my idea, this had better be good.

'Yes please, David!' we all shouted eagerly.

Soon after we set off I told him, a little shyly, about my Big Year. I was worried that this might make him think less of me, as a fellow birder and rugged sort of a man, but he didn't seem fazed. He told us that every week he helped 'bird tourists' see as many species as possible in a short period of time. 'Everyone has their list,' he said, 'even me. I've seen 821 species so far. That's not too bad.'

His father had been curator of these beautifully kept gardens and it was soon clear he'd taught David well. He knew every flower in every bed, every tree and every shrub, and of course, every bird that was flapping about, making the most of this floral smorgasbord.

'OK,' he'd say when he'd trained his own binoculars on a particular tree, 'over there you can see a brimstone canary. To its left there's a swee waxbill. And below that there's an African olive pigeon. Have you got them?'

'Not yet, David,' we'd say, but soon we would.

This was efficient birding. This was prescription birding. This was David's patch and he knew exactly what would be lurking in each corner. He found us Cape sugarbirds and Cape buntings low to the ground, a rufous-chested sparrowhawk and rock kestrels high up in the air. We followed him like soldiers obeying their general. There was no chat, no wandering off. We were on a mission.

Piling into his jeep, we headed off round the Cape Peninsula towards the southern tip of Africa,[124] stopping off to grab olive thrush, Cape white-eye and karoo prinia, amongst others, on the way. Already we'd seen so many species they were blurring in my mind. I couldn't remember what a Cape bulbul looked

---

124 We were heading for the Cape of Good Hope, which isn't actually the southernmost point of Africa. That title is held by Cape Agulhas, about ninety miles to the southeast.

like minutes after I'd seen one. But that wasn't the point of the day. David's job was to get his clients as many birds as possible. Wasting time trying to learn about each one wouldn't help.

We only stopped briefly at the Cape of Good Hope Nature Reserve. 'It's not very birdy here,' he told us, just a touch dejectedly, 'but the scenery is great, and we might get a Cape siskin.'

We didn't get a Cape siskin, and David was irked. Still, we did see a monkey and we were at the Cape of Good Hope, so the four of us didn't mind too much. And if anything, this dip in the day seemed to spur David on. Back on the road, he drove slowly with the windows down, ear just out of the window, listening intently and occasionally stopping when he heard a particular chirrup. 'Orange-breasted sunbird,' he would say and we would wait. Ten seconds later an orange-breasted sunbird would dash out of the gorse. This man was good.

The next stop was Simonstown, a village on the west side of the Cape that had gained fame and prosperity thanks to one particular type of bird, the penguin. There are penguins in South Africa. This was news to me, big and very good news. Penguins! I hadn't expected to see penguins in the wild this year, but here they were, wandering round town. We wandered round with them, as did a thousand other tourists.

This colony of African penguins had turned up here on Boulders Beach in 1985, entirely unannounced. They hadn't called ahead; they hadn't visited the area before. It's almost unheard of for penguins to settle in an area already inhabited by humans. But they arrived en masse and settled in for the winter. Not looking a gift penguin in the mouth, the village sprang into action. Walkways were constructed so the tourists wouldn't disturb the penguins' nests. The penguins were grateful and stayed. In fact more penguins came, bringing with them more tourists. Penguin-themed shops opened up along the streets. Twenty years later, they're all still there. They even have the right of way on the roads. The village is run by penguins.

There are only two other penguin populations on mainland Africa, one on a quiet cove near whalewatching hot spot Hermanus, the other on Robben Island, the island where Nelson Mandela was incarcerated for eighteen years and where Mat, Morri, Rachel and I spent the following day. It was a peculiar experience to be shown round the prison island by a former inmate, seeing where men like Mandela were forced to carry out hard labour in a lime quarry, and trying to comprehend the significance of the place while coming across penguins waddling about. At one point I burst out laughing when one fell over. No one else in the group saw the incident and I looked rather insensitive. Perhaps I was.

Of course, David wasn't content just to show us hundreds of penguins. As the tourists gazed at the fluffy penguin babies,[125] he pointed us towards crowned cormorants out at sea, speckled pigeons in some nearby trees and a yellow-rumped widow (yes, that's a bird too) in a bush. We were up to twenty-six species for the day and I had overtaken Duncton's total for the very first time.

This little landmark seemed to relax David. I think he had taken it upon himself to ensure that I caught up with Duncton. As my guide, it was his duty to help me out. So on our way to our last stop, we were able to chat about his birdwatching life. His life *was* birdwatching. His job was birdwatching, birdwatching was his hobby; everything he knew was birdwatching. He'd been around the world watching birds. When I mentioned Lee G R Evans (as the UK year list record holder), he told me

---

125 Rachel couldn't take her eyes off these incredibly sweet chicks. 'It looks like a little ferret,' she said of one youngster, a quote that I caught on tape and played during my Edinburgh birdwatching show. I think it was something about how reverential she sounded that made everyone laugh so much.

he'd met him at the birdfair a few years previously. 'Does he still run his mobile discos?' he asked me.

'Erm, I think so,' I said, desperately trying not to sound like a dude.

He and his birdwatching friends even had their own unique birdwatching system called a 'Dream List'.

'If you dream you see a bird that bird counts for your list,' he told us with a shy, self-deprecating smile. It had taken all day to win sufficient trust for him to share this secret. He knew I was a comedian. I had told him I wanted to tell Duncton's story on stage. I had stressed I wasn't going to mock birdwatchers, but he was well aware a revelation like this could be a great illustration of the obsessive nature of birdwatchers. I tried to convince him that I didn't find his obsession particularly strange or amusing, that in fact I understood it. During the World Cup, I told him, I dreamed about finding my final sticker, the Tunisian goalkeeper, and sticking him into my album. But I couldn't count him. David could count his dream birds.

Even better, according to his rules, if someone else dreamed that you saw a bird, that also counted for your dream list. So this birddreamingwatching system not only encapsulated the total passion birdwatching arouses in some people, it was honourable too. If you dream about someone else seeing a bird, you have to call them and tell them. And what a strange phone call that must be to receive:

'Are you there?'

'Yes.'

'Hello.'

'Hello.'

'I just thought you should know that you saw a white-tailed sea eagle last night.'

'Did I?'

'Yes. We were riding on the back of a whale along the Norfolk coast. My mum was there too. We only saw it briefly then I was back at school and you'd gone again. I had a fondue for tea.'

'Great, thank you!' *Tick!*

Before long we arrived at our final destination. We'd been out for over eight hours and Rachel and Morri were starting to flag. If I'm honest, I was too. I was looking forward to some more of that fine South African wine. Luckily this was a climactic last spot. 'This,' David told us, 'will blow you away.' This was Cape Town's biggest and best, the one and only, unmistakeably smelly, Cape Town Sewage Works. Mat and I knew how to show our girls a good time.

For some reason, we were the only people there. It was low season, I suppose. There were no tourist shops selling cuddly toy versions of them, but there were loads and loads of birds. Sensing our weariness, David grew even more efficient, and we birded without getting out of the car. It was like my own carbird-watching in Bahrain, except that David knew what everything was. He reeled off species after species, giving us just enough time to see each one as we passed by: 'sacred ibis, red-knobbed coot, southern masked-weaver, purple African swamphen . . .' Our lists grew and grew, the names ever more fantastic. We stopped by the exit for one final scan of the area. Way off in the hazy distance, David pointed out a large group of pale birds. 'Do you know what they are?' he said with a smile. I didn't. Mat did.

'Flamingos!' he said.

'That's right,' said David, 'greater flamingos. And to their right, there are a couple of great white pelicans.' We each took turns on his telescope, looking at these fantasy birds. A true profes-sional, David had saved this treat till last.

But there was time for one more act of gallantry. On the way back to the botanical gardens, Mat told David he was now just one short of 300 birds for his time in Africa. David went quiet for five minutes. A few sharp turns and back alleys later, he pulled over at the side of the road.

'Up there,' he said, pointing up and out of his window. 'See on that awning? That's an Indian house crow. Have you got that yet?'

'No,' said Mat, 'but I have now – 300!'

We all cheered, and looked forward to toasting the total as soon as possible. In the rear-view mirror I saw David smiling to himself: another job well done.

10 September

On our final day in Africa, Rachel and I said our goodbyes to Mat and Morri (by now Mat and I had reverted back to waving rather than hugging) and took the cable car up Table Mountain for a final look down at Cape Town and the seas beyond. As we stood on the table top, contemplating the magnificent city below and our reluctance to go to work on Monday (I say 'go to work' – I mean 'stay at home to work'), I caught sight of two birds of prey gliding round to the east. I had a good look at them through my binoculars, Rachel did too, and together we identified them as black kites. They definitely had forked tails. This was a fine way to end the trip: we'd survived a holiday with birdwatching in it.

I'd seen a total of ninety-six new species in two weeks, close enough to a hundred to make me contemplate calling David and begging him to reveal four more birds, but Rachel said that would be creepy. So I left David alone and Africa behind.

The following day was my twenty-eighth birthday. We went straight from the airport to Midhurst, where Rachel's parents were staying with mine for the weekend, and I think we surprised them all when most of our stories (well, most of mine, but some of Rachel's) revolved around birds.

Duncton, I should say, accepted my new numbers with remarkable composure.

some wood and a hamer
and things like that
some more lego
anther book
anther game
a watch
some bagse
anther picher
a toy plane
a pad of paper

I ♥ BIRDS

My seventh birthday wish list. Despite Duncton's hint in the form of personalised notepaper, none of my requests had anything to do with birds.

17 September

My first birdwatching expedition back in the UK was a little different to David's extensive Cape tour. I was still following the capital's birding scene through the London Birders website, but not much had turned up since my repatriation. I did, however, notice that a man called Tony Duckett was offering guided bird tours around Regent's Park. This was interesting. I resolved to join him on his final walk of the year. After all, he'd written that we might see barn owls and I hadn't yet. I wanted to see barn owls.

I'm quite fond of Regent's Park. It's one of the few places in London I'd always want to show off to a visiting friend. If David ever came to visit, I'd take him here.[126] Not nearly as garish as Hyde Park, the lawns are always manicured, the flowers constantly

---

126 I'm definitely not being creepy, just saying that if he wanted to visit, he'd always be welcome.

in bloom (well, that's how it seems) and, of course, you can see the heads of the giraffes in the northwest corner. It may not quite have the glamour of the Kirstenbosch botanical gardens, but I like it.

Tony, meanwhile, was positively passionate about the park. He'd worked there as assistant bird keeper since 1977, before I was even born, and was currently the park's Wildlife Officer. He was in charge of the wildlife and, in particular, the birds, of which, he told me, 200 species had been spotted in its square mile and a half. Two hundred! In a park bang in the middle of Greater London, next door to Madame Tussauds!

I had arrived at the appointed bandstand ten minutes early for the 8 a.m. start time, as I wanted to impress Tony. Six other hopefuls were already there, loitering. The night's mist had pretty much lifted but we still must have made an eerie sight – zombies with binoculars, lurking in silence.

Tony pulled up in his green parkmobile, looking almost exactly like David. Tall, dynamic, khaki shorts; I thought for a minute that he actually was David, then pulled myself together and told myself to forget all about David.

'Here we are then!' said David – sorry, Tony – confidently. The loiterers snapped into action, transforming themselves into a crack squadron of birders. Most people had their own binoculars, and Tony handed out pairs to those who didn't. Everything was looking good.

Unfortunately, by the time we were ready to set off, our numbers had swelled. More and more people had arrived, attracted, like me, by the promise of owls. Tony counted the group. He didn't want to lose anyone on the way round. We were his responsibility.

'Mmm, sixteen. Possibly a bit too big,' he muttered. I agreed.

But the size of the group wasn't our biggest problem. Our biggest problem was that a quarter of the group were drunk. I couldn't quite decide if they'd been up all night or had risen early with the aim of treating the walk like a morning pub crawl, but either way four friends – three women and a bloke – were oozing alcohol from every pore. I hoped we hadn't been quite so intoxicating when we'd arrived at Kirstenbosch. The smell of booze hung around them like an alcoholic cartoon cloud. What's more, they'd actually brought a bottle of sherry with them, and as we walked they passed it amongst themselves, glugging enthusiastically. At one point they offered it to the rest of the group. The bottle got handed about politely but no one else had a slug.

Despite these boozy shenanigans, we did manage to find twenty-nine species of birds in our allotted three hours. Well, Tony found them and pointed them out to us. If I'd been on my own I probably would have struggled to get into double figures, so was pleased to have got up at dawn on my Sunday morning for this bird lesson. With Tony's help we'd seen a long-tailed tit, grey heron, goldcrest, little grebe, great spotted woodpecker, chiffchaff, and the two pirates, whitethroat and blackcap.[127]

But we hadn't seen any birds I needed for my list. We hadn't seen the redwings, spotted flycatchers[128] and fieldfares Tony was hoping for and we hadn't seen my barn owls. I blamed this on the drunks but I couldn't really be cross with them. I think they had a terrific morning birdwatchingdrinking, staggering round, rolling increasingly poor-quality cigarettes, and finding the whole thing more and more amusing. As their giggling increased, the rest of the group found them funnier and funnier. We were birdwatchingdrinkingwatching and we bonded through

---

127 The park also boasts an ornamental waterfowl collection, with about sixty different species from around the world. They were captive birds so not countable, but I didn't know that at the time. I got very excited when we arrived at the manmade lake on which they live. 'Tony,' I cried, 'take a look at these!' He dealt with the situation professionally.

128 By now I'd realised that 'spotted' birds were always (and ironically) the hardest ones to spot.

our observation. We exchanged sly glances when the sherry bottle became wielded with more abandon, subtle smirks when one of the ladies had to 'freshen up' in a bush.

It was an odd morning. It didn't go quite how Tony expected and wasn't nearly as smooth as David's tour, but it was free, it was in London and it was memorable. Two members of the group were tourists from America and Italy[129] respectively and I watched their reactions with pride. By the time we staggered off on our separate ways I was even fonder of Regent's Park than ever before.

25 September

I've mentioned before how easy it is to procrastinate when you're working from home. Just before writing that sentence I checked what the weather was going to be this coming weekend – not because I've got plans, but because it meant I didn't have to write that sentence for another minute or two.[130]

The internet is the most useful implement in my procrastination toolbox. I could while away hours in front of the TV, but I'd feel guilty. I could put off work by tidying my desk, but I prefer it messy. Browsing the internet is a much more satisfactory way of dawdling, because it very nearly feels like work – I'm at my computer, I'm typing. So, as my Big Year progressed, I started to check the London Birders website every half an hour. It was addictively diverting. And just occasionally, it paid dividends.

Not much had happened that morning on any of the windows open on my laptop. I'd written very little, the birders had written

---

129 He hadn't heard of *Ali*, the Italian birdwatching magazine. I did ask.

130 Although now that action has been written about, it doesn't really count as procrastination.

very little, it was a slow Monday. But then, at 12.30 p.m., just as I was starting to think about lunch, a message flashed up on the forum:

> Barred Warbler at East India Dock from 11 a.m. to 12 p.m. No further information. I'm off there now!
> John

I leaped out of my seat. This was the ideal distraction: a rare bird, particularly scarce in London,[131] had been sighted during work hours. I was just a few miles away and I was available. It was my duty to get down there and make the place safe (i.e. see if I could see it too). I rushed into the kitchen, quickly made myself some lunch (I was in a rush but I was also hungry) and checked my emails again. Another had arrived, this time from Birdguides reading:

> 25/09 12:27 LONDON, GREATER: Barred Warbler, East India Dock Basin NR [A] 1st-winter in northeast corner, frequenting rosehips and hawthorn 100m beyond red lifebelt. Parking restricted.

I won't drive then, I thought. I was keen not to get any more parking tickets. I chucked my binoculars and bird guide in a bag, ran out of the house, very nearly bumped into an Italian neighbour and Harry the performing pigeon, and rushed down to East India Dock Basin as quick as my legs and the London transport system could carry me.

Which wasn't very quick. East India Dock isn't easy to get to from Kensal Green. I had to change lines twice, hop on the Docklands Light Railway, hop off at West India Quay and walk a mile in some ridiculously heavy rain. Only the day before I'd

---

131 This was only the ninth ever recorded sighting of the bird in the capital. Not as impressive as the first ever American robin, but still big news for the capital's birders.

been in the post office and heard a lady (probably the same lady as back in July) complaining that it shouldn't be this hot in September: 'It is close isn't it? I mean, it's much more muggy than it should be really. But then I suppose it is a funny time of year . . .' Now, soaking wet and shivering, I wanted to tell her that I didn't find it funny at all.

I arrived at the basin at 2.30 p.m., 120 minutes after being called to arms. I dug out the now soggy copy of the Birdguides email from my pocket: 'northeast corner, frequenting rosehips and hawthorn 100m beyond red lifebelt' I read for the fiftieth time. That was all the information I needed. I could find this bird. I felt, once more, like a spy. 'Frequenting rosehips' and 'hawthorn' could easily have been secret code for enemy agents.

Thirty minutes later, I felt less like a spy. I felt like a wet loser. The rain was unrelenting and I'd found nothing, no birds, no bird-watchers, no rosehips, no hawthorn, no northeast corner. I had found a red lifebelt, but then I'd found another red lifebelt, and another. There were hundreds of red lifebelts. I tried to find one with rosehips and hawthorn just beyond it, but then I realised I didn't know what rosehips or hawthorn looked like. I'm not a dad. I'm not a David. And while I did have my bird guide I'd neglected to pack my British Shrubberies Guide. I was floundering.

But then, just as I was nearing the murky bottom of my ebb, I found hope in the form of two men with telescopes. They were soaking wet and standing in a particularly desolate corner of the harbour, a recess in the north bank of the Thames, surrounded by council flats and drowned by the noise of aircraft taking off and landing at City Airport further down the river. Normally, I wouldn't rush into this sort of scene, but emboldened by the year so far, I strode purposefully over.

Both men had their hoods up so didn't see me coming – they had very poor peripheral vision. They didn't need peripheral vision. Their eyes and scopes were trained on some bushes that I presumed were either hawthorn, rosehips or both. They couldn't hear me coming either because it was raining so hard, so I hovered just behind them.

Now what? I didn't want to make them jump and scare off the bird. But then I didn't want them to find me skulking behind them and think I was a weirdo. I had to do something.

I coughed. One of them spun round wildly, showering me with rain drops. I tried to look like I'd just that second arrived: 'Looking for the barred warbler?' I asked nonchalantly.

'Yeah,' one of the wet men said miserably.

'Right,' I said, 'it is a funny time of year.'

The three of us (they were both big men, one taciturn, the other with a large scar across his face) spent the next forty-five minutes in what I hoped was companionable silence, staring at the dripping bushes. They had deftly attached plastic bags with elastic bands to keep their telescopes dry. I worried that my new binoculars might break in the rain and spent most of the time trying to remember where I'd put the receipt.

Thirty minutes later there was still no sign of the bird, but the rain had let up and more big men started to arrive. Scarface and Quietman barely acknowledged them. I followed suit. I was sorely tempted to share my wisdom ('It's been raining . . .') but didn't want to sound like a dude.

An hour later there were eleven of us lined up a hundred yards from that red lifebelt, gazing at the bushes. Six of them had their own telescopes. There were enough of us to form a football team, but instead we were gawking at shrubs. The final four to join us had all piled out of one car, which they'd screeched to a halt and parked, presumably illegally, in a nearby bay. The driver had an earring and one eye. He was clearly the leader. Within ten minutes of arriving he'd pointed out whitethroats and blackcaps that none of us originals had registered.

At 4.30 p.m. there was the first non-raindrop-related movement in the hawthorn (or the rosehips; I hadn't asked). 'There's something over there,' gasped one of the leader's crew. We all looked in the direction in which his telescope seemed to be pointing.

'That's it,' said the leader firmly. 'That's the barred warbler!'

We all spent the next ten minutes looking through our scopes at what was a hugely unimpressive and unimpressed bird, peaking out from the wet leaves. It was small and brown and warbly. I tried to sound excited, but I'd spent a whole afternoon wasting work time waiting for this moment, and the warbler just didn't justify the build-up.

But during those frantic first seconds, when the bird had first emerged from its hiding place and everyone was straining desperately for a glimpse, I'd felt part of the gang. That brief flutter was something. What's more, in that initial frenzy, one of the group had whispered desperately, 'I can't get it? Where is it? Lee? Where is it, Lee?'

This was all the confirmation I needed. The one-eyed driver was Lee G R Evans, Britain's top twitcher, part-time mobile disco DJ and arch rival of Riley.

'You see that silver birch tree bursting out of the greenery,' Lee said calmly, 'it's just to the right of that. It's stretching. Nice crescentic markings . . .'

That was Lee G R Evans all right. I was far more excited to see him than the bird. I plucked up the courage to ask him for a look through his scope, but what I wanted to do was train it on him. He had made the trip worthwhile. I'd found one of Britain's most famous birders in his natural habitat, without even having to watch a quiz at a birdfair. As I squinted through his lens, trying my best to work out just what 'crescentic markings' might be, he whispered in my ear, 'It's beautiful, innit?' I looked up at his stubbly, yes, weather-beaten face.

'Yes,' I replied, 'it is.'

A few people drifted off after the identification was made,

but I stayed because Lee G R Evans stayed. I wanted to see this man at work.

More people arrived, too. They'd been following the bird's progress on Birdguides and the London Birders forum (Quietman had been texting in regular reports) and as soon as the sighting was confirmed (and they could get out of work) they rushed down to the scene. I'd left by the time Andrew, my Welsh Harp guide, turned up but he added to the forum:

> Got a brief view at 5.45 p.m. then located it feeding in the bottom of a bush at about 6 p.m. It showed well for a few seconds then crashed its way back inside the bush and I didn't see it again. A typical showing by a barred warbler but that'll do me for my London list.

My favourite character (except, of course, Lee) was a jolly man who must have been in his seventies. Swaggering over to the crowd, he took one look at the warbler through some antique binoculars and pronounced, 'Yes, that's it!' He then spent the next ten minutes boasting about a white-crowned sparrow he'd observed from his caravan in Essex for two weeks over the summer. I noticed a few people smirk at this. A white-crowned sparrow had only been spotted four times in the UK before: twice at Fair Isle, once in Yorkshire, and once at Seaforth in Merseyside.[132] Lee could not let it go.

'Oh, that was you with the white crown was it?' he asked gently. 'I went up there a few times, couldn't see it. Are you

---

132 In January 2008, a white-crowned sparrow miraculously turned up in Cley, the Norfolk town famous for its birdwatching history. It had been blown off course from North America and, amazingly, decided to land in this significant spot on the east coast of England, rather than any more logical place further west. Over a thousand twitchers made the pilgrimage to the house of a retired clergyman in whose garden the bird was resting.

sure it was a white-crowned sparrow and not a tree sparrow?'

The jolly man backed down instantly, not expecting his bluff to be called so promptly.

'Well, I guess it could have been a tree sparrow,' he said quietly.

'As a verb, noun and adjective, string describes the act of making up birds,' writes Mark Cocker. 'String is a sin that strikes at the very heart of birding. We don't tolerate it. We seldom forgive it. Once labelled, a person often goes to their grave with the mark, as if it were indelibly tattooed in capitals across their forehead – STRINGER ... Simply to be free of such a taint is as much reputation as many birders ever seek.'

29 September

I ended the month in Dublin, 6,000 miles (as the crow flies[133]) from Cape Town. I was over for a couple of shows in Ireland but my Galway gig clashed with the World International Oyster Opening Competition, so numbers were low. I guess the population of Galway was either celebrating having opened a lot of oysters that day or were practising opening oysters for the next day's exciting event. Either way, the town was full of people keen on tackling shellfish, but the comedy club was empty.

With a whole day to kill in Dublin[134] I opened up my Birdwatcher's Yearbook. To my dismay, the closest nature reserve was ninety miles away, on Oxford Island in County Armagh. I'd forgotten that this was a UK publication and only covered Northern Ireland. I resisted the temptation to write another strongly worded letter to Paul Murphy about the pesky border.

Opting for a quicker and more practical solution, I headed to

---

133 Which it couldn't.

134 Just in case you're wondering, I don't mean that I had twenty-four hours in which to commit a murder in the capital of Ireland. You probably weren't wondering that, but if you were, that's not what I meant at all.

the nearest internet café and Googled the Irish equivalent of the London Birders forum. Sure enough, I soon found www.dublinbirding.ie and a very helpful section on where to see birds around the city. I scribbled down the details of 'Booterstown'– the first place on its bird-site list – and made my way to the nearest metro station.

By 11 a.m., I'd arrived at Booterstown. I didn't know what to expect from Booterstown. In my haste to get birding, I hadn't read anything about Booterstown. I didn't even know where Booterstown was. As it turned out, Booterstown was by the sea. I hadn't expected that. I just knew I liked the name Booterstown.

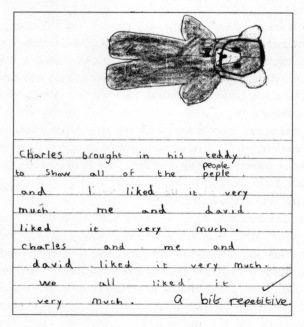

Charles brought in his teddy.
to show all of the people.
and I liked it very
much. me and david
liked it very much.
charles and me and
david liked it very much.
we all liked it ✓
very much. a bit repetitive.

This is one of the only stories I wrote in my writing book that doesn't involve birds. It does, however, employ the same advanced literary technique as I've done in the paragraph above. It might be 'a bit repetitive' but, like I said, I liked it (both Booterstown and Charles' teddy) very much.

Only two other people got off the train at Booterstown. I watched them closely and was disappointed to see that neither of them was sporting binoculars. By now, I'd admitted to myself that I was at least as interested in birdwatchers as in the birds themselves. Again it was the variety I liked: the flamboyance of an Oddie, the calm of the Davids, the confidence of Evans. I was beginning to see how well Duncton fitted in to this community. He was neither robin stroker nor ornithologist. He acknowledged the gaps in his knowledge, and strove to keep learning. Duncton was not a dude. Duncton's place was bang in the middle of the birders' spectrum, at the heart of the birdwatching tribe. Duncton was a birder.

But it seemed that I was the only person at Booterstown with any interest in feathers, and so I plodded off in search of some alone. After my trip to South Africa, and the various high-class reserves I'd visited in the UK like Pulborough Brooks, Sandy and Sevenoaks, I had lofty expectations, expectations that were soon to be dashed.

Unable to see a sign for a nature reserve, I asked a lady in the train station ticket office where it might be.

'A reserve for birds?' she asked.

'Yes,' I said.

'Birds?' she asked again.

'Yes,' I said. 'Birds.'

'No,' she said. It was Bahrain all over again.

'Oh hang on!' She called me back. 'If you turn right you'll see a waste ground. I think most of the birds are over there. But there's no specific building or anything . . .'

I thanked her and went out and to the right. There were indeed birds on the muddy waste ground. I could make out oystercatchers in the distance. A wren touched down briefly in front of me. Fine. But this can't be the reserve?

Checking that I'd written Booterstown down correctly, I saw

that I'd also scrawled a phone number. I didn't know whose number it was, but I decided I had nothing to lose, so I gave it a try. An enthusiastic woman answered: 'South Dublin tourist office! Hello!'

I did my best to explain that I had come to Booterstown to look for birds. She couldn't quite believe this. She was from Booterstown herself, but had no idea there might be a bird sanctuary there. Unfortunately she was the only person in the South Dublin tourist office – she *was* the South Dublin tourist office – so we were a bit stuck.

'Do you know what you could do?' she said. I didn't. 'You could go up to the Tara Towers Hotel, it's a big tall building – it's nice for lunch by the way, or a snack – and ask in there. They should know.'

'Great,' I said.

'Oh, and there is a little area down there just out of the station where you could see the birds. It's a sort of waste area. But where the sanctuary is, I don't know. Or, do you know what you could do?' I still wasn't sure. 'You could go into The Punchbowl, it's a pub on the corner – they do good sandwiches – you could go and ask in there . . . Bye!'

I couldn't fault her knowledge of Booterstown's food options, but it hadn't been all that helpful a phone call. I chickened out of going into a pub and asking where I could watch birds, and headed up to the hotel. On the way I passed a defunct bus stop called, 'The Bird Sanctuary Bus Stop'. I felt as though someone was playing a trick on me.

The hotel receptionist was as helpful as everyone else.

'Birdwatching? Are you sure?' he asked.

'Oh yes,' I said, 'I'm sure.'

'Well, there are some seats and a bit of grass down there by the waste ground. I think there used to be a sign with various things on, but I'm pretty sure they took that away.'

I went back to the waste ground, realising once more how good Brent's Welsh Harp was and how hastily I'd slagged it off. From a solitary bench I watched a couple of curlew and a few sandpipers digging away in the mud but my heart wasn't in it. I needed information, I needed help. I was still a novice birdwatcher and I needed signs with pictures and descriptions. More importantly, I needed other birdwatchers to point me in the right direction.

I decided to abort the trip. But just as I was nearing the station once more, a miracle happened: I found a birdwatcher. He emerged from the station like a binoculared angel. Impossibly tall, he wore a bright yellow shirt with a pen tucked into the breast pocket. This was not typical birdwatching attire, but I didn't care. I rushed right up to him and pleaded for help.

'You're a birdwatcher are you? Well, come this way.'

With these words he led me to the corner of the station carpark and we clambered into a bush. 'Out there,' he pointed back to where I'd just come from, 'that's the bird sanctuary. You see the railings at the end and that bench? That's the viewing area. And out there,' he gestured to the famous waste ground, 'out there you've got dunlins, greenshank, curlews, sandpipers – that's about it. That's my patch. That's Booterstown.

'You probably want to see more,' he continued.

I nodded.

'And you're travelling on foot? Yes?'

I was still nodding.

'Well I'll tell you what you should do – if you want to watch birds in Dublin for a few hours, go to Bull Island. Get the train now – it's an incoming tide, full tide is in four hours' time, so you should be fine – get the train now to Raheny then walk down the causeway to Bull Island. That's the best place. In the high winter you get pintails, long tails, tufties, wigeon, pochard, shoveler; they all come there. About 25,000 birds winter in Dublin Bay. Not many of them will be there yet, but the Brent geese should be coming in soon. They normally arrive in the first week of October so you may get a couple. Does that make sense? Good man,' and off he went to his viewing area.

I stopped nodding, breathed out, and hopped on the next train back into the city then out north to Raheny. By 1.15 p.m. I was strolling down the causeway towards the sea. This was more like it (and less like waste ground). I was determined to find these Brent geese. Any new species at this late stage of the year would consolidate my lead. I looked up the species in my guide (they looked a little bit like Canada geese, a bit more like barnacle geese, but smaller than both) and kept my eyes well and truly peeled.

Ten minutes later I'd crossed over on to Bull Island, the sun was high, the tide was low and I was somewhere in between. Out on what looked to me very much like severals I saw some assorted gulls, more curlews and more oystercatchers. I also found a visitor centre but it was closed. 'Opening hours, 10.15 a.m. to 1.30 p.m.' read the sign. I had missed it by minutes. Oh well, at least I could concentrate on these geese.

By now the causeway had turned into a path and the grass had become dunes. I made heavy weather of walking over large tufty banks of sand, but eventually reached the final ledge and sat looking out to sea for the umpteenth time that year (not an exact number, but way more than in a normal year). I spotted more gulls and wee willie wagtails, but no geese. I watched people drive up to the seafront and potter around, making the most of their lunch hour, but there were no binoculars. I waited and waited, hoping for another miracle, praying that the Brent geese would choose this moment to arrive.

But they didn't. An hour later the tide started rising and I was forced back into town. I hadn't got another bird but I'd had another adventure. I'd explored the town and seen far more than its shopping centres and cinemas. Everything was fine.

CHAPTER 10

Soggy Fish and Chips

'I was far removed from the person who began the year and yet further from the one who was to finish it.'

– Adrian M Riley

Alex: 254 species
Duncton: 209 species

1 October

For the first time in the year, I began the month as leader. With just the measly last quarter to go, there were now forty-four species between me and Duncton. That's a big bird gap. But I couldn't help feeling a little uncomfortable in my metaphorical yellow jersey. I'd certainly put the hours in, I'd definitely stayed within the rules of our game, and I was closer now to a birdwatcher than I'd ever been before.[135] So why did I feel like I'd cheated?

At first I told myself I'd simply been trying too hard; I was embarrassed by how seriously I'd been taking the whole thing, and envied Duncton's cooler approach. But that wasn't it. I hadn't really tried that hard. I'd been on a few walks and visited my brother in Africa, but I hadn't done anything that was genuinely arduous.

So maybe that was it. Maybe I was embarrassed because I hadn't done anything gruelling or onerous. It had all been too simple. I'd overtaken Duncton's hard-earned total with relative ease, and looked like I might romp home by several humiliating lengths.

But it hadn't been all that easy (although it hadn't been hard either – it had been fun). I had sacrificed a lot, I had got up at the cracks of several dawns, I had neglected Rachel at weekends and I had made birdwatching my priority for nine long months. Then again, I'd also taken shortcuts. I had originally intended only to visit places near to where I was working, so I shouldn't have gone to South Africa and hired a guide for a day. Duncton's approach seemed a whole lot more honourable than mine. While he was plugging away at his local patch, I'd flown over to Cape Town and paid a man to show me his birds. Sure, Duncton had spent a week or two in Romania, but even that seemed more

---

135 This 'birdwatcher' could be Duncton, or it could be me – either meaning is fine, and I quite like the ambiguity.

admirable, since he'd worked hard for what were often quite unspectacular birds. I'd been chauffeur driven to penguins and pelicans.

I didn't feel worthy of my lofty perch. I'd somehow got myself into a laudable position which I didn't feel I deserved. I felt slightly ashamed and just a little bit awkward. And this wasn't the first time in my life I'd felt this way.

About twenty years earlier the Horne family arrived in Kemsing near Sevenoaks for one of our reasonably regular visits to Duncton's parents, Granny and Grandpa (Trader). I must have been about seven or eight years old. As we now know, Trader was into his rocks and he'd often show us a couple of his favourites, just as he had with Duncton as a child. Mat, Chip and I would gather round and he'd let us examine amazing stones, all different shapes and sizes, some jagged like quartz, others as smooth as glass. I remember in particular two nuggets, each about the size of a golfball, that were incredibly heavy. Grandpa somehow cut one of them into three pieces (one each) and showed us its shiny core. It had fallen to the earth from the sky in a meteorite shower, he told us.

Their home, South Cottage, seemed massive to me as a child. Then, one day, I grew up and the house shrank. I remember walking in when I was about sixteen, having to duck through a doorway, and looking at the place as if for the first time. It was like when you talk to an old family friend at a wedding and suddenly see what they look like. All your life you've known this person, they've always been there, but you've never before examined their face. Now, for some reason, you notice their laughter lines, their unmanageable eyebrows, the twinkle in their eye.

South Cottage had a porch where Granny and Grandpa hung their coats and keys. On a shelf on the right hand side, Grandpa had placed a small collection of his stones. That was where his meteorites lived. When I was little they were high above my head, only just within reach, a treasure trove to gaze up at with wonder. As I grew taller, they became easier to see, but I stopped noticing them. They became just a bunch of stones on a shelf. I wanted to get inside my grandparents' house and play a game or eat crisps.

On this particular trip to Sevenoaks all those years ago we must have grabbed our coats from the porch as we left South Cottage for a walk in the hills. We probably aimed for Toys Hill or Doctors Wood, places that were devastated by the storm of 1987, but were then still huge and magical forests in which we kids could get lost.

As we walked across one rubbly field, I dropped behind the rest of the family. Duncton strode on far ahead as usual and everyone else was meandering along, gossiping, bickering, laughing. It was easy to fall back unnoticed.

A stone had caught my eye – a smooth piece of what looked like pottery, perhaps about four inches long, with slightly curved edges and a satisfying feel. It was the sort of pleasing object every little boy would pick up and treasure. I rushed back to the group to show them what I'd found. Mum took my discovery seriously and congratulated me. She suggested we go and show it to Grandpa to see what he made of it. Grandpa was even more earnest, turning the small piece over and over in his grand-fatherly hands. 'It's old,' he said wisely. 'Yes, well done Alex. This could be quite a find.'

Back at South Cottage we all had a closer look. Grandpa declared that it might possibly be a shard of a Roman pot. Everyone told me I'd done very well to spot it. Mum suggested we take it to the local museum to see if they'd be interested. I carefully tucked the fragment into my pocket and held it safe all the way back to Midhurst.

A couple of days later Mum drove me to Haslemere, the closest town with its own museum, and I reluctantly handed the piece of pottery over to a kindly curator who agreed with the rest of my family that it was fascinating. A month or two later she rang to confirm that it was indeed part of a fine Roman pot, about 2,000 years old. The museum would like to display it. Once again everyone congratulated me; I was the centre of attention. But I felt a little uncomfortable. I felt like I'd cheated somehow. Yes, I'd found this interesting thing, but that was it. I hadn't known it was anything special – that was all thanks to Grandpa.

So, this year, I had seen a lot of birds, but I hadn't known anything about them. That was all thanks to the two Davids.

I may have been in the lead, but I still didn't feel like a proper birder. My birding had been unnatural. Duncton was the real deal. He hadn't needed an artificial race to get him into the hobby. He'd found his birds all by himself, all through his life. Grandpa had given him a helping hand, but only in support. Duncton didn't pretend to be passionate about rocks. He was too busy being passionate about birds.

What was I passionate about?

23 October

What am I passionate about?

Summer seemed to have turned straight into winter. I'd somehow missed autumn. This was disappointing. I like autumn. I'm not passionate about it, but I like it.

People tend to watch comedy less often in the summer than in the winter, especially when there's a World Cup on. It's more fun to snuggle up and giggle (or scrum down and heckle) when it's cold and dark outside. So as the year hurried along, I found myself doing a lot more gigs and a lot less birdwatching. Opportunities to spot new species were dwindling anyway, and I was fairly content to sit on my lead, despite the mild discomfort it was causing me.

Duncton, meanwhile, seemed typically unfazed by the

dramatic change at the top of our tiny league table[136] and was also birdwatching steadily rather than frenetically. Instead of following Birdguide's advice and driving over to Essex to chase a recently arrived little auk or down to Devon to pick up the seabirds he still hadn't found, he was infuriatingly happy to go about his normal birding business in the vague hope of picking up a couple of unusual birds without leaving his own patch. Intrigued by this optimism and not wanting to miss a grizzled birder's trick, I agreed to join Duncton on one of his RSPB 'starling shifts' and witness his tactics first hand.

In addition to pointing out peregrine falcons to unsuspecting passers-by in Chichester, Duncton's role as an RSPB volunteer occasionally takes him further east along the coast to Brighton, where each autumn one of Britain's greatest natural phenomena goes pretty much unnoticed. Unfortunately, the day I chose to accompany him was a particularly wet one. Rain is good for watching birds (birds tend to shelter in trees or on the ground instead of flying far out of sight) but bad for birdwatching (birdwatchers tend to shelter in homes or in the pub instead of getting wet). Half an hour after I'd bought my £17.50 return ticket from Victoria and ten minutes after the train had chugged out of the station, Duncton phoned to say the RSPB were calling off the outing.

I was outraged. 'They're stopping it because of a bit of rain!' I grumbled quietly into my phone, wanting to express my disgust while being mindful of my fellow passengers. 'Pathetic!'

What could I do? I was on a direct service to the coast, so had no alternative but to end up in Brighton – save for jumping out of the window in a symbolic but painful gesture of frustration.

---

136 Just by the way, as well as tremendous birdwatching, the Isles of Scilly also boast the smallest football league in the world featuring just two teams. Woolpack Wanderers and Garrison Gunners play each other sixteen times a season and compete for two cups as well as the league title. I wonder who I'd have supported if I'd been brought up there.

Thankfully, Duncton is a noble sort and not at all pathetic, so he offered to come to Brighton and do the tour for me alone. I was to be his one member of the public.

While at school at Lancing College, my friends and I would escape by train from Shoreham to Brighton whenever possible, but I hadn't been back for years. Now, waiting for Duncton at the station, I looked around and was struck by how small the place looked. Like my grandparents' home in Kemsing, everything had shrunk. I couldn't have grown all that much since leaving school, but perhaps my outlook had. This had been such a significant place, our gateway to freedom, the threshold of the real world. Like the bridge to my primary school in Midhurst, this was briefly such an important landmark. This was where we would meet before getting turned down in a pub, where we gathered before my first ever rock concert (well, Status Quo's Christmas Extravaganza – our family went three years running), where Chip received the Hornes' only criminal conviction to date by 'forgetting' to pay his train fare then 'hurrying' away from an inspector back when he was still, legally, Christopher. It all seemed such a long time ago. Once again I felt my perspective subtly shifting.

Duncton's train soon pulled in and the jizz of his familiar bearded face shook me from my daydreams.[137] 'It's brightening up,' he lied cheerfully and we splashed down to the seafront under a single umbrella, him generously taking most of the rain just as I do when sheltering Rachel. It was tipping down and I could now, grudgingly, see the RSPB's point. Nevertheless, we managed to find our way to the embarrassingly garish Palace Pier without drowning and Duncton found a suitable spot for us to stand and wait for the spectacle.

---

137 Yes, that is an odd sentence. Jizz is a birdwatching term which apparently derives from US slang for 'General Impression of Shape and Size'.

I didn't really know what that spectacle was to be. I'd had a soft spot for starlings ever since they'd mobbed my fig tree back in May, and the superb and glossy varieties I'd seen at London Zoo and in Africa made me like them even more. But I wouldn't have called them spectacular birds. A swift movement half a mile to our right was to change all that (and cause the humble starling to top my Favourite Bird Chart at the end of the year by quite some margin). For, swooping over the charred remains of Brighton's pitiable West Pier was a flock of starlings so huge I couldn't literally take it all in.[138] I certainly couldn't understand why no one else was standing open-mouthed, gawping at the sky above the sea. OK, the rain was bucketing down, but just yards from the shore, a cloud of birds, like that weird smoke creature in *Lost*, was doing loop-the-loops.

The wonder we were witnessing is called a murmuration and involves thousands and thousands of starlings coming in to roost for the evening. You might remember a Carling advert in which footage of such an event (actually shot by Oddie for *Springwatch* but not credited here because, I guess, he's never really going to be cool) was played with some uplifting rock music before the rather confusing slogan 'Belong' was slapped on the screen. I don't know if the advertisers were going for a rhyming association between Starling and Carling or just liked the pictures, but for some reason the sight was deemed impressive enough to sell beer.

Without taking our eyes off our birds, Duncton and I all but skipped along the shore towards the pier to get a closer look, eventually finding shelter a hundred feet or so away beneath the awning of an ice cream shop, closed in the rain, which we

138 When I say 'literally' here I mean with my eyes. But I also couldn't have 'taken them all in' to my house or 'taken them all in' for questioning. However literally you take the phrase, it remains true.

shared with a teenage couple as focused on snogging as we were on the murmuration. We stood there for about half an hour, rain dripping round us but not on us, as 5,000 starlings performed for our eyes only.

As the light faded, hundreds more starlings joined the group while others dropped away like ash on to the burned pier. They rose and fell as one, creating surreal shapes and patterns, swelling, shrinking, silently flowing. It was as impressive a surge of movement as the start of the London marathon but faster, more graceful, and they were in the air. Apart from the passionate pair beside us ('I'm bored with them now,' he muttered with uncharacteristic impatience), Duncton was mesmerised. 'More than last week,' he whispered quietly.

Then, at exactly 4.15 p.m., as abruptly as it had begun, the display came to an end. As if cued by their leader, the group fell as one from the sky onto every available surface of the structure. And then there was nothing. The fireworks had finished. They'd had enough, and so had we.

'Fish and chips,' said Duncton. It was more of a statement than a question.

'Sounds good,' I said.

Ten minutes later we were sitting, sodden, in an old-fashioned chippie, tucking into a couple of pieces of cod and a single portion of chips. (We really are getting old.) Duncton had mushy peas. That's one taste I don't think I'll ever share.

Unlike a lot of proper birdwatchers, I love London's immigrant parakeet population. I find their squawking exotic and their lurid greens exciting. I don't mind all that much if they scare off a few sparrows, they're Fun Birds! I particularly like the urban myth that when Jimi Hendrix died in London in 1970, his two pet parrots were released into the London sky and went on to propagate the current 10,000-strong population. It's one hundred per cent untrue, but I think that rock'n'roll tale suits them.[139]

Nearly everyone in America, on the other hand, has an active dislike of their most populous immigrants, the starlings. The anecdote surrounding their arrival is geekier, but in my eyes just as charming.

In the 1890s an eccentric gentleman called Eugene Schieffelin decided that it would be in the best interests of New York City if he was to introduce every bird that features in the works of Shakespeare to his home town. And so Schieffelin released sixty pairs of starlings into Central Park, thanks to a brief reference to the starling's mimic-like qualities in *Henry IV* (Part I, Act 1, Scene 3): 'Nay, I'll have a starling shall be taught to speak nothing but "Mortimer".'

They liked New York. Today, the starling is America's most populous and least popular bird, having noisily overthrown the likes of the beloved bluebird. I'm sure there's a meaningful allegory about colonisation in there somewhere, but it's definitely a true story and quite amusing in a Schadenfreude sort of way.

27 October

Duncton had done his bit to lift my wintry gloom. But it wasn't till I looked out of my kitchen window and saw the familiar face of my fat robin that I really got going again. After a four-month summer break he'd come home. This was his home. I'd made

---

139 It's most likely that the parakeets are simply descendants of domestic pets which managed to escape from their cages and survive in the urban wild of London. But one other story that might just check out is that they were actually extras from the film *The African Queen*, starring Humphrey Bogart and Katharine Hepburn. A flock of about twenty birds did, apparently, vanish from the set's aviary in Shepperton Studios in 1951. The film also featured blood-sucking leeches, mosquitoes and crocodiles, so if the tale is true I suppose London was rather lucky.

him feel welcome. I'm sure it was the same bird; he looked at me, I looked at him, *we had a moment.* I resolved to get back into my birdwatching.

Unfortunately, I'd so far been on fewer birdwatching trips in October than I had during the World Cup. I hardly did any birdwatching during the World Cup, so that's a really small amount of birdwatching in October. Maybe my lead was making me cocky; maybe I was bored of birdwatching. Either way, I wasn't impressed with myself, and I hate not being impressed with myself. So I decided to try to impress myself.

For the past few weeks I'd been ignoring emails from Birdguides telling me about a long-billed dowitcher that had turned up in Kent. I'd never even heard of a dowitcher before (which made me think it must be pretty rare) but I liked its mischievous-sounding name. I'd also really appreciated that spoonbill (also in Kent) back in May, so perhaps I'd enjoy the look of this one too. I'm a bill man, I thought, and headed off five hours early to a gig in Shoreditch (Kent is more or less between northwest and east London).

Long-billed Dowitcher, Oare Marshes NR [A], 1st-winter still on east flood

read the Birdguides message, and when I arrived at the Swale estuary for the second time in the year, I saw that this mysterious bird had attracted a fair number of hopeful birders. Forty or fifty lined the track that separated the carpark and the water, mostly retired gentlemen in fine retired gentlemen's attire, and all very cheerful.

'There's a jack snipe here too, apparently,' one said to me as soon as I stood next to him.

'Brilliant!' I said, with genuine enthusiasm.

Ten minutes later neither was showing, so I headed off for a patrol round the water's edge. I had less time on my hands than these older birdwatching colleagues (in the short term, anyway) so wanted to keep moving. The second I sat down in the first hide, the gentleman beside me (again, retired, apparently) asked me if I'd seen the dowitcher.

'Have you seen the dowitcher?' were his exact words.

'No,' I replied.

He grunted quietly. I had become used to this hide etiquette. In general, birdwatchers are a friendly bunch, emitting a cheerful 'hello' when they pass another human. But inside a hide the rules can be different. Birding conversations will often start and finish without a hello or a goodbye. These frivolous phrases are unnecessary when there's serious birding to be done. If there's a rare bird about, it's business time. And businessmen don't say hello or goodbye. They just get on with it.

Things were tense in the hide. My neighbour was part of a car load of birders who'd driven down from Northampton in the early hours of the morning to see the bird. They'd been here for a good ten hours and there was still no sign. I think I'd have been tense too. One of the group was clearly a non-birder – he didn't have any binoculars and was reading a newspaper – but he looked the happiest by far. 'I'm just pleased to have been invited!' he told me, before asking for help with his crossword: 'OK, four down, three words, four, six, and nine letters – invisible mythical bird!'

'It's only two words, you moron,' came the not quite so playful reply. 'Long-billed has a hyphen.'

I decided not to reveal that I was also a novice birdwatcher. Instead, I joined in their nervy vigil, doing my best to work out in my head what the numerous other birds on the marshes were while we waited for the dowitcher to show its long-billed face. No one was commenting on anything that wasn't the dowitcher, so it was a good chance for me to practise my skills. I surprised myself with how many species I could recognise, almost instantly scribbling redshank, little egret, cormorant, green sandpiper, wood sandpiper, lapwing, avocet, godwit, little grebe and pochard down in my note-book. The man next to me asked me what I'd just seen. When I read him my list of admittedly common birds, he looked at me with an expression midway between disappointment and disgust.

Ten minutes later he became mildly animated when he saw a ruff. I hadn't seen a ruff yet, and had to contain my almost all-consuming excitement.

'Where?' I asked at once.

'Oh, it's out there on the flood just by the teal,' he replied begrudgingly. I couldn't remember which ones were teals and was afraid to ask. My pride got the better of me. I'd just about been accepted as a birder.

I pretended I'd seen the ruff.

Half an hour later I left the Northampton men to it. I'd not seen the ruff, the jack snipe or the dowitcher and I wouldn't for the rest of the afternoon.

Back home after the gig I had a look on Birdguides and saw that for the first time in three weeks the dowitcher hadn't been spotted all day. Those men from Northampton couldn't have been happy (although while I was with them, they did seem to revel in their grumpiness – a typical British male trait, I suppose).

I looked up the ruff too, to see what I'd missed. I wasn't happy either. Ruffs are amazing-looking birds, with a ridiculous Elizabethan-style collar that gives them their name. The males in particular looked fantastically ridiculous, and I was gutted. I love ridiculous birds. I might even be more of a ridiculous man than a bill man. Next time, I told myself, just ask the other men. I was still far from impressed with myself.

31 October

The chance for redemption cropped up the following Tuesday in the unlikely guise of a gig at the University of East Anglia.

Minsmere, one of Duncton's favourite haunts (and where he once just missed that Oddie) lies just forty miles south of the students' union. In fact Duncton himself had popped in the day before on his way home from Granny to see his first common scoters[140] and 'some cracking views of a kingfisher from the Bittern Hide' (his words). So, hoping to find Duncton's footprints as well as at least one or two new species, I aimed to get there at lunchtime

I missed. My life got in the way at home – a lightbulb needed changing, some dishes needed washing, quite a lot of jokes needed writing – so I didn't even leave the house till after lunch. If only I could retire now too. Unfortunately, the clocks had changed that weekend so by the time I reached the Suffolk coast, it was 3.30 p.m. and daylight was already fading. Just before I got out of the car rain began to fall, and it didn't stop falling till night had also fallen and I'd got back into my car.

But it wasn't a completely wasted trip. Duncton's trail may have been washed away and I only had an hour to wander round what was clearly a magnificent reserve, but considering the rain, that was just about enough. I didn't ever find the 'Bittern Hide' he'd mentioned, let alone common scoters or kingfishers, but I did recognise curlews, avocets and, to my surprise, a marsh harrier. These birds of prey had only ever been pointed out to me by proper birdwatchers before. This time I noticed the large body, narrow wings, long tail and black wing tips and instantly thought *marsh harrier!* I was impressed with myself.

Despite this achievement, I hadn't seen a single new bird all month. I'd started the month in the lead for the first time, I'd ended it with zero points for the first time. Our monthly phone call would not have made exciting listening:

'Well I didn't see anything new this month,' I said.

---

140 Not, as I first thought he'd said, scooters, 'scoters' are in fact stocky black sea ducks. Without a telescope, they look like debris.

'Ah,' said Duncton. 'Well I got those scoters and a red-breasted merganser at Farlington.'

I noted down his two new birds, relieved that he hadn't taken much advantage of my laziness.

'By the way,' he then said, 'Mum and I are thinking of going out to see Mat too.'

'I know, Duncton, Mum told me. It's mid-January you're heading off, isn't it?'

'Well, that's the thing. I've booked the tickets today. We'll be landing on 30 December – so we'll be there for New Year's Eve which should be fun . . .'

You'll be out there in time for our Big Year, you mean! I thought.

This was disastrous. All that stuff about Duncton birdwatching with honour went right out the window. Duncton wasn't 'plugging away at his local patch' – he was hanging about, waiting for his own trip to Africa! He claimed they were leaving earlier to spend as much time as possible with the eldest son they hadn't seen all year, but I knew it was really only so he could crush his middle son's dreams! At least, that's what I told myself when I started to plot my final two months.

I won't let my dreams be crushed by Duncton. I'll make them shatterproof. I may have failed to see anything new in Suffolk and Kent, but I had spotted the potential. There were loads of birds out there I still hadn't found. I just needed to get one of my birding friends to help me. I got straight on the phone and dialled David's number.

I'll be so far ahead by 30 December I'll already be in next year, I thought.[141]

---

141 I wasn't sure if that made sense. Or, if it did make sense, whether it would be useful to already be in next year. It sounded good though.

CHAPTER 11

Lucky Dip

'It may sound arrogant, but I usually find it inexcusable to miss a bird as I always plan thoroughly, concentrate fully and apply myself completely to the job in hand. How then can I possibly fail? Well, like everyone else, I sometimes do.'

– Adrian M Riley

Alex: 254 species
Duncton: 211 species

7 November

David appreciated the urgency of my situation. When I told him the dastardly Duncton had arranged a last minute dash to Africa he cleared his diary for the following Saturday and started planning our own intensive tour. In the meantime, he stressed that I should be checking my birding websites every other minute for anything that might aid my cause. I was already on the case, but most of the reports coming in were of birds I'd already seen – little stints, a hen harrier, even a puffin at Reculver in Kent – and that I couldn't afford to chase up. But then, one morning at 10.38 a.m. my Batlaptop started flashing:

> London Birders' forum: There has been no mention on this forum yet of a report of a Pallas's warbler yesterday (Monday 6 Nov) in Chiswick. For those who haven't heard but might want to look for the bird, Rare Bird Alert last night reported that it was 'in Hadley Gardens in east side of road in garden near bend briefly at 2.45 p.m.' It's a major London bird, so certainly worth checking out if anyone has the time . . .

I always had time for a major London bird, so dropped everything[142] and sped down to Hadley Gardens. I didn't even waste valuable seconds looking up what this major bird looked like, presuming it was pretty similar to all the other tiny warbling types I'd struggled with all year.

I didn't have a compass and am not a natural orienteer, so when I arrived in Chiswick I couldn't be sure which was the east side of the road and had to peer into every garden along either side of the bend in the road. This was a delicate operation. I didn't want people to notice me peering, but if they did notice

---

142 Just a pen, luckily.

me peering, I didn't want them to think I was peering suspiciously, like a thief. I wanted people to think, that's fine, he's looking for a Pallas's warbler, not checking out our house for burglary potential. I pretended to be having a difficult phone conversation that involved me wheeling around as if in despair, then staring into someone's garden as if in deep concentration. This was fine for one brief recce, but could I do it again without arousing suspicion?

I didn't think so. I pretended to hang up the phone (an easy piece of acting but I think I carried it off well) and walked back to my car, allowing myself just one glance per garden on the way. Needless to say, I didn't see the bird. I did spot a couple of blackbirds and a robin but nothing I didn't recognise (that was my cunning plan for recognising the warbler – by not being able to recognise it). Only one person looked at me suspiciously from their window.

Back at home I got straight on to my Batlaptop and inputted my own bird data for the very first time:

No sign of the Pallas's Warbler between 12 noon and 1 p.m. today. Couldn't stay any longer unfortunately – and no sign of other birders either . . . Alex

Mission sort of accomplished. I hadn't seen the bird but I had contributed to the London birding scene. As Duncton had told me about his butterfly eggs: 'It's sometimes just as useful to not find something.'

I had definitely not seen the Pallas's warbler. I had helped.

11 November

Inspired once more by David, I cleared my whole Saturday for our big bird trip, our last scheduled outing together of the year.

Barely even registering the early hour, I picked him up at 6 a.m. so that we might arrive at our first destination before dawn. I didn't have a gig that evening, so every possible minute would be spent looking for birds. This was a massive deal for me. But for David – and thousands of other dedicated birders – this was just a normal day out.

Like a scout master or a commando (let's go with commando) David had meticulously mapped a route that would maximise my bird-gap-plugging potential.

'You haven't got fieldfare yet?' he'd asked me.

'No,' I'd replied, 'I haven't got fieldfare yet.'

'And you never saw a willow warbler?'

'I know,' I said, 'we've got work to do.'

We watched the sun rise at Cliffe, the same spot in Kent where we'd seen blackcaps and whitethroats back in May. This time we were here specifically to see the little auk that was apparently lingering. I was excited about this bird. One of my good but annoyingly musical friends' surname is Auckland. Our family call their family the Auks. I was looking forward to seeing a little Auk.

We had to walk for a good half hour to find the right spot but David set an impressive pace and we overtook several less pacy birders on the way. This was how it would be today. No messing about. When we found the right bit of the right estuary David silently scanned the water, wielding his telescope like a periscope. After a couple of sweeps he stopped and zoomed in. 'Got it,' he said, 'one little auk for you.' I could only really see its back but that was enough: stocky, cuddly, cool, sometimes noisy – this was definitely an auk.

David didn't tell me till later that this was actually his first ever little auk too. He was thrilled. I was thrilled for him. It was my first ever little auk, but that wasn't quite as significant. And this was a special bird, particularly here in Kent. They're usually found in places like Greenland, and were featured the week before on the BBC's triumphant *Planet Earth* series as being the most numerous species of bird in the Arctic, and here was one having a bath in a lake just forty miles from my house. Often described as the 'penguins of the northern hemisphere', they are charismatic birds. Dressed like puffins but without the ridiculous beak, they strike just the right balance between formal and relaxed. Smart casual, I think, is the term.

After a few minutes' appreciation we moved on. There was no point hanging around – we'd got our first bird, now we wanted more. The next stop was Oare Marshes, scene of my cowardly long-billed dowitcher failure two weeks before. That time I'd been too scared to ask the big boys for help. This time, I was being chaperoned by a rock star (well, former musician, but rock star made me feel pretty bloody cool) and my confidence was restored.

He found the dowitcher immediately, shuffling around only thirty feet from where we'd parked. To me it looked exactly like a snipe.

'No, it's the dowitcher,' said David. 'It's much more slender. It's more like a godwit than a snipe. Of course, it sounds like a cross between a wood sandpiper and an oystercatcher . . .'

'Fine,' I said, 'I believe you. It's a dowitcher.'

There were more birds here than at Cliffe, so David quickly scanned the area, a bit like the Terminator. I tried to copy his actions, but couldn't really pull it off.

'Bar-tailed godwit on the right,' he said, 'have you got that?'

'I didn't,' I replied, 'but I do now.'

'And there's a ruff just behind that, there, see it?'

'A ruff?' I shouted. I was still excited by the picture of the ruff I'd seen in my book.

'Yes, a ruff, right in line with the lifebuoy.'

I looked for several minutes at anything right in line or even nearly right in line with the lifebuoy. I couldn't see anything that resembled my ruff.

'Come on Alex,' said David, not exasperated but nearly. 'It's got a medium bill, plain chest, long quite yellow legs . . .'

'. . . and an enormous Elizabethan-style collar round its neck, I know.'

'Ah,' said David. 'No, I'm afraid you don't know. They do have spectacular plumage during the breeding season, but normally they're just like that bird there.'

I found the ruff and was grateful but disappointed. I'd really wanted to see a bird with an enormous Elizabethan-style collar. But at least I now had a reason to carry on birding until the following breeding season at least.

Stopping only to scoff our homemade sandwiches (no dithering in service stations for us) we raced over to Ferry Lane for another couple of species: rock pipit and water pipit. Pipits look as their name suggests, small and inoffensive. They didn't do much for me, I preferred the little auk, but already I'd seen more new birds in one day than Duncton had in the last four months. What had he been playing at?

David allowed us a strictly limited amount of time to check out each location. We were disciplined, nipping into the Isle of Sheppey to grab a couple of partridges (a grey partridge and one that looked as absurd as our blue-helmeted guineafowl called a red-legged partridge – highly recommended) and a golden plover, then nipping straight out again. I didn't even have time to make my golden plover/yellow jumper joke.

Time was running out. It does that when you're having fun, apparently, so we must therefore, have been having fun. But it also waits for no man and is of the essence – time represents fun[143] but you can't waste it – so we raced down to Elmley Marshes

---

143 And money, and if you put a stitch in it you'll save nine, and its daughter is truth. It also heals *and* takes its toll. But let's not waste too much more of it worrying about all that now.

(previous home of my osprey) for a final march round as dusk settled over Kent. For the first time that day, we found nothing. David had been hoping for a merlin but was denied it and we never found the fieldfares.

But then, on the final stretch before the carpark, a ghost-like vision flapped out right in front of us. 'Shh . . .' said David.

'I wasn't saying anything,' I replied.

'Well shh now then . . . there! Barn owl!'

He was right of course. Not far away, sitting calmly on a fence post was a softly glowing barn owl. It looked fuzzy but fantastic through the binoculars, its big white face beaming out like the moon. 'They really are so wise,' I said, a touch emotional after a whole day's birdwatching. It had been an enjoyable and highly successful day and I was content.

'Well, no, they're not really,' said David dispassionately. 'In terms of the size of their brain they're one of the least intelligent birds around. The trouble is that a third of their head is made up by their eyes. Even a pigeon is cleverer than an owl.'

'Right,' I said, 'but they can swivel their heads all the way round though, can't they?'

'Not all the way, no.'

'But they can swivel them a bit? Their heads are quite swivelly?'

'They are quite swivelly yes, Alex. Let's go home.'

I'm not sure I would have coped if my two owl facts had been dashed at once. Even in my desolate non-birdwatching days I'd been fond of owls, mainly because of their swivelly heads. I liked to imagine the head would be useful for an owl family going off on holiday in their car. The younger owls would be quarrelling in the back, much like Mat, Chip and I may occasionally have done. The owl parents could just swivel their heads round and tell them to shut up. Mum and Duncton would have loved that. Of course, having a younger brother with a swivelly head may have been too much of a temptation for Mat and me. We may well have spent the whole journey testing out the swivel limits of Chip's head, which would have resulted in car sickness. But then again, he would have been an owl, so I presume he'd only have puked up a pellet – easy to clean up.[144]

We saw ten new birds in eleven hours that day, not a great hourly rate but an impressive and invaluable total at this late stage of the game. When I finally got home I drank too much red wine and fell asleep in a chair.

16 November

That, I thought, was my final outing with David for the year. With two kids, his weekends were precious. There were now only six weekends left, including the run up to Christmas, and David would have to spend more time with them than me. I still believed that being able to birdwatch helped you be a good dad, but I also saw that being a good dad did not help you to be able to birdwatch.

But while we were scampering around Kent something amazing had happened down in Devon, something huge, something historic, something that would make headlines around the world – well, around the birding world anyway.

Just before falling unconscious in the sitting room I'd received a text from Tim, my friend and brand new bird enthusiast:

Horne! Was watching the news. Apparently there's a rare merlot about. Thought you should know. Tim.

This meant nothing to me. I'm happy with this cheap shiraz, I thought, and poured myself another glass.

---

144 When I was little, Mat told me owls make that 'twit twoo' noise because sometimes they pick up mice that are too hot. 'Hooo!' they cry. 'Hot! Hot! Hot!' I believed him for ages. Brothers can be bad.

What Tim actually meant to write was 'murrelet', a word of which neither he, nor I, nor predictive texting, had ever heard. A 'long-billed murrelet' to be precise; a Japanese bird that had somehow found its way to Dawlish in Devon. My Batlaptop was buzzing with talk of the bird the following morning. Unfortunately my head was also buzzing with a hangover and I couldn't leave my sitting room. Instead I read as much as I could bear about the murrelet.

It was really rare. Really rare. 'Best bird this decade,' wrote one frantic birder. 'Once in a lifetime stuff,' wrote another. I looked up murrelet in the back of my still shiny new *Collins Bird Guide*. I found 'ancient murrelet' in a section entitled 'accidentals': birds that 'have been recorded only once or twice'. The page included species like a wandering albatross that turned up in Belgium in 1833, some ostriches that ambled into Israel in the 1920s and a masked booby that turned up in Spain in the winter of 1985. But there was no 'long-billed murrelet', because no long-billed murrelet had ever been seen anywhere in the Western Palaearctic before. This was special.

Just how bad is my hangover? I thought, gradually registering the significance of the bird. I tried to get up, felt dizzy and sat down again – there was no way I could drive to Devon, even for a bird that would require a reprint of my guide. Unable to make the trip, I tried to find a picture of the bird in places other than my now out-of-date new guide. Luckily, Rachel's Sunday paper had a couple of amateurish but passable photos of it swimming around happily just off the shingly beach. It looked quite like the little auk David and I had just seen – indeed at first that's what people had thought it was. It was only when pictures were posted on the internet that some more eagle-eyed members of the BirdForum.net website realised it might be something far rarer.

*

The next morning I was fully recovered and raring to go. I checked Birdguides. The bird was still in Dawlish, but I had to be in Lincoln for a gig by 7 p.m. that night. Lincoln is three hours away from Kensal Green but four hours away from Dawlish which was five hours away from London. That's not the easiest way of saying it was possible. But it was. Just. I decided to risk it.

Forty-five minutes later I'd only travelled three miles from my house. Monday morning traffic is never good, but today the roads were even busier than usual. They're all off to Devon to spy on our Japanese visitor, I decided. Lucky them. I wouldn't be joining them today.

I turned back, feeling dejected and foolish, a bit like how I feel when Liverpool are knocked out of some cup competition. I shouldn't have got my hopes up, but up they were, and now I'd missed my opportunity. I had to spend the next two days doing gigs even further north than Lincoln, staying in a couple of disappointing hotels en route, so the earliest I could possibly make it down to Dawlish was Thursday. Surely this would be too late. I did contemplate cancelling the shows, but then I thought about Rachel and what my real job was, and knew I had to go to work. I clearly wasn't a bona fide twitcher yet.

Before abandoning hope entirely, however, I did leave a message with David to see if he was planning a visit. 'Would love to get down there,' he wrote back, 'but don't have a car. Think I'm going to have to miss it.' I told him I was planning to go down on Thursday if the bird was still around and if he fancied a lift he'd be more than welcome. 'I'll be there. You're a star,' he wrote back immediately. David's not a twitcher either, he's a proper birder, but this bird really was very rare. Even Duncton briefly contemplated making the pilgrimage, before deciding he couldn't miss his RSPB duties.

On Tuesday the murrelet was still floating around just off the Devon coast, 6,000 miles from home. More than 2,000 bird-watchers had descended on Dawlish and the newspapers were full of articles describing the amazing sight (the birders, now, not the bird). This sort of thing is easy fodder for journalists. Just a headline like 'The twitchers have landed!' will make most readers shake their head and tut in knowing disbelief. Occasionally this incredulity turns to disapproval, when a paper like the *Daily Mail* self-righteously describes a gang of twitchers harassing a rare bird in the same outraged language they use to moan about happy-slapping hoodies:

'For two days, they pursued the rose-coloured starling from garden to garden hoping to take photographs for their collection,' an article read back in September, 'and eventually they chased it to its death. After repeated attempts to evade the camera-wielding throng, it was left so exhausted that it was unable to fly away before a cat called Mittens pounced on it.'

After eleven months of birdwatching I had mixed feelings about twitching. The act of driving (or flying) thousands of miles to see every single rare bird that alights on these islands is clearly not an environmentally sound one. At a time when climate change is such an enormous issue it seems odd that bird lovers might behave so rashly.[145] That is, perhaps, the heart of the issue – are these people bird lovers? Or are they only interested in adding another tick to their tally? I have to side with the twitchers here. Almost all, I'm sure, are genuinely fascinated by birds. They might be too fascinated perhaps, too keen to drop everything and see a rare species at all costs, but I believe that for most the interests of the birds do indeed come

---

145 I don't want to sound too hypocritical here. With trips to Istanbul, Bahrain and South Africa under my environmentally unsound belt, I know I've not been particularly eco-conscious recently. And I know that my behaviour was certainly twitcher-ish.

first. That poor rose-coloured starling was eaten by Mittens, not Twitchers.

It's too easy to tar all birdwatchers with one faintly patronising brush. There are, undoubtedly, some bad egg(collector)s, but the majority are peaceful, nature-loving, interested, interesting people. And I could understand why many people – who wouldn't dream of calling themselves twitchers – would want to pay homage to something like the murrelet, the birding equivalent of Halley's Comet, an audience with the Pope or an England World Cup win.

So, from a computer in my hotel on Wednesday I checked Birdguides once more with bated breath. I wanted to see the bird. I wanted to see the flock of birders too, but I'd become caught up with the story. I wanted to pay my respects to the long-billed murrelet. Logging on to the website, I was as tense as when I find out a big football score. Unfortunately, on this occasion I'd failed, Liverpool had lost, the bird had disappeared. 'No sign at 6 a.m. or 8 a.m. Weather worsening.' read the message.

But then again, if it was a little stormy, the bird may have headed further out to sea. 'It could well be back this evening,' said David. 'I think we should go.' Who was I to let him down?

I was on stage first at my gig that night and managed to get home at a reasonable hour, which was lucky because I'd invited David to spend the night at our house. You get a lot of time to chat when you're birdwatching for eleven hours at a time and we were getting on well, so I didn't think it was too weird to offer him a bed. But I also didn't want Rachel to spend too long alone at home with a strange birdwatcher I'd met on the internet.

Thankfully I arrived at Kensal Green about half an hour before David, and the two of us retreated to a pub for a drink before grabbing a few hours' sleep. Over our pints, getting up at 4 a.m.

to drive the 207 miles to Dawlish seemed reasonable, sensible even. 'We'll keep an eye on the bird texts,' said David, 'and if it's not around I know a couple of other places we can nip into for a few of the seabirds you haven't got yet.' How is that not a rational thing to do?

But at 8.30 a.m., when we parked the car at Budleigh Salterton in Devon after four straight hours of sleepy driving, part of me did wish I was still in bed. And that part of me was much bigger than the part of me that was happy to be there. My eyes definitely wanted to be in bed, they were sore. My limbs were tired too. I think maybe only my nose and my ears were glad they were here: the birds were singing and I could smell the sea. Apart from that, everything about my bed was better than this.

David was feeling fine. 'If you have a baby,' he told me, 'you'll get used to no sleep.' I tried to pull myself together, the words 'if you have a baby' reminding me why I had started this bird-watching challenge in the first place. That's right, I thought, I need to get used to this. So, trying desperately to get used to total exhaustion, I walked like a zombie behind David as he headed off on a path by some fields, to where he'd heard a cattle egret was lurking.

'So these cattle egrets,' I asked wearily, 'are they called that for the same reason bullfinches are called bullfinches? Are they like normal egrets but with massively wide necks?'

'No,' said David. 'They hang around with cattle. That's it really.'

'OK. So if you see a cattle egret you're bound to find cattle.'

'That's right.'

'And if we find cattle we're bound to see a cattle egret.'

'That's not right.'

My brain wasn't really working yet. We passed a lot of cows but didn't find any egrets. I started singing 'No (R)egrets' by Robbie Williams. I think David may have been regretting ever replying to my email. But eventually he did find the bird, skulking, as he'd promised, amongst a herd of cows looking like they'd also rather be asleep.[146]

On the way back to the car we found a water rail too, another rarish bird that was doing exactly what the bird guide said it would: 'scurrying across a muddy gap in reeds'. The book went on to describe its voice in typically colourful language: 'rich repertoire: a discontented piglet-like squeal, soon dying away, "grüiit grroit grui gru"; a weary, "all-in", choking moan, "ooouuuh"; short "kip" notes when disturbed'. Our one, however, was clearly shy, and scampered off without even a whimper.

The various birdlines were just as silent. There was still no sign of the murrelet. We tried not to contemplate what was looking like a fact: that the rarest bird of our lives may have already packed its bags and headed home. David gritted his teeth and I drove to Dawlish in what I hoped was an optimistic fashion. Perhaps we'd be the ones to find the bird. Now that would be something.

As we drove through Dawlish town centre, I pointed out the black swan still minding its own business on the pond. 'There's a black swan,' I said.

'Yes,' said David, 'that's an Australian import. It's come further than the murrelet but not all by itself. That won't count for your list.'

I later checked in my bird guide, and he was right, of course, so I now had to cross one species off my total. I'd driven to Devon to lose a species. Black swans were in yet another section

---

146 A cattle egret hanging out with cows doesn't sound nearly as exciting as a fork-tailed drongo daringly riding a rhino but it's basically the same thing. Birds often thrive in this sort of symbiotic relationship, and many of these relationships actually involve us. Those gulls chasing tractors, the robin in your garden or my pigeon catching the tube, they're all using humans to help themselves. And by enjoying birdwatching, we can get something out of it too.

at the back of the book entitled 'introduced breeding species and species recorded only as escapes' – 'rule-breakers', in other words, 'rogues'. According to this illicit list, I might also see a California quail, a northern bobwhite or an Indian silverbill wandering round Europe but not one of them would be an acceptable tick. [147]

The rest of Dawlish was deserted. The place we'd seen crammed full of birdwatchers in the newspapers and on TV over the last few days was barren. We needed breakfast badly so went into Geronimo, a bizarrely themed café by the station, for a bacon sandwich. The waitress took one look at us and asked if 'the little bird' was here again.

'No,' said David despondently.

'That's disappointing,' said the lady, summing the situation up brilliantly. 'I had the café shut all week and was hoping to cash in on the extra trade . . .'

Unbelievably, when this small town had been flooded by unprecedented numbers of hungry birdwatchers, she'd decided not to open her café! This made me feel a tiny bit better. We weren't the only ones who'd missed out. And anyway, I was quite pleased she'd picked me as a birdwatcher. I was, admittedly, wearing my binoculars, but this was one of the first times anyone had assumed I was part of that gang – even if, on this occasion, we were a slight and unhappy gang, sitting quietly at a small table amongst rather a lot of American Indian paraphernalia, munching on bacon sandwiches when we really wanted to be watching a long-billed murrelet.

Feeling slightly better after what was a really rather delicious bap, we made our way down to Dawlish Warren and the location of the murrelet's last appearance. We tiptoed up to the

---

147 Although to my mind, these uncountable 'escapes' are actually the wildest birds you can get. They've escaped! And now they're roaming free! That's wild!

exact spot like mourning relatives arriving at the scene of a crash. 'So this is where it all happened,' sighed David.

'I guess so,' I sighed back. We both sighed again.

Slowly raising our binoculars, we looked out to sea. I wasn't optimistic. If it was here, surely someone would have sent out the alert. But then again, we were the only ones here. Perhaps it was here! Perhaps we had done the right thing! Perhaps we were the only ones doing the right thing, the only ones keeping the torch burning for the poor weary traveller?

Or perhaps not. We stood and stared for ninety minutes without success. That's a long time to stand and stare at something without success. Well, it's the same length of time as a football match. So, it was like watching a football match but with no football or football players or other football supporters. It was a bit eerie.

'Let's try the hide,' suggested David.

'Yes, let's,' I agreed. I'd wanted to suggest this myself for the last eighty-five minutes but didn't want to say something inappropriate at a very sensitive time. This was the same hide I'd spied but missed out on with Jamie, Janet and Key at the start of the year, back when I'd only seen fifty species and had never heard of a murrelet. It felt good to finally complete that journey.

The view through the wooden window back over the bay gave us something else to think about for a while. David tested me on various waders; I made plenty of mistakes but did get grey plover, ringed plover and curlew right first time. David was very nearly impressed and rewarded me with three more new species for my list: stonechat,[148] red-breasted merganser[149] and, at last, some Brent geese. I'd been too early to see them

---

148 A name that sounds like what Duncton often had with my grandfather.

149 A name that sounds like a futuristic sports car for the *Nuts* generation.

over in Dublin back in late September but they'd finally caught up with me.

'The Brent boys back together,' I murmured.

'Sorry?' said David.

'The Brent boys – me from Kensal Green in Brent, them, the Brent geese – we're back together!' I explained, wishing I'd never murmured 'the Brent boys back together' at all.

'Oh,' said David. This probably wasn't my best bit of hide banter that year.

We noticed a few more people gathering on the beach, so hauled ourselves off our bench and headed over, hoping a home-coming murrelet had attracted the crowd.

There was no murrelet. There was only a group of birders who, like us, had only just been able to find the time to get off work, drive the many miles down to Devon, and were now putting a brave face on their tired heads. David got talking to a bloke who'd driven all the way along the coast from Brighton and I managed to chip in with some stuff about the starlings. It felt good to be able to talk to a stranger in a reasonably informed way about something that wasn't the weather or football. But then he pointed out a great northern diver way out in the distance, another first for me, my fifth new species of the day (fourth if we're subtracting the black swan).

'Great northern diver?' I said. 'Sounds a bit like a certain Cristiano Ronaldo to me.'

I winked, trying to rescue a poor joke with a subtle reference to the World Cup.

'He's great, yes,' said the Brighton man, 'but he's no diver. That was a foul, I'm afraid. And Portugal were the better team . . .'

He was a Man Utd fan. Typical.

At 2.30 p.m. I was forced to concede. I had another gig that night in Edmonton, North London, and would have to wend my way through the capital's traffic at rush hour to get there. I could tell David wanted to stay longer, but I had to put my foot down.[150] We sped back to London in silence, David asleep, me in a bit of a daze. Should I bring this up at the gig? No, I decided, they wouldn't understand. I didn't understand.

The only real consolation was that the murrelet didn't turn up a couple of hours after we'd left. I was dreading a text saying the bird had miraculously reappeared, and having to decide whether to miss the gig or deny David his golden opportunity. But the murrelet didn't turn up again, not that evening, that week, that year or at any time since. We'd missed our chance. We'd dipped the bird of the century.

17 November

I woke late the next day feeling surprisingly satisfied. Partly I felt smug because it was 10 a.m., I'd had a decent night's sleep and I didn't have to drive to Devon and back or stand on a beach and stare at the sea all day. But mostly my satisfaction was of a deep-seated sort. I was glad we'd given it a shot yesterday, I was glad we'd sacrificed a day of our lives to try to see this bird. We hadn't found it, but it'd been worth the effort.

At the gig in Edmonton I did end up telling the story, in great and probably quite dull detail. I don't think you can really get up at 4 a.m. and spend the whole day doing something like that and then not mention it if you have to stand on stage and talk for thirty minutes the same evening. The audience found the ludicrousness of the jaunt amusing if a little odd; it was, to them, a wacky adventure, funny because of its pointlessness. But that wasn't what I felt. I'd loved our road trip. It was a day David and I will always remember, long-billed murrelet or not. Actually seeing the bird, for me anyway, wouldn't have made

---

150 Yes, in both senses, thank you and well done.

the day that much better. We could always talk about it as 'the one that got away' and that's got to be part of the fun of hobbies. If Liverpool won the Champions League every year, it would (eventually) get boring. The losses make the victories even more enjoyable (perhaps that's why people say it's so good to support a lesser team like Tottenham) and like football seasons, there will always be more rare birds. Maybe there won't ever be another murrelet in the UK but that's fine too, that makes it a better story. I was proud to think we'd done our best.

Twenty years ago in Sevenoaks, I found that piece of Roman pottery, but I felt empty. This time I felt fulfilled. What I didn't mention before, and what I have never dared mention to anyone *ever* before, was that I didn't actually find that piece of Roman pottery in the field. I'd found it on the shelf in the porch by the door to Granny and Grandpa's house. I'd seen it when I was going to put on my coat, I'd picked it up and before I'd thought about what I was doing, we were walking out the door and it was tucked away in my pocket. Impulsively, I'd nicked it.

As we strolled towards the hills I did have time to think. I can't write this off as a moment of madness. I could have smuggled it back to the house and returned it to its rightful shelf, but instead I hatched a plan to pretend I had found it in a field. I wanted people to think I'd uncovered it. I wanted the glory of its discovery. I wanted the attention.

Or so I thought – I was only eight years old, after all. As soon as I got that attention I felt awful. I felt bad at having lied, I felt bad that my lie might be exposed and I felt bad about how nice people were being. Grandpa must have known the piece of pottery had come from his shelf – he'd found it in the first place, I guess – but he let me tell my story. I'm not quite sure why, but he supported me. I've tried to understand what he was thinking (if I'm contemplating fatherhood I might as well look at grandfatherhood too). Perhaps he didn't have the heart to embarrass his grandson with the truth. Perhaps he thought that I would own up myself. Or perhaps he knew that by letting me have my moment, the undeserved attention and unmerited congratulations would become so unbearable I'd learn my lesson the hard way over the next twenty years. Probably he was just being a good grandfather. I was only eight years old after all.

Birdwatching relies on people telling the truth. Unlike fishing, you don't have to produce evidence, you just have to be credible. If you say you saw a rare bird, your story has to add up. The Rare Men have to believe you. If people think you are lying, your birdwatching career will be forever blighted. As Mark Cocker said about 'stringing': 'We don't tolerate it.'

Unfortunately, by this stage of Adrian Riley's far more competitive Big Year, accusations of deception had started to spoil his fun:

Lee (G R Evans) . . . had disqualified me from his tabulations [sic] for, '. . . persistently fabricating sightings from Shetland to Devon,' . . . Of course, I was furious but, at the same time, was strangely relieved. I no longer had to take Lee seriously, as he was satisfyingly in danger of hoisting himself by his own petard by repeating his risible attempts at publicly discrediting his opponents.

Birdwatching can be an emotive hobby. I was happy to admit that I hadn't seen the murrelet, but I'd also insisted I'd seen that lesser spotted woodpecker. Twenty years on from my Big Lie, was I still a stringer?

I don't think so. I think you have to be a proper birdwatcher before you can be a stringer. And anyway, as Duncton taught me as we strolled through those severals down at Pagham in April, there's a big difference between lying and bluffing. Dads must be able to bluff.

25 November

I decided to make another pilgrimage. Without telling my wife or my parents, I used the pretext of a gig in Farnham to make my second ever visit to the Haslemere Museum. I would only be ten miles from Midhurst, but I didn't call Mum or Duncton. I had to see if this time I could find the Roman pottery all by myself.

Once again, the place looked far smaller than I remembered. I think I've now revisited pretty much every significant place from my childhood, so I should soon be over this size fixation.

It was Saturday afternoon and the museum was buzzing. Well, there were quite a few white-haired visitors and there was definitely some noise – more of a mellow murmur than a buzz, but there was something. It's an independent museum, free to wander round and a proud example of British heritage. I promised myself I'd make a donation on my way out.

I asked the wise-looking volunteer on reception where I might find the Roman pottery. 'Very good,' he said, sounding as wise as he looked. 'We don't have an awful lot of Roman pottery on display, but what little we do have is up in the history gallery. If you go up those stairs, past the geology section then through the natural history section, you should find it.' I thanked him and hurried off, feeling, yet again, like a child.

His instructions were spot-on. It's a small museum – more of a cottage than a stately home – but I appreciated his accuracy. At the top of the stairs I found myself surrounded by huge quartz crystals: amethyst, jasper and aventurine, and was immediately whisked back to those days at South Cottage in Kemsing. There were only a few geology exhibits, but the rocks found along the Weald and the Downs between Sussex and Kent were just the things that had captivated me as a child. A couple of large ammonite fossils reinforced these memories.

The geology and natural history sections blurred together.

Dinosaurs stood beside their reptilian descendants. A twelve-foot recreation of a giant moa – a huge flightless bird that wandered around New Zealand up to fifteen million years ago but became extinct in the 1500s – looked down on a stuffed kiwi. I looked down at the kiwi too and remembered seeing one myself somewhere long ago. Suddenly I was back in 1988, on the holiday of our childhoods, when Duncton took four weeks off work, grew his beard and the Horne family trundled around New Zealand in a campervan.

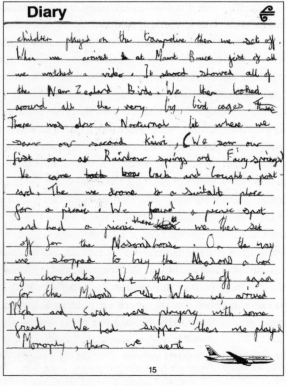

Diary

children played on the trampoline then we set off. When we arrived at Mount Bruce first of all we watched a video. It showed showed all of the New Zealand Birds. We then looked around all the very big bird cages. Then There was a Nocturnal lot where we saw our second kiwi, (We saw our first one at Rainbow springs and Fairy springs) We came both home back and bought a post card. The we drove to a suitable place for a picnic. We found a picnic spot and had a picnic then we then set off for the Masons house. On the way we stopped to buy the Masons a box of chocolates. We then set off again for the Masons house. When we arrived Nick and Sarah were playing with some friends. We had supper then we played Monopoly, then we went

15

New Zealand April 1988.

The natural history section was comprised almost entirely of stuffed animals, mostly Edwardian examples, a few Victorian, preserved by the most famous taxidermists of the time. This was an eerie throwback to the early days of birdwatching, when nearly all research was carried out on recently shot birds. It was stranger than a zoo, odder, even, than Birdworld, but I did get my first ever close up view of a wheatear, a hobby, a cuckoo and a nightjar. The jay looked as beautiful as any bird I'd seen in South Africa, the goldcrest smaller and more fragile than any humming or sunbird. One box contained two great bustards, frozen in the throes of some threatening mating ritual, enormous old British birds with wingspans of up to two metres forty centimetres, interrupted for ever. Gilbert White used to see great bustards while birding in nearby Selborne but, like the moa, they became extinct (in Britain) through over-zealous hunting in the 1800s. But, according to the helpful and well laid-out information printed by the exhibit (probably produced by that man on reception), they were reintroduced to Wiltshire from the Transvolga region of southern Russia in 2004[151] and seem to be doing well. I made a mental note to pop over to the Salisbury Plains when I'm next in the area.

Ignoring the crocodiles, lions and tigers, just as I had in London Zoo and the Addo Elephant Park, I made my way to the history section. Having retraced my own few years I now paced back through the Victorian era, past Georgian furniture, Medieval hats, Norman swords, Viking coins, Saxon shoes, stopping in the small corner devoted to Roman Britain. I scanned the few cases quickly for the piece of pottery I'd held in my hand two decades previously. I could almost feel it, the smooth

---

151 Under EU legislation (Habitats Directive 1992) the UK is obliged to reintroduce species 'where it is considered feasible'. Who knew that? There must be some more fun animals we can get back . . . did we ever have elephants here? Llamas? Mammoths?

rim at the top, the crisp edges, its pleasing weight. But was I remembering the shard itself, or just a memory of that memory? Either way, there was nothing like it in the first display. Instead there were complete urns and perfectly preserved vases, all found in the Haslemere area and dating back to 43–410 AD.

I moved along. There was one more case. This had to be the one: 'Iron Age Britain – 700 BC–AD43'. Again, I skimmed over the exhibits quickly – coins, arrowheads and figurines. Then, next to a small bronze vessel found in Milford, Surrey, was a fairly unimpressive greyish brown piece of pottery without any explanatory notes. I couldn't take my eyes off it. It wasn't quite how I remembered 'my' piece; it was smaller for a start, less rounded and maybe even a different shape – but this could have been it. It did have a smooth rim at the top and crisp edges. As I stared at it, I remembered once more holding 'my' piece in my pocket, wrapped – I now recalled – in a handkerchief, possibly Duncton's, possibly Trader's. A vague memory of 'my' piece snapping in my care flitted briefly through my mind. Was that right? Had I broken Grandpa's pottery as well as stolen it? It was such a long time ago. I remembered Duncton telling me how he'd managed to snap one of Grandpa's magical stones. Had we both done the same naughty thing as children? Or was I just muddling my memories?

Eventually surfacing from my trance, I wrote down the catalogue number handwritten on a sticker on the shard. I'd never looked at anything for so long in a museum before. I felt a bit dizzy. Groggily retracing my steps, I wondered if I'd really found what I was looking for. Something wasn't quite right, and this time I wasn't going to kid myself and say this definitely was the one. I needed more proof. I didn't want to do another lesser spotted woodpecker.

Back at reception, I asked the wise man if it was possible to look up where an item had come from through its catalogue number. He said it was possible – they started keeping accurate records about twenty years ago – but he couldn't help. I'd have to call the Assistant Curator. But she was on holiday. She'd be back in a couple of weeks' time. I thanked the man, gave him my phone number, threw all my loose change (which unfortunately only amounted to about £1.50) in the donations bucket and headed off to Farnham.

Had I dipped for a second time in two weeks? Was I kidding myself again? Or had I found 'my' piece of Roman pottery once more? I wouldn't know till the Assistant Curator got back from wherever Assistant Curators go on holiday.

CHAPTER 12

Countdown

December 18th 2006   Holkham Nature Reserve

'F*** it! I can't be beaten now. If Lee claims he can get to Norfolk in time to see this bird, he truly is a hero and is welcome to it. I'm going to the pub.'

– Adrian M Riley

Alex: 260 species
Duncton: 214 species

6 December

I used to love Advent. I loved the teasing candles and calendars counting down, the volume of carols being turned tortuously up and the garish Christmas lights that suddenly appeared on neighbours' houses as if by tacky magic. It was these potentially vulgar elements that made this the best time of year. It was the build-up, the expectation, the anticipation that I liked best and, like everyone else, I was so wound up by Christmas Eve I would stay awake all night then be too tetchy to enjoy the big day itself.

As a comedian, I now dread Advent. In particular I dread the arrival of office parties into my workplace, and all the vulgar elements they bring. Managers of offices and comedy clubs think it's a good idea to hold Christmas parties at comedy nights, so every year groups of up to fifty people make their drunken way into clubs up and down the country, adorned with tinsel and baubles like slutty Christmas trees. They are all in a good mood. Christmas is coming, they'll have a couple of days off and an added excuse to get drunk. And, by all accounts, office parties are fun, if sordid affairs. I've never attended one as I mostly work by myself. Key and I once got drunk and watched *Takeshi's Castle* in mid-December, but that's about it. I've turned into Scrooge.

As soon as December arrives, so do the festive suits, herded into their seats by the office joker who has organised the event and who considers himself either a comedian or, perhaps worse, a comedy aficionado. They order too many drinks, the club owner rubs his hands together; everything looks rosy.

In the dressing room, at least two of the four comedians sit shaking their heads, knowing what's going to happen next, and swearing they won't allow themselves to be in the same situation next year. They can hear the noise levels increase out in the club, a member of staff tells them they're on in a couple of minutes. They don't feel nervous. They feel a grim acceptance of their grisly Christmas fate.

For, when the 'comedy' starts, these boisterous groups of Christmas revellers are suddenly told to shut up and listen. The fun and banter at the tables is interrupted and they're asked to turn and face the front, baubles and all, and concentrate on me.

For some comedians these conditions are perfect. A great compère can address pithy remarks to every group, insult one member and include the rest, harnessing their exuberance to create a genuine party atmosphere. But then I come on and ruin it with the jokes I've spent all year crafting. I don't like having to engage in conversation with the man at the front wearing Christmassy fake breasts, or listen to 'Jane from accounts' read out her Christmas cracker joke. I wrote my own. I'd prefer to tell them. Or even share a story about my birdwatching dad. But apparently they didn't come here for that. One or two of them did, maybe, but the rest are here for the drinks, the disco, the Christmas *craic*.

There is often a short stand-off. The quieter audience members try to listen, the louder elements start to chat. The quieter elements are too polite to tell the louder ones to shut up. I'm too polite too. And I can't be bothered. By now I'm just keen to take my 'double Christmas cash' and go home. When I get in, ignoring the garish decorations on the front of next door's house, I feel guilty. Next year, I think, it'll be different.

But this year I had a lot of Christmas gigs lined up, mostly in London, the office party capital of the world, and despite the welcome lack of travelling, they gradually sapped my energy and I limped towards Christmas and 2007.

David, my birdwatching crutch, pointed me in the direction of a couple more birds I might still find without leaving London with the following email:

There's a ring-billed gull on the Isle of Dogs at the moment. It tends to show best on a falling tide, when the mud gets exposed – you've probably done your research, but its favourite place is to the east of the slipway at the end of Glenaffric Road, normally with the assembled commoner gulls – chance of yellow-legged there too . . . it's a small example, so you should bone up on the ID features first – it basically looks like a Com Gull, but is lighter on the wings and mantle, with just a little bit of white on the 'tertial step' (sorry, techie talk!) . . . You could try for the monk parakeets at Mudchute City Farm, just around the corner (walk along the high grass causeway between the farm and Millwall Park), and there may be a black redstart at East India Dock bird sanctuary (they're regular there at this time of year) . . .

This is what birders call 'gen': information about the whereabouts of a particular bird. I still wasn't even nearly fluent in the lingo, but picked through it with the help of my bird guide and, for the first time in my life, checked the tides. In a post-Christmas-gig haze, I couldn't really believe what I was doing, but with the help of the tidal section of the *Birdwatcher's Yearbook* I managed to work out exactly when the moon would be pulling the seas back enough to expose the mud and, ideally, a gull with a stripy beak. Accomplishing this made me feel powerful again. I *was* in control.

Unfortunately, when I arrived at the end of Glenaffric Road, there were literally hundreds of the 'commoner gulls' David said would be 'assembled' there. I hadn't appreciated how big a gull assembly would be. A roll call would take hours. I didn't have hours. The tide, like time, waits for no man.

I'd done my best to 'bone up' on its 'ID features' but scanning the myriad seagulls, I couldn't confidently say if one was a bit lighter coloured, heavier bodied, or if its bill was thicker. I also couldn't even hope to see if its bill had a dash of black or if its irises were yellower than a common gull (a notable distinction apparently) because I didn't have the Hubble telescope with me. It was like playing a game of *Where's Wally* in which Wally was hiding out at a *Where's Wally* impersonator convention.[152] They all looked the same! Instead of throwing myself into the Thames (I would only have landed in the exposed mud anyway) I took David's next piece of unlikely advice and tried for the monk parakeets at Mudchute City Farm.

This species was much easier. I walked 'along the high grass causeway between the farm and Millwall Park' as instructed and almost bumped my head on an enormous nest hanging from one of the bare, wintry (non-Christmassy) trees. A couple of squawks later and a bright green bird plopped into the nest, clutching a massive branch in its parroty mouth. He stood out like Wally would have on that beach in Bahrain. I looked at him, he ignored me, and got down to a bit of weaving. He didn't look like a monk, he looked more like the ring-necked parakeets that have settled so well in London – in fact, these birds had also escaped from cages a generation or two ago and had established such a flourishing population that they were also now counted as a British bird. My list ticked over once again.

Not wanting to end my day with disappointment, I decided against looking for David's black redstart. The first bird he'd ever shown me was the common redstart at Walthamstow Reservoirs. Rather than floundering around misidentifying robins by myself, I quite wanted him to show me this one too.

---

152 Come to think of it, if you've been trying to construct a mental image of Duncton while reading about him, imagine an older version of Wally: an older version of Wally who decided to grow a beard in his early forties and is now approaching his sixties but is still as full of beans and enthusiasm as he always was. That's pretty much what Duncton looks like.

I cut my losses and headed home to lie down in a dark room before it was time to stand up in an even darker one.

10 December

I spent most of December cowering in my kitchen, trying to recover from whatever had happened the night before, unable to face the Christmas crowds that were now thronging on every London street.[153]

From my window, I watched my fat robin prepare himself for the winter and found solace. He was joined by the chaffinches, blue tits and great tits that were now so familiar to me, and even, one morning a coal tit. Once more I found myself staring at them instead of the football I'd sat down to watch. I realised that although I would always be a glory fan who revelled in trips to South Africa or Anfield, I could also enjoy the smaller spectacles. When I have kids, I decided, they'll support their local club. I assumed Rachel and I would move out of London when the time came, so I wasn't talking QPR or, dare I say it, Chelsea. I was thinking about the equivalent of my robin, a plucky side who my kids could cheer on. Maybe I'd get behind them too.

14 December

The Assistant Curator of Haslemere Museum called me back.

'I gather you were asking about a piece of Roman pottery?' she asked in a kindly, primary-teacherish sort of way. I told her my story (missing out the bit about me stealing from my grandfather). She said she'd do her best to help and would be back in touch soon.

---

153 And, I should say, just avoiding the 'Kensal Green Tornado' that struck just two streets away from ours on 7 December.

15 December

The Assistant Curator of Haslemere Museum called me back
again. She was so kindly.

'Hello Alex,' she said.

'Hello,' I said. I didn't know her name.

'So, I've had a rummage round in our records and I'm afraid
the name "Horne" didn't come up as a donor.'

My heart sank. I'd got myself quite worked up about finding
that fragment.

'But that's not to say it's not here,' she continued. I perked
up again. This was a rollercoaster ride of a call from Haslemere.

'You see, twenty years ago our system wasn't very well established, so I can't really pinpoint the piece myself. I'm afraid the
donor details almost certainly weren't recorded in the database.
But . . .' – I liked the sound of this – '. . . we do have about 5,000
Romano-British pieces in our reserve collection and you're
welcome to have a look at them. You just need to book an
appointment, then come and see what you can find.'

See what you can find – that was basically what I'd been doing
all year. I booked an appointment for the following week and
crossed my fingers.

18 December

The last gig of the year, like the last day of term, is a wonderful,
silly occasion, for the comics and kids at least. You might start
a little wearily but halfway through you remember how close
you are to your holiday and the adrenaline takes over. You no
longer care what people think. You're going to have a good time
whatever. But instead of heading out to celebrate after mine, I
had to head straight home to bed.

I had arranged to pick Tim up at 4.15 a.m. for our last

birdwatching trip of the year. His school (he's a teacher, remember) had broken up for Christmas the night before and he was up for an adventure. And so, a little wearily at first, we drove out to Norfolk in the December dark, munching a festive turkey wrap as we went.

David's final piece of advice was to get up to Holkham Nature Reserve on the north Norfolk coast before dawn, where throughout winter we could see 20,000 geese on the move. It was an unforgettable sight, he told me. I tried to think of all the other unforgettable sights from my life. There weren't that many. Rachel on our wedding day, Gerrard lifting the cup in Istanbul, those starlings in Brighton . . . these were all treasured scenes. I wanted another. I checked what time dawn would be, feeling confident that even if they weren't going to wait for me, I would at least know how long both time and tide were sticking around.

By this late stage of the year, getting up early was much less of a problem than it had been. As long as I had something I had to do, something I cared about, I was basically fine. A little weary, but fine. And if I'd dragged Tim all the way out here in the middle of the night, it was my duty to appear fine. Maybe that's why dads like Duncton and David seem to have so much stamina, I thought, they just have to.

We parked the car at 6.50 a.m. feeling pleased with ourselves – we'd made good time. But as soon as we opened our doors we heard the honks of what must have been a million geese. We're too late, I thought. They got up even earlier than us.

It was basically still night-time, so we stumbled down to the hide, feeling our way with frozen fingers, thrilled to be so far from home so early in the morning so near to Christmas.

Ten minutes later we were sitting, alone, in the igloo-like hide, watching the sun rise and cast its light on the geese. There were lots of geese. 'Blimey!' said Tim, 'there are bloody loads of them!' We started spotting them slowly at first, a couple on the mudflats, a few in a field; then, as our eyes started to work properly, they were everywhere. Each bit of land had a goose on it, and each goose was muttering to himself, as excited as us by what was already a stunning sunrise.

But I was disappointed. There were lots of geese and that's always nice, but I'd wanted to see them arrive. That's what David had recommended and I'd missed it on my final trip. I'd made Tim get up at 4 a.m. on the first day of his holiday to witness the spectacle but we hadn't got there in time. I'd failed again.

But then, at 7.30 a.m., just as people all over the country were staggering out of their beds towards the kettle, the geese went mental. They started screaming. Our spines started tingling. 'What the hell are they doing?' whispered Tim. I didn't know. It was as if they were all listening to a Norwich match on tiny headphones – perhaps their great Milk Cup final against Sunderland at Wembley in 1985 – and thirty-four-year-old Asa Hartford had just scored his winner, they all went crazy, flapping their wings, shrieking their lungs out and then, unable to stand still any longer, invading the pitch. Inspired by one fearless goose, they all took off, thousands of them, flying as one up into the sky, they swarmed the dawn, swirling this way and that in celebration.

'So are they all just pissing off?' Tim asked me.

'I guess so,' I replied.

I realised I'd misunderstood David. I'd thought the geese were going to arrive at dawn. Actually they were going to leave and we'd had to get here before they departed, en masse, a mighty march across the sky. We watched in awe for another hour as they split into groups of Vs, zooming in and out of the sun like the helicopters in *Apocalypse Now*. It was an unforgettable sight: blue sky, red sun, white frost and a black cloud of 20,000 pink-footed geese and bean geese – not a bad way to start the day or the Christmas holidays. Or, indeed, to end the year. I can still make myself smile by recalling their movement, their cries and

Tim's face. That's priceless. This was my ornithological Istanbul.

As a reward for his loyalty, I'd given Tim my new bird guide to use in the hide so I was looking through Mat's old Collins. As I fumbled my way through to the bean goose page, I found two things in the front that I'd never spotted before. The first, this note to Mat from Grandpa:

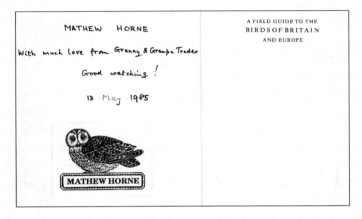

The second was a dedication from the authors:

To our long-suffering wives:

'she laments, sir . . . her husband/goes this morning a-birding'
Shakespeare – *Merry Wives of Windsor*

For some reason these made my spine start to tingle all over again.

Eventually we emerged blinking from the hide and went for a quick circuit of the reserve, alternately walking and jogging to keep warm, spotting the odd bird as we went (including ten curlews flying in perfect formation), mainly enjoying cracking the frozen puddles with our boots.

On the way home we stopped in a town called Swaffham for

an enormous 'double bubble' fry-up, served by terrifying tattooed women clutching babies and cigarettes while cooking. That was also, unfortunately, an unforgettable sight.

I dropped Tim back at his home, got to Kensal Green in time for lunch and went to bed, two more species tacked on to my list. I was now forty-seven ahead of Duncton and far too wound up to sleep.

20 December

Midhurst doesn't have a train station. It did, for ninety-eight years and one day, but after the decline of the railways and the rise of the motorcar, it was closed to passengers in February 1955, then to freight in October 1964. So, whenever I wanted to buy Doc Martens from Carnaby Street or Iron Maiden T-shirts from HMV during my regrettable teenage *Kerrang!* phase, Duncton or Mum had to drive me up to Haslemere and I'd catch the train from there to Waterloo.

On the day of my museum appointment, I felt surprisingly pensive as I made that trip again, in reverse. Speeding down through New Malden, Woking and Guildford, out of the city this time, back towards the countryside I'd hurried away from as a kid, I tried to work out why I was returning, why I was looking for this small piece of pot after all these years.

By the time we pulled in I'd almost worked it out, and as I ambled down from the station, along streets silent but for sparrows, past Haslemere Hall – where we'd all watched *Dances With Wolves* back in 1991 (it came out in 1990 but films always took about twelve months to make their way down to us) – I came to my conclusion. I wanted to identify the fragment myself this time. I wanted to amend the records. I wanted to make it known that this was a shard of Roman pottery found not on the North Downs near Kemsing by an eight-year-old boy, but by his grandfather, in an unknown location. It was important that the real facts were known. I didn't want to be a stringer or a dude.

I reached the museum thirty minutes early for my appointment. This, I should point out, was my first ever 'appointment' at a museum and I was nervous. My palms were sweaty, as if something bad were about to happen – the dentist maybe, or a telling off.

The Assistant Curator came down to collect me.

'Sorry I'm early,' I said.

'That's fine,' she replied. (I'll say it once more: she was so kindly.) 'Let's go.'

This time she led me up a different staircase, through one door marked 'Staff Only', another marked 'Quarantine Area!' (note the warranted exclamation mark) and into the vaults of Haslemere Museum. This was exciting stuff. Vaults! I thought. Modern, functional, well-labelled vaults rather than dark, dusty, Indiana Jones vaults, but vaults nevertheless. The Assistant Curator turned a wheel on one of the large metal doors which slowly slid back to reveal row upon row of neatly stacked cardboard boxes.

'So we've got quite a lot here,' she said modestly. 'But I've got a couple of boxes out over here if you want to start with these. Good luck!'

'Thanks,' I said and gulped.

'Oh yes, and if you wouldn't mind popping on some gloves . . .'

Mind? I thought. Gloves? Brilliant!

'No, of course,' I said. 'I must wear gloves.'

'Cotton or latex?'

'Oh, cotton definitely,' I replied, sounding, I hoped, like I did this sort of thing all the time.

I popped on the cotton gloves, the Assistant Curator popped into her office, and I popped open the first box. Nestled like eggs among layers of protective paper were numerous plastic bags, each holding a shard, sometimes several shards, of what the label said was Roman pottery. Each box contained numerous bags, there were countless boxes and this was just the first locker. There was a lot of Roman pottery here. I gulped again (partly for effect, admittedly – I was having fun).

I began to rummage, carefully. Most pieces I could dismiss with just a brief inspection because they were the wrong shape, size or colour. Some were glazed and marked with a hint of a picture; mine had been rough, grey and plain. But even though I knew they weren't right, I couldn't help but spend a few extra seconds examining each piece, trying to picture the person who'd once used the pot to hold water, ashes, jewellery or, if they were anything like me, worthless foreign change, biro lids and empty Pritt Stick tubes. Or I'd think of the person who'd rediscovered it, who'd been walking, digging maybe, and had noticed, held, appreciated and brought what was left of the pot to the museum, where someone, perhaps the Assistant Curator, had identified, labelled and gently placed it in this box.

Each set of shards was accompanied by a piece of A4 paper covered in rows of neat handwriting in pencil:

'Pottery – handle of pot'
'Miner's lamp with eagle – in pieces'

Or, most commonly, a simple:

'Roman pottery fragment'

Using this as my guide, I looked in box after box, gradually speeding up my (still careful) rummaging, scanning the bags more efficiently, seeking out the familiarity, the jizz, of my piece. I got better at skimming over the bulk of the bits, stopping only when something caught my eye. Even so, one fruitless hour later I'd still barely made a dent in the museum's enormous reserve.

I was tiring. Something had to give. I'd wanted to find the shard on my own this time round, but I was forced to admit that I needed help again. As usual, this meant phoning my mum. She'd know what to do.

'Hi Mum,' I began. 'Do you remember ages ago when I found that piece of Roman pottery?'

There it was again: The Lie. This isn't the moment to admit the truth, I told myself, I'm in some vaults!

'Oh yes,' said Mum, 'on the Downs near Kemsing, I remember.'

I listened for any flicker of doubt, any hint that she might know my secret, but could detect nothing.

I pressed on. 'Well, I'm here at Haslemere Museum now . . .'

'Are you?'

'Yes, don't worry, it's fine . . . I remember us bringing it here together – to be identified – but do you remember anything unusual about it, anything noteworthy that might distinguish it from all the other Roman bits and bobs? Like a handle or an eagle?' Perhaps it did have some marking I'd forgotten about.

'I don't remember much,' she said, 'but I also don't know what you're doing there. I'm pretty sure we brought it home. I'm almost certain we just brought it in for the museum to iden-tify then took it back home and put it in your museum in the playroom. God knows where it is now though, it could be in the loft I suppose. But then I might have thrown it out . . .'

Right then.

I thanked her, hung up and returned to the boxes, half-heartedly (maybe even carelessly) digging around for another twenty minutes while trying to piece together my own cracked memories.

Gradually, it all came back to me. The fragment of pottery had been in our museum the whole time. I could picture it now, on the same shelf as that sheep's skull and all those fossils from Dorset. I'd kept the fragment. The kindly curator had said that it was indeed Roman and that I should look after it. We'd taken it back to Silvertrees, to our museum.

Soon I'd be back in Silvertrees too. Christmas was coming and I could look after it all over again. The only trouble was that our playroom was now Duncton's study, and the museum had been moved to a location even Mum didn't know. I would have to start digging again. The wild goose chase wasn't over yet, and perversely, I was glad. This time, at last, I was putting the hours in – I was working for my Roman pottery. And, inevitably perhaps, the trail was taking me home.

24 December

Once I'd mentioned the shard to Mum, she became determined to help me find it. She didn't question why I needed it – maybe she did know the whole story after all – she just wanted to help, despite Duncton's constant protestations of: 'I'm sure we've thrown it out.'

On the drive down to Silvertrees with Rachel on Christmas Eve I probably wasn't very good company. Again I was thinking about the past and my pot in particular, trying to convince myself that if it had been chucked out, if it had been thrown on to Midhurst's dump, that would be fine. At least then someone else would have the chance to discover it in another thousand years. Luckily there were Christmas songs on the radio, so she might not have noticed.

But then another text lifted my spirits:

Museum found! But not examined. In box in the study. AML Mum xxx

Of course she hadn't thrown it away. She keeps things together.[154]

---

154 She also helped me to find all the scrapbook entries and all my old writing books. 'I don't know why I keep them,' she told me. 'I just can't throw them away.'

In fact, she'd sent Duncton up to the loft and there, in a
corner under some green matting, an old toy castle and a
camping stove, he'd found another cardboard box, this time
with a sheep's skull peeking out of the top.

Back home, alone in the study, I rummaged carefully once
more, putting each piece on the centre pages of the *Midhurst
and Petworth Observer* I'd laid out on the floor: the sheep's skull
from our holiday in Northumberland next to a sea urchin we'd
found in France, a tribal necklace that Duncton had brought
back from Brazil beside a rabbit's skull from the garden, two
large mussel shells leaned against a couple of unimpressive
rocks. But already the box was almost empty. I pulled out a
handful of shiny stones, an Irish coin, possibly a punt, from
1928, and a small blue piece of eggshell – but no pottery. I could
now see the bottom of the box and the only things left were
fossils – crumbly chunks of ancient shell, mostly broken, some
almost dust – and that was it.

But that wasn't it. It wasn't just the pottery that was missing,
it was my spectacular shells, the sharks' teeth, the unbroken
fossils. I ran upstairs and started digging again. Rachel, sensibly,
ignored my strange, probably worrying behaviour and ate a
mince pie with Nana, my mum's mum, in the kitchen.

It only took me about twenty minutes to unearth another
cardboard box from beneath a pile of unread books in a corner
of my bedroom, and this time I knew I'd struck gold (literally).
As soon as I opened the lid I saw what I'd treasured as a kid –
an enormous fir cone from the floor of the Vendeé region of
France in 1981, a ram's horn from Cornwall found in 1986, that
shark's tooth sleeping on a bed of cotton wool in an old black
camera film case marked 'Bracklesham Bay – October 1991', and
a small vial containing a few specks of gold that Mat, Chip and
I had panned for in a place called Shantytown, New Zealand.

There was a guide to shells from the Channel Islands that

we'd picked up from Herm Island in the spring of 1991, and a dozen envelopes marked 'dog cockle', 'cup and saucer limpet' or 'variegated scallops', each containing examples of the various shells. That was a very early obsession. I smiled as I remembered how we'd had to find every shell, how we'd *had* to finish our collection.

There was a compact battered tin with a handwritten sticker that read 'semi-precious stones'. Inside Grandpa, presumably, had placed six smaller pots (marked 'purple', 'white', 'pink', 'orange', 'green' and 'dark') each holding their own delicate selection. In fact, there were several rocks that Grandpa must have given us (I can't have stolen them all) – no moon dust, but those same heavy meteorites that had fascinated us back in South Cottage, one whole and heavy, another sliced into three pieces.

And finally, at the bottom of this cardboard stocking, wrapped in kitchen roll and sealed in a sandwich bag, I found my pottery. It was in two pieces – I remembered it breaking now – but safe. I fitted the pieces together so that they made one smooth rim of a pot, about four inches long, with slightly curved edges and that satisfying feel. I recognised it instantly, just like the red kite, and even though it now looked a little smaller in my hands, even its weight felt familiar.

Before wrapping up my family's presents I parcelled up the museum once more.[155]

25 December

The remainder of Christmas at Silvertrees was rather tense. I'd seen far more birds than Duncton, but he was off to Africa in that surreal post-Christmas, pre-new-year gap, when everything

---

[155] The first box, I remembered now, had contained things we'd deemed unworthy of keeping years before, but which Mum, again, could not bring herself to chuck out.

can change. Meanwhile, we were at a stalemate. I had originally planned to use the holiday as an opportunity to admit the shocking truth about my pottery both to my family and to Rachel, but I couldn't tell them. In fact, I still haven't told them. This book is my signed confession.

It was also Rachel's first Christmas with the Hornes. Almost a year after getting married we'd spent our first in Fermanagh, relaxing with her friends and family, drinking, eating and even sleeping a lot. We'd celebrated Christmas in style and nobody had mentioned birdwatching. Here in Midhurst, we tried not to talk about our challenge but it hung over us like an axe. Birdwatching was the elephant in our already crowded Christmas living room. Sometimes I would catch Duncton gazing out at the garden and would desperately scan the flowerbeds in case he'd seen something new. I'd disappear up to my bedroom at odd times to stare out of my window, hoping to find one last rare species – maybe a magical merlin, maybe an out-of-season willow warbler, maybe that murrelet, back in the UK for a quick dip in our pond.

It's probably odd for a father and son to spend their Christmas surreptitiously birdwatching, each secretly trying to spot birds without the other one noticing, but at least it gave Rachel, Mum and Nana a chance to spend some quality mother-in-law-daughter-in-law-grandmother-in-law time together.

29 December

By the time the magic Christmas dust had settled and the presents and turkey (yes, that did seem a little odd) had all been devoured, neither Duncton nor I had spotted a single new bird. This wasn't all that surprising as we'd also barely left the house – we were lazy and the weather was typically festive fare, wet and miserable. So, with just a couple of days of the year remaining I drove Duncton, Mum and Chip to Heathrow, still forty-seven birds in the lead. They were flying to Accra, the capital of Ghana, where Mat and Morri were to spend the next six months teaching in a small town called Brenu. Morri's parents were taking the same plane over and I waved them all goodbye, wishing them a *bon voyage* and a happy new year, thinking that this must be how fathers feel when they send their kids off on their first trip abroad. But then I remembered that most fathers don't whisper, 'I hope you don't see as many birds as I did,' as they go.

In South Africa, we'd seen forty-six species in a single day thanks to David. My total was easily within reach. He needed about a bird an hour. I was nervous.

I spent my remaining days of the year with Rachel, resolutely not birdwatching. In fact, soon after leaving my family at the airport, we set off to the birdless Alps to spend our wedding anniversary skiing with her lovely non-birdwatching family. Ours was a calmer journey than Duncton's.

The year 2006 ended in foggy fashion in the UK. In fact, there was so much of the blurry stuff over Heathrow in the run up to the new year that British Airways 'lost' thousands of passengers' bags, including Duncton's, in the gloom. The two sets of parents (and Chip) arrived safely in Accra, but several bags (including Duncton's) and several vital holiday items (including his binoculars) didn't. So Duncton (and Mum and Chip and Morri's parents) had to stay in Accra for an extra twenty-four hours until the bags arrived.[156] Duncton only had two days before our Big Year ended. Now he had to spend one of them in an airport, without his binoculars.

---

156 Duncton was one of the lucky ones. Morri's parents weren't reunited with their bags for another two months. A lot has been written about BA's incompetence but that's not going to stop me joining in. They lost everyone's bags for ages! They didn't give them back for two months! That's amazingly rubbish! I'm fairly disorganised, but it would be like telling the set-up line for a joke then forgetting to say the punchline for *eight weeks*!

With far too much time on his hands, Duncton composed a series of texts to keep me up to date. The first, in capitals but otherwise flawless, read:

ARRIVED IN ACCRA. TWO HOURS LATE. BAGS STILL ON THEIR WAY. YOU CAN PROBABLY RELAX – SO DO SO! LOVE TO ALL THERE. D.

31 December

Chip isn't a birdwatcher. In fact he's more opposed to the hobby than I have ever been. While I often wondered why Duncton spent so much of his (now copious) free time watching birds, Chip simply dismissed it without wasting his own (less copious) free time thinking about it. So knowing that I could trust him not to get distracted by any brightly coloured African birds, I had given Chip my microphone and mini-disc player and asked him to record the final hours of Duncton's bird-watching bid.

On the morning of the last day of the year, they finally clambered into a minibus and left the airport for the eighty-mile drive west along the coast. Once more, however, they were thwarted. Seizing the opportunity of another delay and throwing himself into the role of official documentary maker, Chip interviewed Duncton by the side of the road:

'So, it's about 1 p.m. and we've just had our *second* puncture,' he began. Listening back I can picture the scene perfectly: Chip, amused by pretty much everything, Duncton, stoically frustrated. Sorry Chip, you were saying . . .

'A second puncture meaning that our tyre had already been replaced by the spare. And for some reason the spare was very small,' (he now started laughing hysterically) 'much smaller than the other ones,' (still laughing) 'but we put it on and now that one's got a puncture too, so we're standing by the road looking at birds. And Duncton,[157] where exactly are we?'

'Well . . .' Duncton, I noticed as I transcribed the tapes later, begins almost every sentence with this word. It seems to be a useful tactic, adding an element of composure to what might otherwise be an outburst. '. . . we're probably just over halfway between Accra and the Hans Cottage Botel[158] and as you say we're just experiencing our second puncture, which is holding us up, and it's jolly hot out here and we've seen about three or four birds on the way over – well, three or four *identifiable* birds – several birds that were non-identifiable without being able to stop and use binoculars. And I think the sands of time are gradually running out . . .'

They were indeed, and Duncton had suddenly found himself a fish out of water floundering on those fast flowing sands. There were birds all around him, but he couldn't tell what they were. He was in the same position I'd been in at the beginning of the year.

Except that Duncton did have his basic birdwatching skills.

'So Duncton,' Chip continued, 'what birds have you actually spotted so far over here?'

'Well, I've seen black kite, red-eyed dove, hooded vulture and a Senegal coucal, but that's about it. So we've seen a few extras but it's a bit of a measly tally so far and I think Alex can remain confident that he's going to claim his victory. Although we're just at this moment looking at two rather nice little birds and a pigeon on the wires over there.'

'What are the little birds?'

'They're . . . unidentified at the moment.'

---

157 I am doing my best to make everyone call him Duncton. It's a fine name.

158 Where they were all staying for the first few days of the trip. A 'botel' as you may have guessed, is a cross between a hotel and a boat. It's a boat hotel in the same way that a motel is a motor hotel and a gotel is a hotel for goats.

(Chip laughs again.)

'What do you think they might be?'

'Well, I think they're a bit small for bee-eaters, they're the sort of bird that sits on wires. I might be able to work it out but it'd be nice to get some sort of colour on them – with the sun behind they're just silhouettes at the moment. There's also a pigeon to one side which is probably, hopefully, either a speckled pigeon or an African green . . .'

'How can you tell the difference between the pigeon and the two small birds – ooh, two of them have just flown away, which one's left?'

'Well the pigeon's left. It's obviously the pigeon. It's got the jizz of a pigeon.'

'It's got what?!' (Laughing more heartily than ever now.)

'It's got the jizz of a pigeon. The general impression of shape and size.'[159]

'Is that what jizz stands for?'

'Yeah – from the American Airforce . . . jizz jizz.'[160]

'I had no idea.'

'And there's a nice black kite flying right over it which you can tell from its forked tail. It's got to be a kite – ah, there's a very big black butterfly here . . .'

'Butterflies don't count do they?'

'No, butterflies don't really count . . . we might be able to make a case for them if we're really desperate. There's quite a few birds around but what we need is an expert ornithologist – which we had in Romania and which made life very easy, just to say exactly what was what – which I think Alex had in South Africa.'

---

159 Clearly 'jizz' should be spelled 'giss', but that's not how it's pronounced or written by birdwatchers. They definitely call it 'jizz'. I promise.

160 And yes, I do still have the recording of Duncton saying 'jizz' twice in rapid succession – undeniable proof that I'm still not very mature.

'Oh there's another big bird over there!' That was Chip, actually noticing a bird all by himself.

'And what do you think that is?'

'Oh, is it another black kite?'

'Yes, you see the forked tail . . .'

'Yes, and that's what makes it a kite!'

Brilliant. Despite his unfortunate surroundings, Duncton had somehow got Chip birdwatching too. And I bet Chip never forgets that kite.

Duncton summed up this exchange with the following text:

SEEN A COUPLE OF SPECIES BUT STILL NOT AT BOTEL. CHIP AND I HAVING FUN THOUGH. HOPE YOU ARE TOO. LOVE. D.

Two hours later, he followed this up with:

WE'VE FINALLY REACHED MAT AND MORRI – AND THEY'RE ENGAGED. MAT PROPOSED ON CHRISTMAS DAY ON A BEACH! LOVE. D.

Over in the Alps my heart melted (as had most of the snow, but it was New Year's Eve, so we weren't worrying about that). My brother was getting married. Marriage, I knew from personal experience, was brilliant. So is Morri. This was terrific news.

I felt a tiny bit left out of the celebrations. They'd had a nightmare journey down, but were now with Mat and Morri who were engaged. And it was New Year's Eve. They had to be having a fantastic time. I decided to text Duncton a message of goodwill:

That's tremendous news! Send them my love and a big hug. And if you want to have an extension till midday tomorrow that's fine. Call it injury time for the Heathrow stoppage. . . Love, A.

Yes, it was a magnanimous gesture. Well, sort of. There was also an element of me not wanting our challenge to fizzle out just yet. I wanted Duncton to have a fair crack at my total, not just for him, but for me. I suspected that so far he'd been kind to me, too kind almost. A part of me wondered if he'd been letting me win. That is, after all, what dads do. This was what Grandpa had done with the piece of pottery, and look how that had ended up. This time I didn't want to be given any special treatment. I wanted Duncton to at least have the chance to catch me.

Back in Ghana, Duncton embraced the opportunity. He needed thirty-eight more species. He needed an expert. And with Mat's help, he found the phone number of the area's top naturalist, a man called Robert. On Chip's recording you can only hear Duncton's side of the conversation so I've had to guess at Robert's words:

'Hello, is that Robert?'

'Yes, it is, how can I help you?'

'Well, the thing is, I was just wondering if you're around tomorrow. You see I'm trying to see rather a lot of birds.'

'Of course, no problem.'

'What? Well, ah, well great, thank you!'

'What time would you like to set out?'

'Well, I would think we'd be ready to leave at around 10 a.m. or so . . .'

'How about 6 a.m.?'

'6 o'clock?'

'Yes, 6.'

'Well, OK, 6 o'clock in the morning.'

'That's the best time.'

'That's the best time. OK, right, sure, fine – I'll try not to have too late a night tonight!'

'And what's your name?'

'It's Hugh.'

'It's what?'

'It's Hugh – H-U-G-H . . .'

'*Can I just call you Duncton?*'

'Yes, that's fine. Thank you, bye!'

'Well done Duncton! Six o'clock on New Year's Day!'

Those last words were Chip's, no longer quite so amused. Just as in South Africa on the morning after our wine tour, this was to be another 'early start not welcomed by all' for the sake of birdwatching.

1 January

'Morning Duncton!'

Chip can be annoyingly chirpy in the morning.

'Ah, well, good morning.'

Duncton was as calm as ever.

'What day is it?'

'It's still the 31st of December . . . in Alaska.'

Duncton, of course, was right. He may not quite be omniscient, but he's not too far off. It wouldn't be New Year's Day in Alaska till midday. I may have bent our rules, but I hadn't broken them.

Robert was taking the sleepy group to Kakum National Park, a tropical rain forest about twenty miles north of Brenu, home to more than 300 species of birds. Duncton had to see just thirty-eight of them to win. Unfortunately, and quite ironically for him, visibility wasn't great. They were too early. It was foggy.

'The mist will lift as the sun comes up,' bluffed Duncton.

Thankfully for him, Robert knew exactly what he was doing. This was his patch and he knew every inch of it. What's more, he'd guided twitchers before. He knew the score.

Before long, he'd wowed the group – not just Duncton, but the future mothers-in-law *and* Chip too – with an African green parrot, a fire-bellied woodpecker and a yellow-casqued hornbill. Despite the mist, he pointed out violet-backed hyliota, black-winged oriole and even some splendid glossy starlings. On Chip's recordings I can hear genuine (if still slightly groggy) oohs and ahs, accompanied by an earnest 'Oh, that's rather nice,' and 'Oh, gosh yes,' and an 'Oh, that's a handsome bird,' from Duncton.

He was having quite a morning. These may not have been as hard-earned as the Romanian birds, but it's difficult not to be impressed by the likes of velvet-mantled drongo, yellow-billed turaco or, by all accounts the best of the day, a Congo serpent eagle.

But Duncton was not content merely to tick these birds off. He wanted to learn. 'These birds are completely new to me, Robert,' he said, 'all these greenbuls and malimbes. It's great, but they're just so different . . .'

Chirrup.

'What's that one?' Duncton was keen to recognise the calls of the birds as well as their markings.

Chirrup chirrup chirrup.

'Mmm,' Duncton pondered. 'Is that a weaver?'

'No,' said Robert. 'That's a frog. It's a small tree frog. Yes, that's a frog. You can actually see it if you come over here . . .'

'Hey, that's great!' said Mum.

'Yeah, that is quite cool,' said Chip.

Robert clearly registered the general appreciation of a creature that wasn't a bird.

'And that noise there?' he pointed up, ears cocked. Another shriek echoed round the canopy above them.

'Is that a kite?' guessed Duncton, somewhat desperately.

'No, that's a monkey.'

'Yes, I can see it!' cried Mat, a traitor to Duncton's cause.

'Wow,' cried everyone else. 'Did you see it jump?'

'Yes, that's a Diana monkey. They occupy the uppermost leaves. We have five species of monkeys here, including the spot-nosed . . .'

This was what most of the group wanted to see and hear on New Year's Day. In fact, having spent the first couple of hours looking exclusively at birds, it seemed anything else was becoming markedly more interesting.

'What's the tallest tree?' asked Chip, for presumably the first time in his life.

'Well,' said Robert, adopting Duncton's usual tone, 'the tallest trees are the Kantun trees. They grow up to 260 feet. And the squirrels love them. We have more than twenty species of squirrel here, including the biggest flying squirrel – that's like a fox. It's very large . . .'

The tour finished just before midday and the group made their happy, but still quite sleepy way, back to the camp for a nap. But Duncton was too wound up to sleep. He texted me instead:

HAD A FANTASTIC MORNING. SEEN LOADS OF SPECIES. FINISHED ON 243. HAPPY NEW YEAR! LOVE, D.

Back in the northern hemisphere we'd woken late, feeling almost exactly how we had on New Year's Day morning the year before. While heavily washing up in the kitchen, I noticed a small grey bird sliding down a tree outside the house and instinctively shouted 'nuthatch'. I even tapped the window with my knuckle like Duncton always did when spotting kestrels while driving (despite the hot water, my action was carried out in a safer situation). Rachel and her parents peered through the glass and eventually saw the bird too.

'So that's a nuthatch?' they asked.

'Yes it is,' I replied. 'They're fairly common round here.'

Rachel looked at me and smiled. While she must have been pleased my birdwatching year was over, and I wouldn't have to ruin any more weekend lie-ins with dawn trips to meet strange men from the internet, I think she liked the fact that I could now identify at least some of the world's birds. Just as I like to imagine Mum feels about Duncton's birding, I hoped her occasional well-hidden exasperation at my obsessive behaviour was outweighed by some pride in the fact that her husband could now point at a small grey bird and tell everyone what it was called.

Mostly, though, I think she saw that I enjoyed being able to tell everyone what that small grey bird was called. And because she's perfect and I'm a very lucky (and soppy) man, she mainly just loves me being happy.

*

By the time Duncton's text arrived, we were finally out on the slopes, attempting to banish our anniversary hangovers in the mountain air. My attempt hadn't been entirely successful yet and I had to read it twice. On the first occasion I thought he meant he'd seen 243 species that morning alone and felt like a fool for so generously offering him the extra morning.

But then I remembered the small amount of birding common sense I had gained. Even Duncton couldn't see 243 species in one morning, even in Africa. He'd seen 243 species in a year. I'd seen 257. I'd won.

'I'm going to *le pub*.'

Why Did the Chicken Cross the Road?

'Not only is this the opening chapter of my story, but also the opening of a new and exciting chapter in my life.'
– Adrian M Riley, prologue to *Rivals and Arrivals*

What happened next . . .

I sent our complete year lists to Lee G R Evans for verification (David wasn't deemed quite neutral enough).

'Hi Alex, I've studied your year list submissions for the year 2006 and make the following comments,' he replied with appropriate gravitas. 'By UK400 club rulings,[161] feral pigeon is not a valid taxon and is therefore not countable . . . nor is monk parakeet . . . I see too that most birds listed are from outside of Britain and the Western Palaearctic so outside of my jurisdiction.'

Fair enough, I thought. He's never claimed to be expert on every bird in the world. No one is expert on every bird in the world.

Evans concluded that my 2006 British Year list total was 152

---

161 This is the birding club that Evans set up and runs, named after the achievement of seeing 400 species in Britain. He himself is one of the few to have seen over 500 and he's still the Year list Champion of Britain.

species. Subtracting a nightingale and a tawny owl that he'd heard but not seen (we were still sticking rigidly to our three rules) Duncton's 2006 British Year list total was 136 species (the birds we'd both seen in County Cavan had been approved without question, so maybe Paul Murphy had finally got round to moving that border).

These, to me, were highly satisfactory figures. I was sixteen ahead of Duncton, so whether I'd actually seen that lesser spotted woodpecker or not, I'd still won. I was also sixteen ahead of Duncton on our total world lists, meaning that we'd seen exactly the same number of birds overseas. His trips to Romania and Ghana had yielded the same number of birds as my trips to Bahrain, South Africa and the birdless Alps.[162]

I love statistics. Throughout the year I'd enjoyed the meticulous collating of facts and figures, and this statistic convinced me that this had been an absolutely fair contest. I immediately sent our scores to Surfbirds.com, a website that publishes league tables of the year's top listers and where the 2006 Big Year results were soon published.

In the final reckoning a man called Ian Robinson sat at the top of the British list leader board with 349 species including, of course, the long-billed murrelet. Second was a man called Lee G R Evans with 340 species. 'A comparatively disappointing year but clearly made up by new additions long-billed murrelet and Canada Warbler,' he wrote.[163]

If you look up the list today you will still find, in ninety-sixth place, a man called Alex Horne with his 152 species, five places above a man called Duncton Horne. He came 101st, frustratingly

---

162 Although, in the remainder of Duncton's trip to Ghana he did see another twenty species – but that was well into 2007 and so entirely irrelevant.

163 I won't spoil the climax of Adrian Riley's book for you, but during his Big Year in 2001 he did end up seeing more than both these men . . .

close to the top 100 but still an enormous improvement on his real tennis ranking.[164]

'If only I'd made more of an effort to see the seabirds,' said Duncton wistfully when we met up to look over his 30,000 photos of Ghana (far more of which featured birds than my newly engaged brother and his fiancée), but I don't think he was particularly referring to our challenge. Since his childhood trips to Fair Isle, Duncton has always tried to make at least one trip to Scotland every year to see the guillemots, the gannets and the kittiwakes. This year, what with his real tennis, his RSPB work and a son to teach, he'd missed them. He'd really missed them.

I asked him for his birding highlights of the year.

'Just the birds that stir the soul basically,' he said casually.

That sentence, uttered by Duncton without forethought, answered all my questions. That is why my dad watches birds, often for hours at a time.

'As always it's got to be the peregrine falcon,' he went on. 'My last afternoon taking part in the RSPB show at Chichester Cathedral – seeing all five birds fly at once, flying more or less in formation; that was amazing.' Duncton had been watching these particular birds for five years now and had been an ardent peregrine supporter for two decades.

'And, I reckon, well, the best bird really,' Duncton continued, 'was the golden oriole, which was a fantastic sighting, right at the top of a tree on a lovely sunny morning with blue sky. And the long-eared owl that I saw with you. That was memorable.'

Yes it was, I thought. That had been the moment I'd seen his soul stirred and realised, with some resignation, that mine wasn't

---

164 In case you're as interested in statistics as me, the Surfbird.com World list leader board was topped by a man called Jonathan Roussouw from South Africa who saw a remarkable 2,744 species in his twelve months. Andrew, my guide from The Welsh Harp, came in a very respectable twentieth with a total of 1,154 thanks to trips to Venezuela, Montana and Uganda. I always said he was a cracking birder.

even shaken. That was when I saw Duncton as he must have looked as a kid, birdwatching because he loved it. That *was* memorable.

Simply spending time with Duncton was undoubtedly the best thing about my Big Year. Whether in a hide, on the phone or in the vague vicinity of some severals, those were the moments I'll treasure most. At the risk of sounding cloyingly sentimental, I'm so glad I got to have my birdwatching trip with him. I did start to understand why he does what he does and I did get to know him better through birding.

I learned, for instance, that the reason he's called Hugh, his middle name, rather than James (or Duncton) is that his own granny, Trader's mum (my great-grandmother), had started calling him Jamie when he was a month or two old. His mum (my granny) didn't like the name Jamie (as I mentioned several months ago, it's not, in my opinion, a name for a dad), so she started calling him Hugh.

I'd never known that. I'd never asked. Or I'd never listened. But often when you're birdwatching there's little else to do.

'Always happy to engage in conversation. Just to pass the time as much as anything.'

That's what tall, wise Martin had taught me on Hampstead Heath back in April.

I still take some pride in the fact that Duncton saw his first ever long-eared owl thanks to our Big Year. Mat had been with him when he saw his first peregrine falcon, but two decades later, I'd helped him find this owl. In fact, I'd be tempted to say that our challenge breathed new life into his hobby.

Perhaps it's a coincidence, perhaps it was always going to come alive again in his retirement, but the following year Duncton bird-watched with renewed vigour, taking part in weekly garden watches, an annual breeding bird survey, and contributing to an atlas of wintering and breeding birds by comprehensively studying a square mile of land. Before our Big Year, he'd barely made a list (excluding the Birds Seen on or over Silvertrees still bluetacked to the fridge), now he couldn't stop. He's also in the middle of a three-year farm survey for the RSPB for which he has to cover another square mile or 'a substantial chunk of Hampshire', in his words.

'People like me are doing this all over the country,' he told me. He's right, and I think it's great. But I'm not yet like him; I still couldn't comprehensively study my garden, let alone a square mile, and even if I could, I wouldn't want to, yet. But I like to think (again, erroneously, probably), that our challenge had helped him. I'd made him keep a catalogue of his birds – that was one of my obsessions – and he is still doing it now, edging his way up the birdwatching tree in the process.

My mentor and friend David, meanwhile, has been climbing even closer to the top of that tree. He left his job at a film company in October 2007 and is currently studying for a Master's in Taxonomy and Biodiversity at the Natural History Museum. He knows his birds and wants to do something positive with his gen, including offering to painstakingly check all the references to birds in this book. I'm indebted to him.

Mat and Morri got married on 18 April 2008. The wedding was fabulous, they'd chosen African music and decorations that meant so much to them and they both looked tremendously happy. (Mat had shaved.) At dinner, every table was named after an African bird and on the centre of each they'd placed a card with a picture of the bird beside which Mat had written a paragraph, like John Wakefield in *The Strange World of Birds*, 'a tender celebration of all their freakiest features'. I stole (with their permission this time) many of these words when describing the birds I saw in Africa.

Two days after the wedding I received a text from Tim:

I can see a heron. Hope you're having an equally profitable Sunday afternoon, Love Tim x

He's still watching birds too. We really should find the time for another trip back to Norfolk soon – for a double-bubble breakfast special in Swaffham at the very least.

But what am I passionate about?

In the summer of 2007, Rachel and I moved out of London. It was time, we both thought, to at least think about the practicalities of starting a family, and since we were both born and raised in the country, it seemed natural to leave the city behind us. We wanted to nest where we could be comfortable, so moved to a peripolitan town called Chesham[165] just outside the M25, at the bottom of a valley at the foot of the Chilterns and five miles from the home of Lee G R Evans.

It's also not far from the M40 and at least once a week I get to see some massive great birds circling over our garden. 'Forked tails,' I want to say to someone, 'red kite.'

I think I'm now ready to pass on that sort of gen myself.

Meanwhile, the broken piggy bank I gave Rachel, sits on a shelf in my new study, beside two rather grey fragments of Roman pottery. Having spent so long tracking down the troublesome pottery, I now get to see it every day. I had thought about taking the pieces over to Granny in Norfolk but that didn't feel right. It seemed more appropriate for me to keep it – after all Grandpa had, really, given it to me. So I placed the pieces beside the wounded pig on the bookshelf above my desk: a reminder, a memento, a keepsake.

The rest of the museum is still safe in Silvertrees. Mum and Duncton say they aren't going to throw any of it out, not even the sheep's skull. After all, they might be grandparents themselves some day.

*

---

165 Twinned with Friedrichsdorf in German, Houilles in France and Archena in Spain.

On our return to Chesham after spending Easter over with Rachel's parents not birdwatching in Fermanagh, we found, to our surprise, that a funfair had been set up in the field opposite our house – Steven's Funfair, to be precise. We had mixed feelings about this but did our best to look on the bright side. There was a funfair in the field opposite our house.

At the first possible opportunity we made our way over to the gaudy lights and risked our lives on some sort of jerky ride called, simply, 'The Best Machine'. I liked it, Rachel didn't so much. Neither of us thought it could justify such a brazen claim.

Still fairly wobbly, we then moved on to the more stable prospect of those games you're always tempted to play but never win at a fair – coconut shies, hoops over bottles, that sort of thing. The tent we were drawn into was manned by a boy of about nine who brusquely explained that we had to throw four darts at a dartboard, all of which had to land on the board, but the total of which had to be below thirty in order to win a small prize (which included, spectacularly, a golfball taped to a can of lager) or below ten to win a 'special prize'.

This, I thought and hopefully didn't say, is man's business. I swapped the darts for a dink (this, apparently was Steven's Fair Slang for a pound coin) and flung them, one by one, straight into the number two. I was astonished. 'That's right!' I cried. 'Less than ten! I've won a "special prize!"'

'You didn't read the small print,' the nine year old said, presumably for the millionth time. I now read the small print: 'all darts must land in different numbers' it said, in very small print. I shook my head and did some swift mental arithmetic. To score a total of ten or less you had to get one dart in one, one in two, one in three and one in four.

'Right,' I said, digging around in my pocket for another pound. 'I'll have another go!'

Rachel tried to pull me back, as if rescuing me from a fight outside a nightclub. 'Don't!' she yelled, 'it's not worth it!'

'I know what I'm doing,' I yelled back. I think I might have winked but again, I hope I didn't.

I handed the child two demis, he handed me the darts. This was tense. The whole fair, I felt, stopped for a second to watch the action. I raised my first arrow, aimed for the number one, and flung it straight and true. It missed the dartboard completely. The nine year old laughed, betraying some emotion for the first time.

'You can take that one again!' he said patronisingly. I was tempted to walk away. I knew that according to the rules, I had already failed. But he'd handed me a lifeline. What did I have to lose – except my already shaky dignity?

This time my first dart landed bang in the middle of the number one. The next two hit their targets too. Suddenly, only one dart stood between me and glory. I closed my eyes and imagined I was taking a penalty for England. I was a Liverpool player taking a penalty for England. I opened my eyes again (I'm not a complete idiot) and threw.

'You did it!' shrieked Rachel. 'You won a "special prize"!' The nine year old looked with disbelief at the dart, tucked right in the corner of the number four. I had indeed won a 'special prize'. This was the most daddish of all my achievements to date. Still incredulous, the nine year old gestured to the cities of gold-esque area where the 'special prizes' lay.

'You choose!' I said gallantly to my wife. She ignored the enormous cuddly lions and tigers, she dismissed the slightly creepy man-sized dogs, and just as David had done in those fragrant Cape Town sewage works, she pointed straight to a four-foot tall pink fluffy flamingo. 'That's the one I want,' she said.

Steven the flamingo now hangs in a fairly dignified manner from a hook in the kitchen, nervously waiting to be mauled by a toddler or two.

Occasionally true to my word, I told my first version of this story at the Edinburgh Fringe in August 2007. There I witnessed first-hand the breadth of birdwatching's appeal as, after every show, a large and varied group of birdwatchers gave themselves away by hanging around to check the full lists of birds seen by me and Duncton that I put up on the screen at the end. They're on my website (www.alexhorne.com) too, if you're interested.

Edinburgh Fringe 2007.

I never made it back out to Bass Rock during the festival but I am still watching birds, occasionally rather than regularly, often accidentally rather than deliberately. Whichever way I look at them, birds are definitely on my horizon. A year after Mat and Morri got engaged, the Horne family repeated my in-laws' trip to the Alps, and on New Year's Day 2008, our third wedding anniversary, I saw my first golden eagle. My soul was very nearly stirred. It was certainly nudged. Of course it was Duncton, really, who pointed out the undisputed king of birds to the rest of us (all of whom, including Chip, were impressed). Rachel squeezed my hand.

The trouble is, I'm still very much a novice. I'm still amazed that even after a whole year of birdwatching at least once a week every week, I'm still rubbish at it. I really am. When I was eighteen I spent four months in China and picked up a very small amount of the language. I think I still know more Mandarin today than I do birds.

But I do notice birds now. If I'm out walking in the Chilterns I'll hear the sound of birdsong (over my own mutterings). I'll stop to listen to it, I'll enjoy it and just occasionally I'll recognise it, or at least pretend to. I'm still a proud member of the RSPB and, thanks to a particularly persuasive salesperson, I did renew my subscription to one of the birdwatching magazines.

Elsewhere, Liverpool have twice come close to winning the Champions League again but I think I'm fairly safe in the knowledge that nothing will ever beat that night in Istanbul. I can relax on that front. And England kindly failed to qualify for Euro 2008, so I've been able to concentrate on The Good Life in the country without having to worry about whether this will be The Year, or collect stickers to mark the occasion. I've been able to settle down for a few months and write this book. It's been fun. I haven't driven miles and miles to gigs for a while. Instead I've relived my birdwatching adventures and chased up bird facts. I've loved trying to put my experiences into words. Rory McGrath wrote a great book about his birdwatching life which came out as I was writing mine. It was frustratingly good, funny and moving. He got into his birdwatching late, like Duncton's friend Peter, and confesses that, 'word-watching, as opposed to birdwatching . . . has been my constant, passive, background hobby'.[166]

As I wrote this book, I came to understand that words are what I'm mad about too. I'm passionate about lots of things, Rachel,

---

166 McGrath famously knows the scientific name of pretty much every bird on the planet, which makes him, in one way, extraordinary, and in another, quite a typical bloke.

my family, Liverpool even, but words are right up there. Next time, it'll be them I'll chase.

Out in Chesham I also realised that wasting words trying to entertain drunken stag nights wasn't what I wanted to do. I did my last gig in that sort of comedy club on the day I sat down to write about Duncton. Smaller clubs, arts centres, theatres, they're all places I love and where I'll hopefully always tell my jokes and stories, but the others just aren't for me – although I haven't completely given up on hens just yet.

Not long after moving out of London, Rachel and I decided to speed up the process of enlarging our little family by buying two chickens.[167] So although we haven't quite got round to having kids yet I am now looking after two charming young ladies. They're called Beyoncé and Shakira, they live in our garden and they each give us one egg a day in rent. They're our first pets, and I've decided that they're my responsibility. I really am very grown up now.

It's not strictly birdwatching according to the first rule of our Big Year, but as I scratch around for words in my modest study, I do look down from my window at the two of them, scratching around for worms in the garden. I take some sort of encouragement from their gentle clucks. They're another welcome distraction.

Duncton hasn't met the chickens yet. Soon after they arrived, he and Mum went off to Sri Lanka for a honeymoon-like holiday. He saw eighty-five new species in three weeks, but managed to restrict his birdwatching to a sensible level that Mum could enjoy. They watched birds together.

It is, after all, a sociable hobby.

---

167 Female chickens are only actually 'hens' when they have laid their first eggs. Before that, they're 'pullets'. Our pullets were sixteen weeks old when they arrived. To their and our surprise, they laid their first eggs six weeks later. So, the chickens, officially, came first.

One of the birds he found was the Sri Lanka jungle fowl, a distant relative of our own domesticated chickens. As Shakira, Beyoncé, Rachel and I happily pottered about in Chesham, they were roaming wild in the heart of the island's forests.

My dad is a birdwatcher.

Appendix

Horne's birdwatching euphemism bingo

1. We thumbed breathlessly, page 40
2. A huge eighteen inches, page 61
3. Duncton's Dangling Coconuts, page 64
4. All swinging temptingly in the breeze, page 64
5. Buzzing round the nuts, page 70
6. Every gig was now an opportunity to grab more birds, page 98
7. Caught me with my binocs out, page 100
8. This was just me and my woodpecker, page 114
9. I had got a very hard woodpecker, page 115
10. Let me have a go on his telescope, page 165
11. Comparing equipment, page 181
12. I notched up my . . . first shag of the year, page 217
13. Duncton and I both got our first woodcocks of the year, page 226
14. Gesturing . . . at his yard-long prize item, page 247
15. Squirrels wouldn't even get a sniff of your nuts, page 247
16. A jealous birder had been eyeing up my Deltas, page 250
17. I had trouble concentrating on the road with foreign birds flashing all around me, page 252
18. I remember in particular two nuggets, each about the size of a golfball, that were incredibly heavy (not happy about this though – it's Grandpa!), page 294
19. The jizz of his familiar bearded face (when I told this story in Edinburgh I appointed an 'innuendo (wo)man' who was supposed to 'bash his bell' whenever he spotted one. The word 'jizz' always

received mixed responses. Half the audience couldn't believe it was a birdwatching term, the other half didn't understand why it was funny that it should be. It seems to be quite a modern innuendo. If you're in that second half of my audience, try to find someone from the first half to explain what it means, I don't think it's really my place), page 298

20. A really rather delicious bap (getting desperate now), page 321

Famous gardeners that I could name off the top of my head in thirty seconds

1. Alan Titchmarsh
2. Monty Don
3. Bob Flowerdew – perhaps the best example of nominative determinism there is
4. Charlie Dimmock
5. Kim Wilde
6. Lancelot 'Capability' Brown
7. Martha Stewart
8. Don Burke, host of *Burke's Backyard* and producer of *Backyard Blitz*

Prime Ministers that I could name off the top of my head in thirty seconds

1. Tony Blair
2. Margaret Thatcher
3. Winston Churchill
4. John Major
5. Gordon Brown
6. Harold Macmillan
7. Ted Heath

Birdy names

1. Tony Duckett
2. Nancy Gull

3. Mark Cocker
4. Bob Martin
5. Matthew Weaver
6. BILL Oddie

My final top ten birds of the year

1. starling
2. secretary bird
3. penguin
4. puffin
5. robin
6. blue-helmeted guineafowl
7. Harry the woodpigeon
8. bee-eater
9. East Indian wandering whistling duck
10. lapwing

Duncton's pedantic quibbles after reading the hardback edition

p.72, para 2 The jackdaws have the white eye-rings, not the rooks.

p.123, para 1 People tend to think of Woolworths as the home of pic'n'mix – or nick'n'mix. (*This is a wonderful joke from Duncton. After doing a modicum of research, however, I was gratified to discover that WHSmiths has also been known to sell pic'n'mix. A.H..*)

p.178, para 3 *Ali* is a bird conservation journal, produced by LIPU (Lega Italiana Protezione Uccelli), which I support with a small annual sub. See also footnote on p.279.

p.204, para 2 The Fair Isle boat – it's not a ferry – continues to be The Good Shepherd, as far as I know, but I don't know if it's the same boat – it may be a different one and have a new number, i.e. IV or V.

p.227, para 3 Alternatively, the idea is that the hankies mimic the white wing-spots of nightjars, and the birds come to have a look.

p.259, para 2 House sparrows tend not to nibble on worms. Being finches, they're more partial to seeds, grain etc. but may eat small insects (I think!).

p.336, para 2 Monk parakeets visiting a nest in December??? But you may be right, if they're still working to a southern hemisphere timescale (*unlike the lesser spotted woodpecker, I am sure I'm right this time, Duncton*).

p.342, para 3 In fact Midhurst had two stations – for the north-south and the east-west lines respectively.

p.363, para 8 A little about my surveys: the breeding bird survey covers the same 1km square every year (mine is between Redford and Milland, i.e. farmland – fields and woods); the Atlas (of winter and breeding birds) is the current BIG project, covering the whole of both the UK and Ireland and is conducted every twenty years and takes four years to complete. I'm allocated a different 2km square on the Ordnance Survey map every year; last year it was mainly Petworth Park, this year it involves the countryside around Lodsworth. Peter usually helps me, so two pairs of dodgy eyes and ears (see p.364). The Farm Survey is part of the 'Volunteer and Farm Alliance' project, run nationwide by the RSPB in response to individual farmers' requests for info as to what birds are on their land and how they can help with their conservation. I think the farm's a lot bigger than 1 square mile and the survey involves walking round the periphery of every (huge!) field four times during the summer; hard work and very time-consuming, hence a three-year timescale.

For the complete list of birds seen by me and Duncton in 2006, visit www.alexhorne.com

Select Bibliography

The Birdwatcher's Yearbook and Diary 2006, Buckingham Press, 2006

Barnes, Simon, *How to be a Bad Birdwatcher*, Short Books, 2004

Cocker, Mark, *Birders: Tales of a Tribe*, Grove Press, 2002

Cocker, Mark and Richard Mabey, *Birds Britannica*, Chatto and Windus, 2005

Cottridge, David and Richard Porter, *A Photographic Guide to the Birds of Israel and the Middle East*, New Holland Publishers Ltd, 2000

Freddi, Chris, *Pelican Blood*, HarperPerennial, 2006

Fry, Stephen, *Paperweight*, Arrow Books Ltd, 2004

Grose, Francis, *A Dictionary of the Vulgar Tongue*, Papermac, 1981

Horne, J E T and Sir Kingsley Dunham, *Towards the Twenty-first Century. A Discussion Organized Jointly for the Royal Society and the Mineralogical Society*, Royal Society, new edition published 2007

Hosking, Eric and Frank Lane, *An Eye for a Bird*, Arrow Books, 1973

Kaufman, Kenn, *Kingbird Highway*, Houghton Mifflin, 2001

Marren, Peter, *The New Naturalists*, Collins, 2005

McGrath, Rory, *Bearded Tit*, Ebury Press, 2008

Mullarney, Killian, Lars Svensson, Dan Zetterström and Peter J. Grant, *Collins Bird Guide*, Collins, 2001

Obmascik, Mark, *The Big Year*, Bantam Books, 2005

Oddie, Bill, *Gripping Yarns: Tales of Birds and Birding*, Christopher Helm Publishers Ltd, 2000

Peterson, Roger, Guy Mountford and P A D Hollom, *Collins – A Field Guide to the Birds of Britain and Europe* (4th edition), Collins, 1983

Riley, Adrian M, *Arrivals and Rivals: A Birding Oddity*, Brambleby Books, 2004

Wakefield, John, *The Strange World of Birds*, Iliffe, 1963

Acknowledgements

I already gave thanks to some of the people who helped me watch birds for a year in the unashamedly soppy epilogue but that won't stop me offering more to Tim and David, both of whom were great birding companions, and to all my other friends (in London and Midhurst) with whom I've been lucky enough to grow up. Thanks also to Bill Oddie and Lee G R Evans who didn't know it was them being watched this time, and to anyone I know or met in a hide or a pub in 2006 who showed me a bird or told me a story and let me scribble it down. And apologies if I wrote up anything wrongly – I inherited my handwriting from a doctor.

James, Becky and all at Avalon and Ed, Davina, Sophia and everyone at Virgin have all been amazingly (almost suspiciously) encouraging throughout, as were Jonathan, Suzanne and everyone else at the RSPB during Edinburgh 2007. Thank you. My friend Owen also gave me his time, great notes and much needed praise when I called on him. Very much appreciated. Hello and thanks too to Margaret, my first ever copy editor. We've never actually met but I think you're brilliant. This book would have been twice as difficult (and time-consuming) to read if it wasn't for your judicious eye and tactful suggestions.

Finally, thanks to my family – both here in England and over in Ireland. Again, you've all supported me tremendously. Apart from everything else, I really appreciate you allowing me to write about you without once asking to read a word before publication. You're very trusting and I hope you won't have cause to regret anything you said or that I've written.

So particular thanks to Terry and Anne for letting me write in your study in Lisnaskea and then eat so well in your kitchen; to Mat, Morri and Chip for watching and not watching birds with me so entertainingly; to Mum, for being so patient and honest (in the traditional sense) throughout, for finding and keeping scrapbooks and boxes, going to museums and libraries with and without me and just for being a brilliant mum – the next one's for you; to Dad, for being Duncton; and to Rachel, for everything. I can't wait for the next chapter.

Copyright Acknowledgements

The author and publishers gratefully acknowledge permission to quote from the following sources:

Birders: Tales of a Tribe by Mark Cocker, published by Vintage, 2002, © Bernard MacLaverty. Reproduced by permission of the author c/o Rogers, Coleridge & White Ltd., 20 Powis Mews, London W11 1JN; *Paperweight* by Stephen Fry, published by Hutchinson, 1993; *Arrivals and Rivals: A Birding Oddity* by Adrian M Riley, published by Brambleby Books, 2004; 'Mute v whooper swans' by Matthew Weaver in the *Guardian*, copyright Guardian News & Media Ltd 2006.

Photograph on page 368 © Jaimie Gramston